THE WHITE LAKE

FIGHTING FOR A FREE PRESS, JUSTICE, AND A PLACE TO CALL HOME IN THE NEW POLAND

JOHN BORRELL

A CHARLES GLASS BOOK

First published in 2014 by Charles Glass Books
An imprint of Quartet Books
27 Goodge Street, London W1T 2LD
Copyright © John Borrell 2014
The right of John Borrell to be identified
as the author of this work has been asserted
by him in accordance with the
Copyright, Designs and Patents Act, 1988
A catalogue record for this book
is available from the British Library
ISBN 978 0 7043 7332 7
Typeset by Josh Bryson
Printed and bound in Great Britain by
T J International Ltd, Padstow, Cornwall

For Ania, without whom there would be no tale to tell

CONTENTS

CITIZEN KANE

On a freezing winter morning, I rose nervously from the dock of the district court in Gdańsk, Poland, to defend myself against a charge of criminal libel. My lawyer was not sanguine about my chances. Under Polish law, a guilty verdict could mean twelve months in a grim prison where overcrowding and physical assaults, including rape, were not uncommon. Staring at me from across the court was my accuser, the bearded former mayor of the city of Kartuzy. The ex-mayor claimed my newspaper had 'lost him the public confidence required to hold office' and thus made him lose the last election. It was a serious charge. It could mean prison, fines, large legal costs and a criminal record.

The ex-mayor, Mieczysław Gołuński, was right about one thing. My newspaper had campaigned vigorously against him. I was delighted when he was voted out of office. I believed he was high-handed and arrogant. Like many other public officials, he didn't appear to understand that the Communist era was over and transparency and accountability were part of the new democracy. Just prior to the election, the public prosecutor had charged him and other council officials with irregularities in the tender process for building a public school. Judgement was pending. So were the verdicts in scores of other corruption trials involving politicians and businessmen. Corruption was so endemic in Poland that Transparency International, the non-governmental organisation that monitors corruption worldwide, placed Poland's public sector sixty-first in the world for honesty and transparency. This bracketed it with

1

countries like Botswana, Bulgaria and Egypt, not exactly exalted company for a new member of the European Union.

Arbitrary and far from transparent decision-making by ex-mayor Mieczysław Gołuński and others in the local cabal had angered me so much that I launched my own newspaper, *Express Kaszubski*. It was a feisty twenty-four-page weekly produced by an enthusiastic team of young Polish journalists and published weekly in the city of Kartuzy. Nearly fifteen years earlier I had settled with my wife and sons next to a nearby lake called Jezioro Białe [The White Lake]. Like many who had lived in exile during the grey years of communism, my Polish wife had been thrilled to return to the country of her birth after the system crumbled in 1989. We were ready to share the risks and excitement of creating new enterprises from scratch. It was harder than we expected, or than it needed to be.

Doing anything meant constant battles with officialdom. The more we stood up to the bureaucrats, the more hostile they became. We soon learned how closely interwoven and intact was the Communist-era *układ*, a cabal of public officials that helped one another and ganged up on outsiders and anyone challenging them. Once I was left bleeding and dizzy from a physical attack by a neighbour, who cracked me on the back of my head with a fence post. Although the assault might have left me dead or brain-damaged, police said my injuries were not serious enough for a proper investigation. The public prosecutor refused to lay charges of assault on the illogical grounds that I had not suffered permanent disability. Would you not arrest someone, I asked the police and the public prosecutor, who had shot at a person and missed? Had I attacked my neighbour with a fence post, I was certain the police would have taken me away in handcuffs. The prosecutor would almost certainly have charged me with aggravated assault.

The local state-owned television station weighed in with a biased documentary that demonstrated little more than the reporter's lack of professional integrity. When presented with the facts, the station's management neither retracted nor apologised. They threatened to take me to court for challenging their staff's honesty. I urged them to do so, but they did not file a lawsuit. The local fire chief refused to help in an access issue that meant his fire trucks might not be able to reach us in case of a fire. Even the local priest warned his parishioners not to help us in the dispute involving the neighbour. Most of them disliked the neighbour as much as we did, but they could not ignore their priest.

I knew from reading Polish newspapers that the local *układ*'s hostility towards me was not simply because I was a foreigner. Poles too suffered indignities and worse at the hands of public officials schooled during the Communist era and unwilling to change their ways. They were aided by laws which seemed out of a place in a member state of the European Union. Public prosecutors and courts could keep people in jail for two years or more without charge. Those who were not prosecuted received neither apology nor redress. In one celebrated case, the head of a regional tax office and his public prosecutor friend conspired to keep two businessmen in jail for nine months while they searched for evidence to charge them with corruption in a business deal involving state property. No evidence materialised, but the businessmen were ruined by the time of their release. Both officials kept their jobs. One was promoted.

In standing up publicly to the local *układ*, I had put myself at risk. They hated my newspaper. It published stories that others would not touch. We ran trenchant editorials. We asked tough questions of local officials. We bludgeoned some of them with uncompromising headlines and opinions. We did what newspapers should do but usually don't. We probed, we exposed, we embarrassed. I headlined one editorial about Mayor Gołuński with a single word: 'Liar!' We refused to back down when a former member of the Communist-era riot police threatened us.

Now, on that freezing morning in a court near the Gdańsk shipyards where the battle for Poland's freedom had been waged in the early 1980s, the judge demanded that I justify my newspaper's reporting and editorialising. Ex-mayor Gołuński eyed me with hatred. 'This case is all about freedom of the press and the accountability of public officials,' I told the judge. I knew it also might be about my own freedom, something I had taken for granted when I gave up life as a foreign correspondent and arrived in Poland with energy, enthusiasm and ideas. That seemed a lifetime ago.

RED KITE LODGE

Fifteen years earlier in the spring of 1993 I had stood on a small hill beside an old birch tree looking down the rough track scratching its way between tiny fields of rye, oats and potatoes. The track petered out at a small escarpment, beyond which a lake danced impishly in the freshening breeze. On the far shore, half a kilometre away, a forest patrolled the water's edge before marching off, ridge by hazy ridge, into the distance. Behind me, a rough dirt road ran through the six houses and various barns and outbuildings that comprised the hamlet of Sytna Góra. Two of the houses were made from the rough, homemade concrete blocks widely used during the Communist era. The others were traditional single-storey cottages with steeply pitched roofs and small windows. The oldest, nestled up against a giant lime tree, was more than one hundred years old. It had a thatched roof and half-timbered walls in the manner of a Tudor cottage in medieval England.

Professional ennui, serendipity, and the recent shift in the tectonic plates of European history had brought me to this hamlet in Kaszubia, a region of post-glacial lakes, forests and subsistence farms near the Baltic Sea in northern Poland. The bleak, post-war years of Communism were over. I had recently given up my job as a foreign correspondent for an American news magazine. My last assignment had been covering the collapse of Communism in Eastern Europe and I knew that on the scuffed, down-at-heel fringes of the New Europe, a little capital and a willingness to take risks opened up opportunities seldom found in the plump, comfortable economies of the Old Europe. This was the new frontier for dreamers and gamblers like me.

I was building a hotel. It would probably be the first boutique country hotel to be built in Poland since the beginning of World War II which, I reminded myself, had started just forty kilometres away in the city of Gdańsk. That was also where the shipyard strikes of 1980 had exposed the frailties of Communism and the limits of Soviet power. A decade later, the post-war Soviet empire in Eastern Europe had disintegrated and Poland became free for the first time in half a century. The shipyard strike leader, Lech Wałęsa, was now president and Poland was on course to become a member of NATO and the European Union.

My eyes that spring morning took in the view only as far as the mounds of sandy soil which a squat little bulldozer with a red cab was creating. Until this year, potatoes, rye and beets had been grown rotationally in the field. Now, beside the busy bulldozer, grey concrete blocks, bags of cement and a rusty concrete mixer were being unloaded from a battered blue Jelcz, an almost comic Communist-era truck named after the small town in southern Poland in which it was manufactured. This Jelcz didn't look sturdy enough to have carried such a load from the nearest town, Kartuzy, eight kilometres and several steep hills away. As soon as the bulldozer finished, the men in faded blue overalls unloading the truck would begin building. First the foundations would go deep into the sandy soil. Then the steel-reinforced basement floor would be poured, wheelbarrow by wheelbarrow, the mixer churning nonstop throughout the day. After that the basement walls would go up, brick by brick, the trowels smoothing and scraping the thin layers of grout. Then the ground floor and more walls, yet another floor and finally roof trusses and brick-red roof tiles imported from France.

Providing the next winter wasn't too harsh, within a year it would be all done. I planned to call it kania Lodge, *kania* being the Polish name for the beautiful red kite *Milvus milvus*, a rare diurnal raptor with a wing span of more than a metre. It is indigenous to this part of Poland, and I had first seen it gliding gracefully above the field where the lodge was being built. It seemed an omen. When the first stage of the project was finished, the lodge would comprise two imposing buildings with nearly a thousand square metres of floor space, electricity, running water, central heating and, not least of all, splendid views.

The main building would be south-facing, with French windows leading from the ground floor onto a large terrace. From the terrace the land sloped gently for fifty metres to the escarpment which fell sharply, almost perpendicularly, to the lake. The steep escarpment was held in place by a forest of mature beech trees, some more than one hundred years old. At the edge of the forest were several wild cherry trees, beautiful when they blossomed in spring and heavy with small, sweet cherries in summer. There were two venerable oak trees at either end of the escarpment, itself about two hundred metres in length and rising twenty-five metres above the water. Along the water's edge were a rough path and a fringe of alder trees.

I planned to create lawns and gardens, put a tennis court on the land sloping away from the terrace and to fell two trees to open up a view to the lake. Then I would put in steps down the escarpment and build a jetty in a place where the lake bed was sandy so that we would have a private swimming beach. It was positioned to retain the summer sun from mid-morning until well into the evening. The White Lake was so clear and clean that you could not only swim in it, but also safely drink the water. Created when the glaciers retreated 10,000 years ago, it was fed by springs bubbling up from nearly fifty metres below the surface. Its moods changed with the seasons, shimmering with reflected sunlight during the spring and summer and turning deep and moody in the autumn when the trees around it slowly lost their leave. Each winter it froze and was kept a pristine white by successive snowfalls. Without the lake we would probably have not settled here or dreamed of building the lodge. It gave everything a focus and nourished our souls.

Because the land on which we were building was in fact a small promontory pushing out into the fifty-hectare lake, we sited the second building at right angles to the main dwelling to give all rooms a view of the lake. In fact, the second building would overlook the larger part of the lake which was about half a kilometre wide. The escarpment here started ten metres from the building and, steep though it was, had been cleared of trees during the Communist era. It was now covered in grass and young fruit trees that we had recently planted.

At the top of the escarpment there was a shady place under a coppice of beech trees where tiny wild strawberries could be picked in the summer, and another where the wild parasol mushroom, also called *kania* in Polish, was to be found in the autumn. When coated with egg and breadcrumbs and pan fried, it made the most delicious of breakfasts. The tiny wild strawberries were sweet and full of flavour and you could eat them singularly or collect a handful and before long have juice running down your chin. It was here that I'd lounged in the grass on a brilliantly clear, sunny and warm autumn day a couple of years earlier. A skein of geese was flying overhead, honking as they headed south. The deep lake was so still that the forest on the far side cast a mirror image on its surface. Nobody else was about, not even on the lake. I had recently been reporting from Sarajevo where a new war was starting and, as I luxuriated in the sunshine and silence, I dreamt of a different life far from the death and destruction I had spent more than two decades chronicling. It would be wonderful to live in a place like this with a house with big windows looking out onto the lake and lawns and gardens leading down to the shore. But what would I do for a living? Why not build a luxury lodge here, I mused, and share the sunshine and silence with paying guests? Quickly the idea took hold and after covering the first US invasion of Iraq, I boarded a flight to New York to hand in my resignation.

Yet as I watched the bulldozer at work in the spring of 1993, I felt uneasy. What was about to go up was mine; it was being built with my money, almost all that I had. I was forty-five and I had just given up a successful career in journalism. I now had no income apart from the occasional cheque from freelance writing. Poland wasn't my country, nor Polish my language. Sandwiched between Russia and Germany, the country in which I was planning to settle was on one of history's most unreliable political fault lines. Armies had marched east and west, north and south across the country for centuries. Germany and Russia had been the last invaders, devastating the country only a few years before I was born.

The first shots of World War II had been fired from the German battleship *Schleswig-Holstein* into a Polish garrison at Westerplatte near Gdańsk, or Danzig as it was then called. Sixty kilometres away to the east was the largest brick castle in Europe, the medieval fortress of the Teutonic Knights. After being ousted from the Holy Lands by the Moslems, the Germanic order held sway in northern Poland, Latvia, Estonia and what is now Kaliningrad, for nearly two centuries. It was finally defeated by a Polish-Lithuanian army in a bloody battle at Grunwald in 1410. Since then Poland had been invaded by the Swedes, Germans, Austrians and Russians. For more than one hundred years it ceased to exist, its territory divided up between Russia, the Austro-Hungarian Empire and Prussia, later to become part of the unified German state. Occasional rebellions were crushed with great cruelty and exile to the frozen wastes of Siberia became a rite of passage for successive generations of nineteenth-century nationalists. Poland was re-born at the end of World War I and a Polish army defeated the Russian Bolsheviks near Warsaw in 1920. Stalin took his revenge during World War II when he colluded with Hitler to carve up the country again. Hundreds of thousands of Poles were forced into unheated cattle and cargo wagons on trains bound for Siberia. In 1940, Stalin murdered twenty-two thousand Polish officers, soldiers, police and landowners and buried them in mass graves at Katyń, twenty kilometres west of Smolensk in Russia.

Hitler's World War II depredations in Poland were on an even grander and more inhumane scale. Up to three million Jews perished, either starved to death in ghettos or gassed in Nazi extermination camps like Auschwitz and Treblinka. Another two million Catholic Poles were also killed. Even today you will not travel far in Poland without coming across a plaque or gravestone commemorating the victims of extermination, forced labour and starvation. When the war ended, Poland's suffering continued under Soviet tutelage.

The post-World War II Soviet domination of Eastern Europe collapsed suddenly in 1989 and Poland elected a government with strong leanings towards the West. I had met and interviewed many of the leading figures, including Wałęsa. Once, when I talked with him in his union's headquarters in Gdańsk, he was wearing carpet slippers and looked as if he had just got out of bed. I had also known Tadeusz Mazowiecki, the first post-Communist prime minister, and the brilliant Leszek Balcerowicz, Minister of Finance and possibly Poland's greatest hero of the early 1990s.

You could trust these people: they were democrats and wanted a liberal, free-enterprise society. In 1993 though, it seemed likely that rabid nationalists like Vladimir Zhirinovsky might come to power in Russia, and dictators still held sway in neighbouring Ukraine and Belarus. Poland's own former Communists were enjoying a resurgence of popularity and the old guard, reactionary, corrupt and larcenous, looked like retaking control of the local council, or *gmina* as it is called in Polish. This was the first and most intimate layer of government I'd have to deal with as I built the lodge and got the business up and running.

Nuts, I thought, you're nuts. This, clearly, was not the ideal time and place to be spending one life's savings. Politics and history aside, why was I committing myself to living next to a lake at the end of a dirt road in Kaszubia, a regional backwater even in the poor and unsophisticated country Poland then was? This wasn't Tuscany or Provence, where a country retreat nestling amongst vineyards and olive groves was the dream of many a weary corporate warrior in London or New York. Mediterranean tradesmen might be fractious, but there was compensation in things like a long lunch in a restaurant which served spectacular food. In France or Italy you could still be sitting out on your terrace at times of the year when people in Northern Europe wrapped themselves up and scurried from centrally-heated house to equally warm office. Even in winter, snow fell rarely enough in Tuscany or Provence for it to be exciting. In northern Poland it was something to be endured.

The first hints of spring in Mediterranean countries come as early as February, not late March or April as on the shores of the Baltic. At 54° north, Kaszubia is on the same latitude as Newcastle-upon-Tyne in Britain and Vladivostock in Russia. It is three degrees further north than Calgary in Canada and eight degrees closer to the North Pole than Invercargill, the most southerly city in New Zealand, is to the South Pole. In Kaszubia the snow sometimes arrives in October and is still there in April. The lakes freeze so solidly that it would be possible to drive a tank over them. In mid-winter the sun rises lazily after 8am, creeps furtively along the horizon and sinks without trace by 3.30pm. On my first visit to Gdańsk in January 1986 it was -25ºC when I arrived after a flight from Cairo on a Russian Tupolev via Bulgaria to Warsaw. Comically, one side of the aisle was designated smoking and the other non-smoking. Almost everyone smoked, as they did in Eastern Europe in those days, and the entire cabin was soon enveloped in tobacco fog. In the Soviet sphere for the first time in my life, I changed to a propeller-driven Antonov for the flight from Warsaw to Gdańsk. It vibrated so violently I was sure the rivets would pop out. Even more menacing were the two soldiers in winter camouflage sitting at the back of the plane. They were there cradling Kalashnikovs to thwart hijackings by people seeking freedom in the West. You had to ask the stewardess for permission to use the lavatory and even just to stand up. I'd been told it would be cold and had dressed for it. Or thought I had. I was dressed for Cairo cold, and spent the entire visit in a borrowed coat, gloves, scarf and hat, staying indoors most of the time. The Baltic Sea around Gdańsk froze that year and there were snowdrifts up to two metres high blocking country roads. Deer starved to death.

It wasn't quite that cold every winter, but each year the thermometer fell well below -10ºC for long enough to have everyone yearning for warmer weather. Spring arrives coyly and uncertainly, the weather in late March and early April flirting with the yellow and purple botanical crocuses and small white snowdrops which are the first flowers to make an appearance. One day it is sunny enough for the flowers to open up, the next they are buried under a new fall of snow. Summer comes in a rush of colour as cornflowers and poppies colonise the edges of fields of rye and potato. The days lengthen quickly and by mid-summer there are more than seventeen hours between sunrise and sunset. Daytime temperatures can reach more than 25ºC but they drop quickly at night, and eating outside on a terrace in Kaszubia is possible just a few weeks of the year.

When we arrived in Poland, eating out was still not something many people did. As a result there were no little restaurants in our area serving interesting local food with a bottle of wine. There weren't even many restaurants in the cities then, although things were improving. On my first visit to Warsaw in the dreary days of Communist rule, it was virtually impossible to buy a sandwich. If you weren't a foreigner staying in one of a handful of big state-run hotels, there was no such thing as a restaurant. The closest was a *bar mleczny* [milk bar] serving cheap and generally greasy food. Chipped, formica-topped tables, aluminium spoons and forks and unsmiling counter service by plump, surly, middle-aged women were the norm. Even in a top hotel, fried meat, boiled potatoes, cabbage or carrot salad and a glass of vodka were standard fare.

When one thought about it, and that's what I was doing as I watched the bulldozer with the red cab work away below, this probably wasn't the best place in the world to build a country lodge. Would a handful of well appointed rooms, good food and wine in an inviting environment with proper service and a smile or two from staff, be enough to persuade people to visit? Were people here ready for the kind of cheerful, friendly place you found in the southern hemisphere, especially New Zealand where I'd grown up. There were no such places in Poland at that time, fifty years of Communist Party rule having virtually stripped the countryside of anything – or anyone – remotely cultured or civilised.

During the Communist era the cities offered some music, film, theatre and a lively intellectual life in the privacy of small but meticulously kept apartments of the country's middle class. Class was then measured more by education and background than by money. No one had much of that and it was not much use to those who did have it. There was little to buy, almost nothing to do and it was difficult to travel anywhere. In the countryside, nothing remained of the landed gentry or even the middle class. Old manor houses with pianos and libraries, once home to spirited conversation, had all been ransacked by the Communists after 1945 and divided up to house people who often could barely read the label on a vodka bottle.

The nearest manor house to where I was building was just ten or so kilometres away. It was a modest yet beautifully proportioned wooden building with a pillared porch, large windows and a steeply pitched roof. But nearly forty years of Communist neglect, indifference and hostility had taken their toll. It hadn't been painted in decades, shutters hung askew at several of the windows and there were holes in the roof. It was so run-down it was hard to imagine that once there was probably a piano in the salon and a library where the owner might have retired after dinner to pen a letter or read Flaubert in French. It wasn't just the owners of manor houses who had been dispossessed. The state requisitioned all the big farms and estates after 1945. Farm workers squatted in the grand old houses or lived in tiny apartments in hastily constructed tenement buildings nearby, all with peeling paint and squalid stairwells. The managers, Communist Party appointees, lived a little better thanks to party perks but were generally dull, plodding people who toed the line and either met their quotas or blamed someone else when they didn't.

If they weren't dull they were tragicomic like Andrzej Lepper, the xenophobic, Eurosceptic and anti-Semitic former state farm manager with an Elvis-style quiff and sunbed tan. When he found he couldn't farm successfully in a free market, he created the *Samoobrona* [Self Defence Party] in 1992 and set about blocking roads and roughing up opponents in pursuit of his statist vision. Since he was also a big admirer of Alexander Lukashenko, the Stalinist

14

dictator in neighbouring Belarus, it was unnerving to see him garner votes and seats in parliament. Fortunately, the closest he came to power was a brief period as deputy prime minister and minister of agriculture in a coalition government in which *Samoobrona* was a junior partner. In the end, after being found guilty of a sexual assault on a party worker, he committed suicide.

Apart from the big state-owned farms which comprised roughly twenty per cent of the agricultural land, there were around a million peasant farmers in Poland. Stalin pushed for them to be collectivised too, but post-war Polish regimes, fearful of massive unrest, left the peasants alone. Sixty per cent of them had landholdings of less than five hectares (just over twelve acres) so did little more than subsist on the land, and often took part-time labouring jobs to supplement their meagre earnings. Villages were poor and run-down, lacked piped water and proper sewage and were accessible only by dirt roads which often became impassable in the winter.

Sytna Góra, the hamlet where I was building the lodge, was typical. Only one farmer owned a tractor. The rest ploughed their fields with horses, planted rye and barley and were lucky to wrest a ton or two of grain from a hectare of the poor, sandy soil. Potatoes were their staple food and they planted and picked the crop by hand, the whole family inching down the rows on their knees during harvest time and dropping the potatoes into wicker baskets which were later emptied into a cart.

Each farmer had two or three cows, some pigs and poultry. The cows were milked by hand, often while they grazed in a meadow. It was common to see the ample bottom of a farmer's wife spilling over the edges of a three-legged stool as she milked. Since there were no fences or hedgerows, the cows grazed tethered to iron pegs. Summer days were punctuated by the sound of the pegs being beaten into the earth with stones as the cows were moved to new grazing. Water was drawn from wells in buckets and carried to the houses, none of which had a proper bathroom or running water in the kitchen. Bath day was Saturday. The following morning everyone set off to church, some walking, some cycling and some in horse-drawn carts. The lucky ones crowded into the ubiquitous *mały* [little] Fiat, one of the smallest cars ever produced.

By then I knew these farmers and their families. I had bought land from five of them, twelve small pieces in total, enough to give me a contiguous five hectares right next to the lake. Negotiating with them had not been easy. It had taken me nearly three years and countless bottles of vodka to put it all together from the patchwork of meadows, ploughed fields and forest the five of them owned. There were no discussions without a bottle of vodka, and I had dutifully plonked one down on the kitchen table of the farmhouse before discussions began. Despite eating several thick slices of bread spread thickly with butter beforehand, drinking with the farmers was hard work. Once we started, custom required that the bottle be drained to the last drop, a lot of vodka for two people to consume at a sitting.

By the time the bottle was empty, I sometimes had trouble remembering whether I was buying or selling, not to mention the way back to the caravan by the lake which was temporarily our home. Fortunately for the negotiations, after a bottle of vodka most of the villagers could also not remember whether they were buying or selling. I persevered, my Polish improving along with my negotiating skills, and slowly, piece by piece, I got the land on which I planned to build the lodge and create gardens, lawns and a park. The farmers sold in the end because I was paying well over the going rate and they wanted to buy tractors. Having watched them wrestle heavy ploughs behind a pair of massive horses, I understood why. Within days of signing the deeds in the notary's office and being paid cash in US dollars, they were driving second-hand Ursus tractors, no-nonsense machines assembled in a Communist-era plant on the outskirts of Warsaw. Not only did the tractors quickly replace horses for ploughing fields and hauling hay wagons, but some farmers also used their new purchases to drive the four kilometres to church in the village of Prokowo on Sundays. As many as five people packed themselves into the tiny cab, their breath fogging up the windscreen.

I understood why farmers were willing to exchange land for tractors but I doubted that any of them understood why a foreigner like me would trade life in a comfortable Western city, Vienna as it happened, for a new start on a piece of poor agricultural land at the end of a dirt road on the fringes of Europe. Few would have appreciated why I was tired of doing what I did for a living. Being a foreign correspondent and covering political upheavals, wars and famines had seemed a glamorous, exciting way to earn a living when I'd left New Zealand as an ambitious young journalist. Twenty-five years of living my dream had left me tired of the constant travel and of being under pressure of unforgiving deadlines.

After a brief foray into Asia as a young reporter, I'd gone to Africa and covered the slow overthrow of Emperor Haile Selassie in Ethiopia. I had also spent months of my life in Angola and Mozambique as Portuguese colonial rule ended, been one of just a handful of reporters to have witnessed the war in Rhodesia from the side of the black guerrillas and reported on the rise and fall of despots like Idi Amin. At times it had been a swashbuckling existence. I had crossed the border from Cameroon to Chad by canoe to report on one of Colonel Gadaffi's invasions and flown with a French bush pilot from Bamako to Timbuktu. During this time I had made homes in Nairobi, Lusaka and Harare and briefly owned a small farm in newly independent Zimbabwe.

Later I lived in Beirut for two years and chronicled the aftermath of the Israeli invasion, America's intervention in Lebanon and the rise of Hezbollah. I watched, crouched on the balcony of my apartment, as the militias drove the Lebanese army out of west Beirut. I was there, too, the night the battleship *New Jersey* shelled the hills around Beirut in a final, spiteful, show of strength as the US pulled out of Lebanon. The flashes from the ship's triple turrets lit up the horizon as shells weighing more than a ton sailed overhead, exploding somewhere in the mountains with a muffled roar. Countless times I had driven up through the Shouf Mountains and Bekaa Valley to Damascus, or boarded flights in Beirut to cover stories in Iran, Tunisia, Libya and Egypt. I had chased hijacked planes and ships around the Mediterranean and once I had made a hair-raising 2,500 kilometre dash by road from Tehran to Instanbul. Flights were full and I needed to file a scoop which would have landed me in jail, or worse, had I written and dispatched the story from Tehran. Later, when kidnappings made it impossible to live in Beirut, I moved to Cairo and an apartment in Zamalek with a fountain on the balcony. Ania, the Polish artist I had met three years earlier when she taught art at the University of Nigeria, joined me there when we married near the end of my time in the Middle East. It was Ania who introduced me to Poland; without her I would never have dreamt of building the lodge, let alone have realised the project.

After the Middle East, we spent two years in Latin America. I covered the war in Nicaragua between the Sandinistas and the American-backed Contras, drug wars in Colombia and illegal immigration and drug smuggling on the Mexican-US border, as well as the unpredictable General Noriega in Panama. I was seldom at home. When I was, I was generally recovering from a gastro-intestinal bug picked up on my travels. It was not a great life for a new bride and, after more than twenty years of covering the Third World, even I longed for a posting somewhere where the water was drinkable and where I could read the *International Herald Tribune* on the day it was published. In the spring of 1989 I persuaded my editors at *Time* to transfer me to Vienna and arrived by a stroke of good luck, perceived as cleverness on my part by some at *Time* in New York, at just the right time report on the collapse of Communism.

It was a whirlwind of a year which started with talks between the Communists and Solidarity in an old palace in Warsaw. The negotiations led to elections and the Polish Communist party's crushing defeat. They also led to the rapid dismantling of Communism across the rest of Eastern Europe. By Christmas, when Romania's long-time dictator Nicolae Ceauşescu was executed, even the Berlin Wall had come down. The Soviet Union's European empire was no more.

Yugoslavia then disintegrated and I made my way regularly to Belgrade, Ljubljana and Zagreb to chronicle the unravelling of this hotchpotch of Balkan states. Next was Sarajevo, the picturesque capital of Bosnia where frost blanketed the parked cars and fresh snow covered nearby Mount Trebević when I flew in from Belgrade for the first time. The most devastating conflict in Europe since the end of World War II, a conflict in which more than one hundred thousand people would die, had yet to start. But the coming war could be felt.

The previous summer I had gone to Kosovo with the Serb leader Slobodan Milošević and listened as he told thousands of Serbs gathered in a dusty field not far from Pristina that Kosovo was an integral part of Serbia. That was what the belligerent Serbs wanted to hear and they cheered him hoarsely, their defiance echoing over hills where the Turks had defeated them in battle centuries earlier and brought an easy-going and tolerant version of Islam to the shores of the Adriatic. Moslem Slavs in Bosnia were part of that Turkish tidemark of history. The Serbs hated them, a primitive, visceral hate that presaged the massacre of men and boys at Srebrenica, the rape and murder of women and the shelling of crowded streets and market places in Sarajevo. When you met and talked to their leader, Radovan Karadžić, you knew that bloodshed was not far off.

When I wrote that war was on its way, I sensed that it would be every bit as brutal and bitter as the conflict in Lebanon a decade earlier. I was living in Beirut then and had witnessed the cruelty and ultimate senselessness of it all at close quarters. I had also been a witness to history unfolding in blood and gore elsewhere in the Middle East, as well as in Africa and Latin America. The images wedged most tightly in my head were of innocent suffering: the small child squatting next to his dead mother, a fly-infested exit wound the size of a tennis ball in her back; the mangled remains of a family in a mortared home, twisted, broken limbs and eyes that stared reproachfully in death as if I, the witness, had launched the mortar. Even cleaned-up images of war's death and destruction were dispiriting: the tearful family washing the gravestone of an eighteen-year-old soldier in a cemetery on the outskirts of Tehran; the neatly laid-out row of body bags in Colombia that looked like kit waiting to be collected; the blackened ruins of a burnt-out house in Africa with bougainvillea already clambering up the remains of a brick fireplace which had kept a farmer's family warm in July.

Did I want to cover another war? Perhaps my number would come up as it had for some of my friends and colleagues, most recently David Blundy in El Salvador, where we had reported together. Was someone else's war worth losing your life for? Wasn't being a witness a waste of time? Weren't you just a voyeur, peeking in on someone's tragedy and then moving on? Your stories didn't change anything, not enough, anyway, to help those you wrote

20

about. There had to be more to life than being constantly on the move, climbing on and off aeroplanes as if they were local buses, spending months of every year in hotels and pounding out stories when normal people were with their families or out with friends sharing a bottle of wine or two with dinner.

A few years earlier I had rushed off to Romania from Vienna on Christmas Day when the news broke that the dictator Nicolae Ceaușescu and his wife had been tried secretly and executed. William and Johnny, two young sons from a previous marriage whom I rarely saw, had come to stay with me and Ania in our grand nineteenth-century Viennese house. It was to be our first Christmas together for years, and they were rightly crestfallen and uncomprehending as I rushed out the door.

If inconvenience and risk had been the only things nagging at me I'd probably have soldiered on until my pension or redundancy cheque came along. But, at forty-five, I was troubled by the fact that not only did I not belong anywhere, but I had also not created anything more than words on paper. The closest I had come to belonging since leaving New Zealand was in Africa, where I had played cricket for Zambia and later owned a small farm in Zimbabwe.

Potatoes and onions grew in the rich red soil of my land in Zimbabwe and I had battled to keep a resourceful python away from the chickens. I had planted and nurtured trees, built houses for the workers, and provided them with running water from a resurrected borehole. I had also built environmentally friendly dry toilets, previously unknown in their villages. In the evenings I had sat on the veranda of the house and watched the wood smoke rising from the huts below and the hills stretching out towards the Mozambique border. Sometimes I had imagined that this was home. But Africa offered no long-term future for white people. If I

21

needed a reminder that Zimbabwe was no different from elsewhere, it came in the form of distant drumming on still nights when there were only a few pinpricks of light in the vast plain below.

The subliminal message of danger and reproach that the drumming carried across the still, silent veldt was that you were the outsider, an interloper in the lives of people who had foraged across and farmed the sun-baked vastness of Africa long before white people like me had settled there. It didn't matter that we had improved the land, made farms work and bettered the lives of those working for us. In the end we were all – Indians, Europeans and sometimes even the Africans themselves – hostages to the whims of men like Idi Amin or Robert Mugabe or the capriciousness of nature itself. Africa was not my home and I was lucky to have sold my farm long before the expropriation of white farms began in 2000 and individual farmers, not to mention the country as a whole, left devastated and penniless

New Zealand was also not home any more. I had left it when I was just twenty for OE (Overseas Experience), a rite of passage for young New Zealanders that helps exorcise the cultural cringe often inherent in those who come from a small, distant place with a colonial background. Most of my generation spent a few years in London or elsewhere in Europe before returning home to marriage, children, mortgages and a pension plan. But many stayed on abroad, pleasantly surprised that they were as good as, and sometimes better than, their metropolitan cousins. As travel became easier, swifter and cheaper during the last decades of the twentieth century, more and more young people did not return from their OE, at least not permanently. They could get good, better-paying jobs, not only in Europe and America, but also in Asia. They could always fly home for Christmas and put off thinking about returning for good until they were older, richer and worldlier. By 2012 nearly twenty-five per cent of New Zealand's population, about one million people, lived outside the country. Only Ireland and Luxembourg in Europe have comparable percentages of their citizens living abroad.

I lost accent and innocence by degree over the years. While I enjoyed holidaying at home from time to time it was, as my wife put it, a long way out of town. New Zealand was wonderful when the pohutukawas were in bloom, there was fine, warm sand between your toes and a decent bottle of chilled Sauvignon Blanc waited in the cooler. But summer is almost as fleeting 'down under' as it in the northern hemisphere. Winters in New Zealand, especially in places like Taranaki where I had grown up, could be long, wet, chilly and windy. The climate, of course, was only a minor consideration. I would not be going there to retire; I was far too young to be thinking about ending my days in the sun and I hoped I would always be too young to want to gravitate towards a deckchair. My trouble with New Zealand was that I didn't fit in anymore because it was a different country and I was a different person.

So here I was, in 1993, under a birch tree on a small rise overlooking The White Lake in Kaszubia, Poland, with uncertainty gnawing at the confidence I had felt when I abandoned corporate life and spurned the opportunity to return to the country where I'd grown up. I was less sure now about the wisdom of either decision. A nice little *bach* [summer house] on a beach somewhere in New Zealand and lashings of familiarity and comfort suddenly seemed attractive. Even a job with a monthly cheque would be something. If only that bulldozer would stop ferreting about and the workmen in blue overalls and knitted woollen caps would just pack up and drive home in their Jelcz, we could call the whole thing off. I could then do something sensible with my life.

NOT WANTED ON VOYAGE

By early spring the following year I had largely forgotten about my moment of panic. Perhaps the stones and shells from Kaipara Harbour in New Zealand that we had buried in the foundations of the building were a reassuring link with the past. Perhaps my confidence had been bolstered by the fact that the building had gone up on schedule and to specification, and even the roof was on before winter set in.

Whatever it was, I was more excited than concerned as dawn broke one morning in early April with me prowling the forward deck of the cargo ship *Inowrocław* as it brushed aside a thin Baltic fog and slipped quietly past rows of cranes to a berth in the port of Gdynia near Gdańsk. Not far from where the ship docked there is a sail-like stone monument to Józef Teodor Konrad Korzeniowski, better known to English speakers as Joseph Conrad. His gaze is not out to sea, as one might expect of a seafarer who went on to write some of the most enduring books in the English language. Instead he is looking towards the city of Gdynia and the low, forested hills behind it. An inscription in Polish may explain why his back is to the sea: '*Nic tak nie nęci, nie rozczarowuje i nie zniewala jak życie na morzu.*' It's a line from *Lord Jim*, one of the best sea and redemption stories ever written. 'There is nothing more enticing, disenchanting and enslaving than the life at sea,' is how Conrad wrote it in English, his use of the definite article 'the' a tiny clue to the fact that English was not his first language.

Since there are no definite and indefinite articles in Polish, Poles have as much trouble deciding when and how to use these small words as Anglo-Saxons like me have with declining Polish nouns. I am reminded of this every time I fly out of Gdańsk airport. The standard airport warning not to leave bags unattended is followed by the sentence: 'The unattended bags will be destroyed.'

Conrad's mastery of written English was amazing for someone whose mother tongue was Polish and whose first foreign language was not English but French. He left occupied Poland when he was sixteen and spent two decades at sea during which he sailed frequently to the Far East and also to Africa and South America. His sole command was of the 345 ton barque *Otago*, named after a province in the South Island of New Zealand. Soon afterwards he left the sea and settled in England to write. I had been equally rootless as a foreign correspondent for a similar period and was now settling in Poland. It was not the first time our paths had crossed distantly and obliquely. As a correspondent I had visited and written about many of the places that inspired Conrad's best-known books, amongst them the Congo (*Heart of Darkness*), Colombia (*Nostromos*) and the Far East (*Lord Jim*).

The *Inowrocław* was not a sleek or pretty ship, grace of line having been sacrificed to the bulbous midriff and squat stern which enabled it to engorge or discharge hundreds of containers in a matter of hours. But, in the three days since we had boarded her in the northern British port of Middlesborough, I had grown attached to her chubby cheerfulness and stolid working-class disdain for frippery. The half dozen passenger cabins on the ship were large and simply furnished with the kind of plastic wood veneer that was found everywhere in Poland during the Communist era. The food was simple but plentiful. We seemed to be fed at least four or five times a day, starting with scrambled eggs, cheese and cold cuts of pork at breakfast and followed at regular intervals with soups, *pierogi* (a dumpling similar to Italian ravioli), *gołąbki* (cabbage leaf filled with rice and meat), roast pork and countless varieties of cake.

We had taken the *Inowrocław* across the North Sea and through the Kattegat into the Baltic because I had just emptied out and let my parent's house in a small village in Northumberland, only a dozen miles or so from where my mother had grown up and I had been born. My father had died the previous year and I had moved my mother to a smaller, more suitable place in the same village. I was bringing a lot of my father's things with me, everything from his paintings – watercolour landscapes of Northumberland and the English Lake District that had provided him with a living for the last twenty years of his life – to a chair he'd had in his architectural practice in New Zealand. I also had the cabin trunks with which we had sailed across the Atlantic to New York in 1950 and then the Pacific two years later when we sailed to New Zealand from the United States.

In bold letters on one of the trunks were the words 'Not wanted on voyage.' They had perturbed me as a child because I thought our family hadn't been wanted on the ship for some dark, distant and grown-up cause. When curiosity got the better of me years later and I asked, it was almost disappointing to find out that it was the trunks and not we that had not been wanted on the voyage from Vancouver to Auckland. Instead of being taken to our cabin somewhere close to the waterline, the trunks had been stored in the ship's hold.

With the same trunks stored in the hold of the *Inowrocław*, I held our six-month-old son Harley in my arms as I leant on the rail and looked out at the warehouses, factories and apartment buildings beyond the port. I suppose ships' rails and foreign ports are traditionally places for reflection. I thought of my parents on the deck of the SS *Ruahine* in 1952 as it slipped past Rangitoto Island and into Auckland Harbour. It was delivering them and their three small children to a new life far away from England and America, where my youngest brother had been born.

26

As my parents had no doubt done with us, I wondered how Harley would make out in this new land. It would probably be easier for him than for me. Polish would be his first language. He would also naturally assimilate the culture and spirit of the place as the children of immigrants mostly do. I would find it harder. However, I had lived enough of my life being tossed around in other languages and cultures not to be phased by it. Harley had been born only a few miles from the terraced house in the western part of Newcastle where I'd drawn my first breath. He had been baptised in the same church in Newcastle as me, in the same silk, hand-embroidered baptismal smock that I, my mother and two earlier generations of our family had worn. It was so old that my mother had to 'borrow' it from the museum in Northumberland to which it had been donated a few years earlier.

'Just make sure that you don't spill anything on it,' she fussed as Ania prepared Harley for the christening. 'The cloth is so fine and worn that we won't be able to wash it.' Harley promptly brought up part of his last feed and was whisked off to the bathroom by Ania while I diverted my mother's attention. There was further continuity in the fact that my new son had been given my father's name and spent the first few months of his life in the same house in which my father had spent the last years of his. But Harley's mother tongue would be Polish, not English. I wondered whether one day he would be embarrassed by his father's accent and mistakes with Polish grammar or, even worse, that his father spoke to him in English. I remembered Basia, the Polish girl I had known as a child in New Zealand, and how embarrassed she had been whenever her parents spoke to her in Polish in front of her friends.

I remembered, too, other immigrants who had found their way to New Plymouth, not we Britons who endured little more than the stigma of being *Poms*, but those to whom the English language, not to mention culture and tradition, were so alien. They were people with names like Imre or Atilla who had fled Hungary after the abortive 1956 uprising, or the Václavs and Jiřís who had forsaken Czechoslovakia after 1968. They wore flamboyant clothes, smoked pungent cigarettes, brutalised the English language and jabbered incomprehensibly amongst themselves. As children we ignorantly and smugly derided them, secure not only in the knowledge that God was an Anglo-Saxon and that New Zealand was God's own, but also in a lingering conviction that Britannia, or at least its offspring, America, still ruled the waves.

Now here I was brutalising someone else's language, stumbling verbally over groups of consonants that seemed to have been thrown together so haphazardly that when pronounced, they sounded like the swish of feet on a ballroom floor. How, for example, to pronounce Wrzeszcz, the name of a town not far from where the *Inowrocław* was docking and the place where the Nobel Prize-winning author Gunther Grass had been born and much of *The Tin Drum* is set? And how to get a firm grip on the slithery nouns of the Polish language, nouns that not only had a nominative form but an accusative, genitive, dative, locative, instrumental and vocative form. Even proper nouns had their own regulated metamorphosis. So 'John' in the nominative (i.e. the subject of the sentence) becomes 'Johnem' in the instrumental form (as in, *I went to Warsaw with John*) and 'Johna' in the genitive (as in, *John isn't here*). Dictionaries were not much help if you looked up nouns in other than the nominative case. Dog is a good example. In the nominative case it is *pies* (pronounced pee-ess). But it becomes *psa* in the genitive (as in, *there isn't a dog*) and *psem* in the instrumental (as in *I went for a walk with the dog*). There is no separate entry for either *psa* or *psem* in a Polish dictionary.

Unlike the Polish, Hungarian and Czech immigrants to New Zealand after World War II who were forced to use English, I found many Poles willing to speak to me in my own language. Some were keen to improve their English, others to spare themselves my waywardness with their own language. I was a privileged immigrant and I wasn't poor, tired or yearning to be free. I was looking for adventure and, when we docked in Gdynia in 1994, Poland was one of the world's new frontiers. Fifty years of Communism had laid waste to the land and the human spirit. When the system collapsed in 1989 everything was overgrown, run-down and dispirited. Poles were rebuilding their country with energy and enthusiasm. It was exciting for me to be joining them in pushing back the frontiers, just as immigrants to the Americas and the Antipodes had done at different times and in different circumstances.

The frontier beckoned as much for my wife as it did for me. Ania had left a Soviet-dominated Poland to teach art at the University of Nigeria just a few weeks before martial law was declared in 1981. She was lucky to have left when she did. When martial law was declared, the borders were closed and it was months before travel became possible again. Since World War II it had never been a simple or risk-free matter to leave or return to Poland and, once back, you had to turn in your passport. Holding one was not a right but a privilege the state could withdraw at any time and for any reason.

I was with Ania in 1987 when she returned to Poland from our home in Mexico City to visit her parents. She dutifully handed in her passport and then immediately applied to get it back, since we planned to leave in just a few days. She was in tears when she returned to her parents' house from the passport office. 'I had to go to a meeting with the police special branch,' she sobbed. 'The man told me I could have the passport only if I agreed to help them by getting information from you and giving it to their people in Mexico City.'

'What sort of information?' I asked in disbelief. When Ania related what had happened I was even more astonished. At the passport office in Kartuska Street in Gdańsk she had been ushered into a sparsely furnished room with a desk, a filing cabinet and two chairs. Behind the desk sat a middle-aged man in a grey suit. A file containing Ania's passport and other documents was open in front of him. He leafed through the papers and told her that they knew she was living in Mexico City and that her husband was a correspondent with *Time* and responsible for the magazine's coverage of Latin America. They would like her to find out what I knew about certain things and people and relay the information to their man in Mexico City. She would use the code name Dolores when calling the Polish Embassy in Mexico City to set up a meeting at a shopping mall not far from where we lived. Her handler would be reading a copy of the newspaper *El Universal* and there would be a password and response so that she could be sure she had made contact with the right person. Ania was being asked to spy on me and to pass on information to Polish intelligence. If she didn't want to co-operate, the man told her, there was no certainty that she would get her passport back and be able to return to Mexico City with me. Whatever she decided, he warned, I was not to know of their approach.

At first I was angry. Asking someone to spy on their husband seemed grubby spy-craft. Threatening to withhold Ania's passport unless she co-operated was crude blackmail. I thought of complaining to the press office at the Polish Foreign Affairs Ministry in Warsaw and, if that didn't work, asking someone at the United States Embassy to talk directly to the Minister's office. But the code name, newspaper and password seemed such parodies of spy-craft that my anger turned to amusement. If they'd done the simplest of checks they would have known that Ania would be a terrible spy. She was far too honest and loyal to poke around in my notebooks or attempt to extract information from me in whispered pillow talk. In any event, I knew nothing that could possibly be of interest to Polish intelligence. All my reporting about Latin America finished up in stories available to anyone who took out a fifty-dollar annual subscription to *Time*.

'Look Ania, here's what you should do,' I said. 'Go back to them tomorrow and tell them your husband is happy to tell the Polish Ambassador in Mexico City everything he knows about politics in Central America. I only have one condition; that the ambassador buys me a decent lunch. Emphasise the good lunch part.'

Like other foreign correspondents, I frequently had lunch with diplomats from different countries at which we swapped notes about everything from a president's health to the implications of a recent cabinet reshuffle. Sometimes I'd find out something really interesting and it would form the basis of a story, occasionally even a scoop. Sometimes I had information that I was about to publish that was interesting to a diplomat. Journalists and diplomats were all supposed to be well informed and we fed off each other. I'd have been happy to have the Polish Ambassador as one of my contacts, but the low-level apparatchiks who were blackmailing Ania probably didn't know that this was the way things worked in the West.

The next day Ania returned with a smile. She'd met the *Służba Bezpieczeństwa* (SB), or State Security man, and told him what I proposed.

'What did he say?' I asked eagerly.

'He didn't say anything except that I could have my passport,' she said.

31

I was never taken to lunch by the Polish Ambassador to Mexico and Ania was not contacted by anyone from Polish intelligence or even the embassy. It's probably just as well. However innocent lunching with the ambassador would have been, it was the kind of encounter that might have set malicious tongues wagging at some future stage of my life, especially now that I was planning to live in Poland. The Polish Parliament had passed its first lustration bill in 1992 and the hunt was on for all those who had co-operated with the SB during the Communist era. I could imagine the difficulty of explaining away, as many innocent Poles found themselves doing, an entry from a special branch file which read something like this: 'Borrell has agreed to supply information to our ambassador in Mexico City. The fact that he has a Polish wife who returns periodically to Poland and needs a passport to travel abroad makes him a willing and possibly useful informant.'

Amongst those suspected of working for Polish intelligence during the Communist era were journalists like Ryszard Kapuściński, whose reportage from Africa, Iran and Central America brought him considerable literary success in the West. I first met Ryszard during the civil war in Angola in 1975. This was long before publication in 1983 of the English translation of *The Emperor*, the book on Ethiopia's Haile Selassie which made him famous. In 1989 I lived next door to him in Warsaw and we met occasionally to talk about what was happening in Poland. I once commissioned him to write an essay for *Time* on Lech Wałęsa and the Solidarity trade union movement which had played a pivotal role in bringing the Communist era to an end. The piece he wrote was a big disappointment to me and an even bigger one to my editors in New York. It was never published. Ryszard did not even mention his own decision to quit the Communist Party after Solidarity was proscribed and martial law declared in 1981. He

32

also didn't explore, as I had suggested, the dichotomy of the Soviet Union's support for liberation movements in Africa, some of which Ryszard had eulogised in his reports, and Soviet hostility towards those seeking freedom closer to home.

Ryszard was uncomfortable with subjects like this. He had joined the youth wing of the Polish Communist Party in 1948 and became a fully fledged member a few years later. Being a Party member helped land him a job as a correspondent abroad for *PAP*, the state-owned news agency. Before he went to Africa in the 1960s, he was briefed by Polish intelligence and asked to keep an eye on American companies and institutions in Africa. He would be able to identify Polish intelligence personnel abroad, he was told, because they would approach him with the salutation 'Greetings from Zygmund.' He was to reply 'Has he sold the car?' before passing on any information he had. There is no evidence from files released during the lustration process that he was ever approached in this way in Africa or that he fed any information to Polish intelligence. The files suggest however that he did write reports for them when he was living in Mexico City. That was long before I was assigned there and Ania was asked to spy on me, so our paths never crossed in Latin America.

Much has been made in Poland of this collaboration but his detractors seldom put his limited assistance to Polish intelligence in any sort of context. For someone born in 1932 in Pinsk, then on the eastern border of Poland and now in Belarus, becoming a Communist after World War II was more natural than people today might imagine. As a child he watched first the Soviets and then the Nazis murder and deport Poles from the borderlands. He had been poor, hungry and terrified and had learned that standing up to implacable forces got you nowhere. You survived by being quiet, going with the flow and applauding whoever happened to be driving by in the victory parade. Brave, principled people got killed or went to jail, generally a death sentence in itself. Once the Communists came to power, plum jobs went to party members who were expected to be loyal to all the organs of state, including the intelligence services. Had he not been willing to work with them, Ryszard would not have been sent abroad. But I doubt that he made a much better spy than Ania would have been, or that he was ever in possession of any more secret or sensational information than I was privy to.

My ruminations at the ship's forward railing ended as the *Inowrocław*'s engines went silent and the bow opened up to discharge the cargo of containers and a few vehicles, our Jeep amongst them. It was stuffed inside and on the roof rack with boxes and suitcases. We must have looked like refugees as we drove ashore and, after clearing customs, the forty kilometres to Sytna Góra. It was a beautiful spring day, warm, still and bursting with new life. Fruit trees were in blossom and there were splashes of yellow dandelions in meadows and on roadsides. Fields of rye which had lain dormant during the harsh winter were greening up. Black and white cows grazed in the fields. I wound the windows down and said to Ania: 'Go on, breathe deeply. It's your first Polish spring for years.'

Ania hadn't been with me when I'd returned to Poland during the autumn and winter of 1993 to keep an eye on progress at the building site and to release successive tranches of money to the builder as the work progressed and our architect signed off on it. Having seen photographs of the work in progress, she knew what to expect as we crested the hill near the old birch tree. Still, she gulped and said: 'Is that ours? It looks so big.'

Considering there'd never been anything there before, there was indeed a lot of building in the field below. It was still a construction site with a large yellow crane and a workmen's cabin in what was to be the courtyard. But the piles of soil which had once been everywhere had been levelled out to make a large terrace. There were two buildings, both with burnt-orange tiles on the roof and whitewashed walls. We'd built them at right angles to each other to take advantage of different lake views and to create a courtyard which would later be closed in by a third building. The winter had been too harsh to work through, but doors and windows had been put in after the thaw and the two structures looked more or less finished from the outside.

The access road had been improved in the autumn and was now more than just two tracks running through a field. We drove down it slowly, neither of us saying anything. Marek, our architect, was waiting for us. He had been at school with Ania, and had been patient with us as he translated our rough, back-of-the-envelope ideas into something buildable. He had also obtained all the necessary permits and approvals, not an easy matter in a country where many council officials, especially then, expected bribes in return for their signatures and official rubber stamps. Marek, like us, opposed the paying of bribes. He had simply worn the officials down. He greeted us effusively, kissing Ania three times on the cheeks, ruffling Harley's wispy hair and shaking my hand firmly. 'Come and see the interior, Ania,' he said. 'They are still working on it so careful where you step.'

Inside, walls and ceilings were being plastered, a wet, messy job that had to be done before the floors were laid or interior doors fitted. We stepped around plastic containers of plaster to get to the French windows leading to where the terrace would be. Two beech trees had been felled in the winter to create a gap in the trees that grew on the escarpment. The lake sparkled in the sunshine and we stood there for some time admiring the view and feeling a little smug at having chosen such a perfect place to build.

While Ania and Marek checked out the two buildings room by room, I drove to the farmhouse of the Frankowski family. A year earlier I had persuaded Janek to build a large garage next to his barn. I'd paid for all the materials and his labour and had agreed to turn the whole thing over to him once we moved into the lodge. In the meantime, we were using it to store all the furniture we had trucked up from our last home in Vienna. It also garaged the nine-metre-long caravan that had been our temporary summer home in a meadow by the lake while we were buying land and getting ready to build. This year I wanted to set up the caravan on a flat piece of ground behind the house. We would live in it until we could move into the lodge.

Janek was the son of Leon Frankowski, a hard-working and resourceful farmer who had wrested a living for his family of six from the sandy Kaszubian soils. He set up his two sons and a son-in-law on farms around Sytna Góra; no mean feat during the Communist era when being a success incited envy and could attract the attentions of local party officials. Leon was now in his seventies but he still farrowed fields with a horse and got down on his knees at harvest time to help the family gather in the potatoes. He would also take a sledge drawn by two horses to the nearest shops during the winter, the bells on the horses' collars tinkling as he went.

Once, when I had just driven to Poland from France, I met Leon in the narrowest part of the lane just outside Sytna Góra. I wound down the window to say hello and proffered my hand. 'Where are you coming from this time?' he asked.

'France,' I replied. 'We've been in Normandy.'

'Normandy,' he replied, 'I've been there.'

I wondered whether I had misheard him. Many people of Leon's age in Kaszubia hadn't even been to Warsaw, let alone abroad. If he

36

had said he'd been to Germany I'd have been less surprised yet still curious. But France? Normandy?

'You've really been there?' I asked.

'In 1944,' he said. 'I remember it well.'

'What were you doing in Normandy in 1944,' I asked.

'Chasing French girls and shooting at the British and Americans,' he said, a twinkle in his eye. 'I wasn't very good at either.'

And then it clicked. Leon had been one of the tens of thousands of young Poles drafted into the *Werhmacht* during World War II. The Pomeranian region where he was born was part of Germany at the start of the war. The uncle of one of Poland's longest-serving prime ministers, Donald Tusk, had also been drafted into the *Werhmacht*. During one election campaign an opposition politician had tried to make an issue of it, suggesting that Tusk's family had been traitorous. Fortunately most Poles are more conversant with their history than the politician and he was thoroughly, and rightly, ridiculed by the press and even by politicians in his own party. Tens of thousands of Polish-speaking Pomeranian farm boys like Leon had simply been called up shortly after the start of the war and spent the next five years in German uniforms.

'You are lucky they sent you to the Western Front and not to the Eastern Front,' I said.

'I wouldn't be here today if I'd been sent to Russia,' he replied. He knew that, if he hadn't been killed in Leningrad or Stalingrad, cold or hunger would probably have got him. If he'd fallen into Russian hands he would have been shot.

Janek, the diminutive of Jan or John, was Leon's oldest son. He had inherited much of his father's resourcefulness. With just twelve hectares of land, he was the farmer with the largest landholding in the hamlet of Sytna Góra. But what really set him apart from his neighbours was his skill with his hands. He repaired his own tractor and the rest of his farm machinery and had just built himself a new two-storey concrete-block house to replace the thatched *chata* [cottage] in which he'd grown up.

'So you've come back,' Janek said as I shook hands with him in the kitchen where his wife, Teresa, was clearing up after lunch. 'We were wondering when you would come.'

They made me coffee and I sat with them while I drank it, telling them about England and the voyage on the *Inowrocław*. Neither Jan nor Teresa had been much further than Gdańsk and Gdynia so they were happy to hear of other places, and details like the price of food and clothing and how much people earned.

Like other Poles at the time, especially country people, they thought everyone from Western Europe and America was rich. In Kaszubia, they even used the word *Ameryka* as an adjective in place of 'beautiful' or 'wonderful' to describe anything that was fancy, well-made or unobtainable. That was the word Janek had used when he saw the caravan I had bought in Vienna, a sleek aluminium capsule with a bedroom, kitchen, shower room and dining table. '*Ameryka*,' he exclaimed, not once but several times, as he opened drawers and cupboards and folded down the table to make another bed.

Now I was asking him to hook the caravan up to a tractor and tow it two hundred and fifty metres to the flat patch of meadow on the other side of the house. This meadow had once been Janek's and he had sometimes planted potatoes there, ploughing the steep sloping parts with a horse. At other times it had been a pasture whose steepest parts had to be cut with a scythe. Janek had struck a hard bargain for the meadow and adjacent strip of forest, forcing me at the last moment to raise the price. By then I had learned that a handshake didn't seal a deal, as it probably would have done in New Zealand. A deal was not a deal, especially when it came to buying or selling land, until you sat down in front of a notary public, signed and paid.

The caravan, parked and hooked up to the electricity, was going to be our home until mid-summer when the lodge would be finished and the builders would hand over the keys. There was a lot to do to get the caravan ready, especially as we would be sharing it with five-month-old Harley, a fussy eater and poor sleeper. He suffered from colic and a skin rash and the well water was going to be too hard and full of minerals for his delicate skin. So I would haul buckets of soft water up the hill from the lake for his bath and to wash his nappies. The lake water was so soft and pure that local people swore by it for washing, using their horses to haul big metal barrels of it back to their houses.

PICKLED CABBAGE

A large awning, custom-made to fit onto the side of the caravan, doubled our covered living area and made our temporary home comfortable. One part of the covered outdoors was turned into a laundry, where we washed Harley's nappies in the plastic baby bath. There seemed always to be nappies hanging on the line outside to dry, and there were occasions during the first month when we thought we would give up on towelling diapers and switch to disposables. It seemed a particularly good idea when I had clambered halfway up the steep escarpment from the lake with two large buckets of lake water for the third time in one day.

Once, as I paused halfway up the escarpment, my heart pounding, I remembered wash day on the farm at Mangorei near New Plymouth, which had been our first home in New Zealand. With three children under the age of five, one of them still only a few months old, my mother did a big wash twice a week. This meant firing up the old copper in the outhouse. One of my earliest memories is of the crackling of dry macrocarpa kindling as the fire under the copper took hold. The macrocarpa (Monterey Cypress in California) is a big, sprawling, untidy tree which was grown in windbreaks on most New Zealand farms in the 1950s. A dark, gloomy plantation shielded the milking shed on our farm. I hated walking through it in the early morning half-light because the huge branches creaked and groaned in even the lightest of breezes. I was sure it was haunted and that one day a gnarled branch would reach out and pluck me off the path. The best place for macrocarpa, I felt, was in a fire.

While the water in the copper heated up, my mother would soak the clothes in soapy water in two large galvanised iron tubs. Then she would take the most stained items, nappies amongst them, and rub them vigorously on a wooden washing board before depositing them into the now boiling copper. Fifteen to twenty minutes later, she would remove the steaming clothes with a stick and plunge them into a concrete tub half-full of cold water, pumping them up and down with gloved hands. At this stage the 'blue bag', which made whites 'extra-white', would be added to the water. Finally everything would go into another tub of clean water for the last rinse before the wash was pegged out on rope lines in the back garden. Doing a wash took all morning and had to be done while at the same time ensuring that three under-fives didn't get too near to the boiling copper, crush a sibling's hand in the mangle or wander off and fall into the septic tank. Despite her vigilance, my middle-brother, Peter, did manage to impale his foot with a pitchfork on one occasion and let us all know with piercing screams. By the time my father came home in the evening, the laundry would have been taken from the line, folded and damped down ready for ironing after supper, if my mother still had the strength, or more probably the following morning. My mother ironed everything, nappies included, and would have been ashamed to put a creased t-shirt on one of us, even though she knew it would be stained and ready for the wash again within hours, sometimes just minutes, of slipping it over our heads.

Remembering my mother's wash days on the farm made me ashamed of my momentary twinge of self-pity at the steepness of the hill, the heaviness of the buckets and the frequency with which my son soiled his nappies. We had decided on towelling nappies for Harley because it seemed ridiculous that millions of tons of disposable nappies, diapers to Americans, finished up in landfills each year. I washed the nappies by hand in cold or slightly warm water since there was no copper to fire up. There was also no washing 'blue' to add to the first rinse. I didn't mind if the nappies weren't lily-white and I certainly didn't iron them.

Disposable nappies, long in use in Western countries, were only just becoming available in Poland. I'd met an American venture capitalist a little earlier who'd told me they were buying into a company that was planning to make and market some of the first disposable diapers in Poland. I told her that I didn't think they would take off, that people wouldn't pay the extra money for the convenience. I should have known better. One of the main reasons for Communism's demise was the system's inability to produce consumer goods in sufficient quantity and of a high enough standard to keep people happy. Most people, I believe, would have swapped lots of personal freedoms and rights for shops full of things like toilet paper, nappies and sanitary towels.

On my first visit to Poland in the winter of 1986 I had brought expensive whisky, chocolate and oranges with me from Cairo as presents for Ania's parents, my future in-laws. Poles could get cognac and chocolate in the state-owned Pewex stores which sold luxury goods for foreign exchange, which the family had after working in Ghana and Nigeria. But oranges were mostly unobtainable. An orange in Communist Poland went a long way. First you ate it, probably not all at once as people elsewhere might have done, but in small pieces. You could impress friends by decorating a cake with it. The peel wasn't thrown away; it was chopped up finely and dried for use later as flavouring in cakes. It could also be sliced into strips and boiled, once to get rid of the bitterness and then again with a little sugar to make a syrup. You could also pour 94% proof alcohol over the peel and let it steep for a few months to make a spirit drink Poles call *nalewka*.

42

Since few foodstuffs were consistently available in the shops, Poles had become proficient at making and storing food at home. Ania's parents had two kitchens in their house, one on the first floor, next to the dining room, where meals were prepared on special family occasions or for guests, the second down a narrow flight of stairs in the basement whcre the family ate at a large pine table. The kitchen and table were also used each year to prepare copious amounts of pickled and bottled food for the winter. A two-hundred-litre barrel of *kapusta kiszona* [pickled cabbage] was prepared each October or November. It was a big undertaking. The cabbages had to be shredded finely and then packed in salt in the barrel. Juniper berries, caraway seeds and bay leaves were added and the barrel left for a month or two in a dark place while the contents fermented. Every so often foam on the top had to be skimmed off and the fermenting cabbage stirred. The smell of fermenting cabbage used to pervade Polish houses in the autumn and often throughout the winter, but not any longer. Very few people make their own *kapusta kiszona*, now that it can be found in shops and supermarkets throughout the year.

In September, hundreds of bottles of pickled cucumbers and mushrooms were sealed and put away for the winter. Mushrooms, especially the coveted *prawdziwki* (*boletus edulis* in Latin, *cep* in French or *porcini* in Italian) were sliced, dried in an oven or a warm place and bottled or sealed in plastic bags for use in soups and sauces during the winter. Fruit of all kinds was also sliced, boiled with sugar and bottled. Nothing that grew in the garden or in the gardens of friends or neighbours was wasted. Even the petals of the wild dog rose (*Rosa canina*) were collected, ground up with a pestle and turned into a sweet jam filling for *rogaliki*, little pastries which were served with tea. Rose hips from the dog rose were also collected in October after the first frost. They were cut in half and the seeds scraped out before being cooked with sugar and then bottled. The bottles for preserving were all of different sizes and were used year after year, the original labels slowly disappearing until the jars became anonymous.

My own family used to have a pantry full of bottled fruit by the time winter set in. As a child in the late 1950s I would accompany my father on what we called 'expeditions' to the lower slopes of Mount Taranaki to pick blackberries from unruly wild patches along the sides of quiet country roads and in farmers' fields. We used small aluminium milk billycans to collect the blackberries, which my mother boiled with added slices of apple and some sugar before bottling. Throughout the winter, blackberry and apple pie served with lashings of cream was a family favourite, with fierce competition between my brothers and me for the crispy pastry on what we called the 'bone', the glass cone which held the pastry up in the middle of the dish.

By the 1980s the amount of preserving done by families in the West had declined dramatically, especially amongst city dwellers and professionals. Preserved fruits and jams as well as pickled cabbage or beetroot could all be bought in shops and supermarkets. Unless vast quantities of any of these things were required, it was cheaper and a lot easier to shop for them than to prepare them at home. That wasn't the case in Poland and the rest of the Communist bloc, where state-run factories and distribution chains were unable to maintain a reliable supply of consumer goods. No one knew whether there would be strawberry jam in February or pickled cucumbers in March or toilet paper, even the roughest and scratchiest kind, at any time of the year.

People like Ania's parents, both architects and part of Poland's *inteligencja*, grew as much of their own fruit and vegetables as they could and rolled up their sleeves each autumn for the hard work of preparing cabbage, beetroot, cucumbers and fruit of all kinds to be preserved for the winter. They were used to hard work and getting by on very little, as were most Poles who had been children during World War II. Two periods abroad as architects in Ghana and Nigeria had enabled them to save enough money to buy a Mercedes and a plot of land on a lake in Kaszubia, where they were building a summer house for their retirement. Marian, Ania's father, was doing almost all the work himself, as he had many years earlier when he built the family home in the Gdańsk suburb of Oliwa. The walls of the ground floor of the summer house were made of stones he had hauled up from the lake, faced with a stone chisel and then plastered into place with such skill and precision that even today people are amazed at the quality of the work. It was a constant battle to get cement, timber or other building supplies in Poland at that time. In the summer I would find Marian sunburned and in an old pair of shorts, carefully straightening bent and slightly rusty nails with a hammer and a small metal plate.

'What can you say about a system that can't even produce enough nails to satisfy demand?' he would sigh. 'We make and even export steel, so we have plenty of the raw materials for nails. But you can almost never find them for sale anywhere. Maybe we send them all to Russia or somewhere else.' Years after Marian died, Ania and I found a box full of bent and rusty old nails that he had been planning to straighten.

It was therefore a luxury for us to be debating the merits of towelling nappies versus disposables in 1993. The latter were at last available, if not widely so. Four years since the collapse of Communism, private enterprise was slowly filling stores with goods that had previously been unavailable. At first, they had been hauled into Poland in private cars and vans as budding entrepreneurs with a little capital drove to Germany and paid cash for consumer goods they felt could be sold for a higher price in Poland.

A friend of ours who started out this way was later so successful that he sold a car leasing company he had developed from scratch to General Motors. A few years later, after the crash of 2008 when General Motors needed cash, he bought it back at a price which left him with a big profit. Even today he shakes his head in disbelief when recounting the story. 'If someone had told me in 1989 that I'd one day buy a company from General Motors, I'd have thought him completely crazy.'

Later on, more conventional import and distribution channels were developed and foreign companies like Johnson & Johnson and Procter & Gamble began manufacturing and distributing household-name products throughout Poland. Coca-Cola and Pepsi arrived more or less at the same time and foreign breweries swooped down on old state-owned companies up for sale because they needed massive modernisation. French and American companies battled each other for a foothold in the telecommunications market which took off in the early 1990s. Within a short time French and German supermarket chains were opening stores in Poland. Ikea was an early arrival too, perceived then as a purveyor of luxury home furnishings. We bought French tiles for the roof of the lodge because those made in Poland had a reputation for falling apart after a decade or so. We also bought a French fireplace for the guest lounge in the main building and Danish stoves for the three apartments in the second building. To buy the cast-iron French fireplace we had to contact the importer in Warsaw, three hundred and sixty kilometres away, since no one in Gdańsk had them. Trust being in short supply in the business world in 1993, payment in advance was the rule. I eventually persuaded the supplier to collect the cash at the time of installation, even though that still meant me making a special trip to Warsaw to withdraw the money from my bank.

I banked in Warsaw because a bank there offered accounts in both US dollars and Polish złoty. Having a US dollar account was important. The farmers I was buying land from had little faith in the złoty and insisted on being paid in US dollars – and in cash, since none of them had bank accounts. They had good reason not to trust the złoty. High inflation in the 1980s and early 1990s meant that by 1992 the Central Bank was printing one and even two million złoty notes. Big denominations were hard to find. If you needed to withdraw a sizeable sum, the bank gave you bundles of smaller denomination notes. One American dollar was worth close to ten thousand złoty in 1993. I would have needed hundreds of millions of złoty for a single land transaction and a small suitcase to carry it in, so I was used to making a four-hour train journey to Warsaw to withdraw dollars, once nearly twenty thousand dollars in one hundred dollar bills. I was always careful to ensure I wasn't followed when I left the bank.

When Ania and I started buying furniture for the apartments in the lodge that summer, there was still little choice in the shops. I was pleased when I found a state-owned furniture producer in the nearby city of Słupsk. Almost everything it produced was exported, which meant that its range was better designed than anything made solely for the Polish market. But it was still trapped in the time-warp of Communist-era quotas, disdain for customers and a reluctance to sell. A long trek through the Dickensian factory in the company of a grumpy salesman ended in a dusty warehouse, where beds and other furniture were unwrapped for inspection. When I placed an order, the salesman said I could pick up the beds the following week. I called him a week later and the beds were indeed ready. But there were no mattresses. 'Call back in a week,' he said. I did. 'Sorry, we have the mattresses now, but there are no beds.' It was a month before beds and mattresses were available at the same time.

When I eventually picked up the order, the salesman couldn't bring himself to apologise for the delays. His elegy for Communist-era central planning was eloquent enough though: 'Don't worry. The factory is being privatised. Things will get better.'

On my way back from Słupsk one day with a trailer-load of beds, I found a small company making couches and lounge chairs for export to Germany in an old chicken shed outside a small village. This was not a former state-owned firm, but a private enterprise start-up. They were keener to sell than the state-owned factory and even offered me tea before I went into the factory to choose the fabrics. This level of customer service was almost unknown, even in big cities like Warsaw. I ordered some couches and they were delivered on time.

Cristy, a banker friend in the capital who was a frequent visitor to the lodge soon after we opened, told me of her experience in visiting the glitzy main street store of one of Poland's leading fashion houses: 'The two assistants carried on talking to each other when I entered the store – no good afternoons or anything like that. In fact the only words they spoke to me during the ten minutes I was there were *nie ma* [there aren't any] or *nie wiem* [I don't know], in response to my questions.' We agreed that it was so unusual and refreshing to be treated courteously as a customer, you almost felt obliged to buy when it happened.

The fledgling enterprises like the furniture factory that were then popping up all over Poland had their roots in the small private businesses tolerated during the Communist era. Carpenters and blacksmiths, for example, existed in towns and villages across Poland. They made everything from furniture to window frames and doors. If you needed a wooden floor or ceiling they cut and prepared the boards. Many of them did very high quality work and were the antithesis of the state-run concerns that turned out most of the country's manufactured goods. There the attitude was, as workers themselves would often say only partly in jest, 'They pretend to pay us, and we pretend to work.'

In the nearest village to us, Pomieczyńska Huta, there was both a carpenter and a blacksmith. Czesław Szwaba, then in his sixties, was in the process of turning over his carpentry business to his only son, Wojciech. The business was small. There was a kiln for drying timber and then four rooms with lathes, saws, and planers of various kinds. When I went to see Szwaba one day he invited me into the kitchen of the small, single-storey house next to the *stolarnia* [carpentry shop] where he lived with his wife, Helena, and Wojciech. We sat at a small table with a plastic tablecloth and drank thick, soupy village coffee made by pouring boiling water over ground coffee and leaving it to soak up water and sink to the bottom of the cup. If you sipped too early, you would get a mouthful of coffee grains.

'So, *Pan* John, how is the building coming along. Have they finished the plastering?' Szwaba asked, sliding a sugar bowl towards me and turning down the volume on the small radio on the windowsill. *Pan* and the female counterpart *Pani* are honorifics. Literally translated, they mean lord or lady. Since everyone is a *Pan* or *Pani*, they serve the purpose of Mr or Mrs in English. However, moving from the *wy* (formal you) to the *ty* (informal you) in Polish, and therefore from the honorific *Pan* or *Pani* to first names, is complicated. It is even more complicated than moving from the formal *vous* to the familiar second person singular *tu* in French. It is not good form in Poland to say 'Hello Jacek' to someone to whom you have just been introduced, as an American or Antipodean would do. Getting on first name terms is often only achieved after several meetings and even then after the third or fourth glass of wine or vodka. One person will say, 'I'm Piotr, may

I call you Jacek?' Once that hurdle is jumped, you are not only on first name terms, but can use the more familiar second person singular rather than the formal second person plural. The stiffness and formality of the honorific is slowly breaking down, especially among younger people. Back then, by calling me *Pan* John, Szwaba was already moving our relationship from the formal (*Pan* Borrell) to a halfway house of familiarity.

Michael Kaufman, a fellow correspondent I first met in Africa, had grown up in New York speaking Polish in family settings. His Jewish parents had luckily emigrated from Poland just before World War II. After his assignment in Africa and another in India, the *New York Times* posted Michael to Poland where he was surprised to find that he could cobble together whole sentences in serviceable Polish. But since he had only ever used Polish within the family, at the beginning of his posting to Warsaw he astonished government ministers, well-known dissidents like Lech Wałęsa and prominent priests by addressing them in the familiar second person *ty*. The equivalent would be a reporter using *tu* rather than *vous* in addressing a minister in the French government. Michael very quickly learnt to use the formal second person plural in the appropriate setting and was an impressive best man at Ania's and my wedding in a state registry office in Wrzeszcz in 1986.

His mistakes were considerably less egregious than mine. Soon after arriving I asked my wife for the Polish word for envelopes. '*Koperty*,' she told me. The following day I set off to Kartuzy to buy two big envelopes. '*Poproszę*,' I said to the girl in the stationery store, '*dwie duże kobiety*.' She looked at me, stunned. Someone behind me sniggered. I repeated my request, pointing to a box of envelopes behind the counter. '*Koperty*,' she said, smiling and clearly relieved. The customer behind me laughed. '*Kobiety*,' I suddenly remembered, was the Polish word for women. My malapropism was embarrassing but funny. I had asked for two big women instead of two big envelopes.

Other linguistic and cultural differences were revealing themselves to me as we prepared to open the lodge. Service everywhere in Poland was indifferent and, in public offices, often unhelpful. When I wanted to renew my permanent residence card, I called the immigration office in Gdańsk to ask exactly what documents I would need for the application. I turned up with all the documents they had asked for only to be told that I needed two additional papers. 'Why didn't you tell me when I called?' I asked, exasperated. 'Because you didn't ask,' was the reply. An American friend, Laura Sokol, assured me that there was nothing unusual about this response. Laura wrote a book in the early 1990s on cultural differences between Poles and Americans which became required reading for foreigners keen to master Polish manners and better understand the country's customs and culture. In Poland, she told me, information is never given freely and helpfully. 'You have to go and find it. You have to ask. And most importantly you need to know whom to ask and what to ask. Even then you'll often come away empty-handed. Americans expect people to volunteer information. Poles expect people to extract it from them.'

Years earlier, while studying Spanish with Ania in Cuernavaca near Mexico City, I battled with reflexive verbs. Ania mastered them almost instantly, instinctively understanding that if you broke a glass you would say '*se me rompio la copa*' [the glass broke itself to me] rather than '*yo rompio la copa*' [I broke the glass]. In Polish too, the reflexive verb is used to remove any direct responsibility for a mishap. No one in Poland would say '*stłukłem kieliszek*' [I broke the glass]. They would exclaim '*stłukł się kieliszek*' [the glass broke itself]. I found this frustrating and wondered whether the buck-passing I ran into so often was less a legacy of Communism, as everyone claimed, than something embedded deeply in Polish culture, language and Catholicism.

Even my dealings with the kindly Szwaba could be frustrating. I wanted him to make some furniture and other fixtures like kitchen cupboards and work areas. I especially wanted a big oak table for the kitchen, a place where we would eat and socialise. My father-in-law had warned me that the carpenter, while he was a meticulous tradesman, was often late in finishing projects. He admitted this himself. 'I always tell people that the job will be completed *po niedzieli* [after Sunday] and it always is. I just don't tell them which Sunday.' He was late in finishing the work for me, but not too late. I visited him every day to remind him of the deadline. My pestering paid off; Szwaba worked overtime to finish the table.

A hundred metres or so from the *stolarnia* [carpentry shop], the village blacksmith worked in a small, soot-blackened shed with a forge and anvil in the middle and bellows, horseshoes and iron rods hanging from the walls. A big part of Brunon Pakur's business was shoeing horses. At that time almost every farmer owned at least one, and generally two or three, massive brown draught horses with pitch-black manes. They were used for ploughing, tilling and for hauling the high-sided carts every villager owned. Like Szwaba, Pakur was in the process of handing over to his son Geruś, a tall, gangly lad who already had a good reputation for the quality of his wrought-iron work. Working in a different shed with his own forge and anvil, Geruś was making balustrades and fences for new houses that people were starting to build. Some of the pieces I saw in his workshop were elaborate, with intricate, flowing designs and whimsical reliefs. Like the Szwabas, Geruś was sometimes difficult to pin down time-wise, but visiting him every few days to enquire about progress speeded up the work.

Talking to Szwaba and Geruś nearly every day was good for my Polish and for learning about the people amongst whom I had chosen to live. *Kaszubi* are probably the most distinct regional ethno-cultural group in Poland. They are descendents of the original Baltic Slavs who settled in the region long before the first written acknowledgement of their presence in the thirteenth century. That was when the Pope ratified possession of the region by the Teutonic Knights, a Germanic order which had recently been expelled from Jerusalem by the Moslems.

Their Slavic background and association with Germanic culture and administration over the centuries has led to the development of a language spoken today by no more than one hundred thousand *Kaszubi*. It is largely incomprehensible to most Poles. In *The Tin Drum*, Gunther Grass describes the Kaszubians as 'not German enough for the Germans and not Polish enough for the Poles.' The Germanisation of Kaszubia and other areas of Poland at different times over the past millennia, and the spread of Protestantism in the nineteenth century in particular, made the Catholic Church an important source of identity for the *Kaszubi*. It remains so today and Kaszubians are probably the most overtly religious in Poland. Big wooden crosses can be found every few kilometres on country roads. There are at least ten within walking distance of the lodge, as well as several roadside chapels. Farmers and their families gather around them on summer evenings for prayers, singing and reflection.

Czesław Szwaba visited the little chapel in the village of Pomieczyńska Huta almost every day and listened to *Radio Maryja*, a stridently xenophobic and nationalistic radio station which was especially popular with older people in rural areas like Kaszubia. I skipped as deftly as my Polish would allow around any conversations of a political and religious nature, aware of *Radio Maryja*'s views. *Radio Maryja* listeners probably saw me as an interloper, someone who had bought Polish land and was bent on undermining native morals. It helped a little, I am sure, that I was from distant New Zealand and not from neighbouring Germany. 'When was the last time New Zealand invaded Poland?' I would ask jokingly if conversations became tense. I would also remind Szwaba occasionally that New Zealand was the second country in the world, after Britain, to declare war on Germany when it invaded Poland in 1939. The only other New Zealanders hereabouts, I'd tell him, were in the Commonwealth War Cemetery near the Teutonic castle at Malbork, eighty kilometres from the lodge. The youngest of the New Zealanders buried there was just nineteen when he died.

On All Saints' Day on the first of November, Poles pay homage to the deceased at cemeteries across the country, including the Commonwealth War Cemetery in Malbork. I once watched a bent and arthritic old lady place single flowers on graves at this cemetery. She shuffled from grave to grave with the aid of a walking stick and crossed herself when she laid the flowers. It was a touching scene and I wondered for how many years she had been doing it and what had happened to her during the war to make her so respectful of the Commonwealth casualties. Family fealty on All Saints' Day is equally touching. Relatives begin tidying up the burial plot and cleaning the gravestone days in advance of the public holiday. Gravestones are festooned with yellow chrysanthemums, millions of which are grown especially for the occasion. Candles are lit and cemeteries glow warmly, familiarly, in the November gloom.

With both buildings now up, the lodge had become something of a tourist attraction. It was bigger than anything in the neighbourhood and stood out. Rumour had it that the owner, a foreigner, was going to build an airstrip next to it to fly in tourists. He must have money and influence, people gossiped, since a big section of the dirt road leading to the lodge from Prokowo had just been sealed. In reality, there is nowhere nearby where you could even contemplate building an airstrip. The two-kilometre section of new tarmac was part of the local council's road improvement plans and had nothing to do with me.

That spring and summer scores of people came to look at the lodge at weekends as it neared completion. They walked down the access road or found their way up the escarpment from the lake. Since the building site was deserted at weekends and most of them were unaware that we were living in the caravan, people would press their noses against windows and try to open doors. Some would even come to gawk at the caravan, trying to catch a glimpse of what was going on inside. Others would stroll past talking about us as if we didn't exist or weren't at home. We could tell by their accents that some were local people, a few of whom I even knew by sight. But most were city folk. Some apparently felt that the Communist era wasn't over and that there was no such thing as private property in the countryside and that they were free to roam as they pleased. As the numbers grew I began to turn people away, telling them this was private property and that they were welcome to view the site from the hill above. I didn't want them wandering about what was, after all, our home. Most people accepted this graciously, but a few of the city folk wanted to argue with me.

'I've been walking across this land since I was a child,' one man told me. 'And anyway, who are you, a foreigner, to tell me where I can walk in my own country?' One day a woman, told that she couldn't access the lake through our property, hurled invective at me for five minutes as I stood my ground and prevented her and her husband from proceeding any further. When it eventually became clear to her that I wasn't going to allow her to carry on, she turned and spat over her shoulder: 'You dirty Jew. You have stolen our sacred Polish soil.'

I was surprised to be called Jewish. My religion was clearly not relevant to anything and there was nothing Semitic in my appearance or in our family history. The Jewish population of Poland at that time would not have amounted to more than a few thousand people and, despite whispers and scare stories in right-wing newspapers, there was no evidence of Jews returning in large numbers to reclaim property they had owned before World War II. The lady was of an age which made it possible, perhaps even likely, that she had never met a Jewish person in her life.

I was conversant with the sometimes tortured history of relations between the Slavic Catholic majority and Jewish minority in Poland. As a journalist, I had listened to people complain that one of Poland's first cabinets after the 1989 election was made up of a 'bunch of Jews' when only one of them, in fact, had any Jewish connections at all. I also remembered that Gabriel Narutowicz, Poland's first president after World War I, had been vilified and then assassinated by nationalists who claimed that he was only 'half Polish' (he came from on old and distinguished Slavic Polish family) and was too friendly with Jews, Germans and Ukrainians.

But this was the first time I had been verbally abused in such a way. I thought the outburst xenophobic rather than specifically anti-Semitic. The Jewish part may have been shorthand for someone, even a fellow Pole, who was disliked. The writer Eva Hoffman, whose book *Shetl* traces the history of the Jews of Brańsk, a small town in Eastern Poland, was astonished to find anti-Jewish lists circulating in Brańsk in the 1990s. The Jews of Brańsk had all been rounded up and murdered by the Nazis during World War II, so the majority of its present inhabitants had probably never met a Jewish person. But the lists contained the names of dozens of so-called Jews supposedly 'harmful to the interests of Poland.' Amongst the names were many important non-Jewish Polish politicians, people being stigmatised in the same way as Narutowicz had been in the 1920s. Hoffman saw this as the symbolic rhetoric of a new anti-Semitism that allowed anyone whose influence or views were objectionable to be labelled Jewish. 'The Jews were Poland's grand paradigmatic *other*,' she writes. 'Anti-Semitism, in the Polish psyche, is the paradigm of all prejudice; it stands not only for itself but for the more unpleasant strains of chauvinistic arrogance and defensive exclusionism.' Whatever the cause, the woman's outburst was certainly unpleasant.

I had just finished washing a baby bath full of Harley's diapers at the time I'd got into the spat with the woman. When I returned to the caravan and set about hanging them out to dry, I realised that choosing between traditional towelling diapers and modern disposables might be one of the more straightforward issues I'd confront in my new life in Poland. Whether or not I was Jewish, I was different. In rural Kaszubia that was not insignificant.

CLICKITY-CLACK

That night I was woken by the slow clickity-clack of a passing goods train and then the blast of its klaxon as it approached a level crossing in the forest on the other side of the lake from the house and our caravan. I heard it regularly, but for the first time I could remember there seemed to be menace in the way the train crept through the forest and something sinister, too, in the blast from the klaxon. The woman who had called me a 'dirty Jew' had reminded me that the Nazis had murdered three million Polish Jews during World War II. Another two million ethnic Poles also perished at the hands of the Germans and Russians.

It was mass murder on an unprecedented scale, so big, brutal and industrial that even words like genocide seem too puny to reflect its enormity. It was as if the entire population of New Zealand, Ireland or Norway had been wiped out. The Jews were taken to the death camps in cattle cars and freight wagons drawn by steam engines. At the Auschwitz camp in southern Poland, which has been kept as a monument to the Nazi genocide, railway tracks still run through the camp's main gate. Just fifty kilometres from Gdańsk is the Stutthof concentration camp, where as many as one hundred thousand people, roughly half of them Jews, were murdered during World War II. Like Auschwitz and other camps, Stutthof was chosen by the Nazis because of its isolation and the fact that it was served by a railway line. Trains played a key role in the Nazis' mass extermination and many of the victims spent their last days in the appalling conditions of the crowded cattle cars and freight wagons. They would have heard the clickity-clack of the wheels on the track and the screech of the engine's whistle at level crossings as the trains approached the camps where the gas chambers awaited them.

The train creeping slowly through the forest near us not only reminded me that so many Jews had been murdered but that my overpowering image of their fate centred less on the concentration camps than on the trains that transported them there. I imagined them in cattle wagons, crushed and unaware of what awaited them. On one of my first visits to Poland, in the depths of a particularly cold winter, I took an overnight train from Warsaw to Gdańsk. The train crept through stations with names full of consonants and in one it stopped next to a goods yard where snow was falling and ghostly cattle and goods wagons were waiting silently on other tracks. History had rendered them so sinister that not even a buffer of nearly half a century stopped me shivering inwardly in my overheated compartment.

Several years later, just after the massacre in Rwanda of some eight hundred thousand Tutsis and moderate Hutus by rampaging Hutu militias, I flew into Kigali and checked into the Mille Collines Hotel where, in happier times, I had stayed while on my way to write about mountain gorillas. This was the hotel where more than one thousand Tutsis and moderate Hutus had sought refuge from the marauding mobs and had been protected by the manager, Paul Rusesabagina, himself a Hutu. George W. Bush awarded him the US Presidential Medal of Freedom for his bravery, and the academy-award nominated film, *Hotel Rwanda*, was based on his story. When I checked in shortly after the massacres even the new paint in my room could not mask the lingering fear. I imagined the terrified occupants peeking out through the curtains and seeing gun-toting and machete-wielding mobs in the street beyond. Listening to the radio for news, they would have heard rabid

Hutu announcers urging people to 'crush the Tutsi cockroaches.' In Rwanda I felt the same frisson of fear I had experienced on the train to Gdańsk as I watched a gardener at the Mille Collines cut grass with a machete next to the swimming pool which had supplied guests with drinking water during the massacre. Machetes no longer seemed innocent tools for cutting grass.

In Poland during World War II, limbs were not savagely severed with machetes in wild orgies of killing as in Rwanda. The cruelty here was much more measured and calculated. Grandparents, university professors, doctors, shopkeepers, factory workers, pretty young girls, babies in their mothers' arms; they were all rounded up, forced into stinking railway wagons and taken to be killed. Before the start of World War II, Poland's three million Jews compromised roughly ten per cent of the population. Only a few thousand survived the war, some by fleeing before they could be captured. Others, like the film director Roman Polański, stayed alive because they were taken in and protected by Catholics, despite the fact that aiding or hiding a Jew was punishable by death. While there were anti-Semites, cowards and opportunists, there were also many heroes amongst the Polish population.

Slavs and Jews had lived together for centuries in Poland. Relations between them had often been difficult, not unusual between two ethnically, culturally and religiously different peoples, one a minority and more recent arrival. The Nobel Prize winner for Literature, Isaac Bashevis Singer, gives a sense of the touchy relationship between Jews and Catholic Poles in *The Family Moskat*, a saga which spans the period from the late nineteenth century until World War II. He writes of the poor, religiously dogmatic and hermetically sealed Jewish *shtetl* [village or small town] which is never going to change or merge into the Polish mainstream. He also captures the colourful, diverse Jewish communities in big cities like Warsaw. They were often divided over whether to assimilate, maintain their religious and cultural identity or simply emigrate to the United States or Palestine. Between the wars, Jews were certainly discriminated against in schools and universities and in many other aspects of daily life as Europe in general became less tolerant, more nationalistic and less subject to the rule of law.

Like the Poles, I get angry when I read of 'Polish' death camps. Auschwitz and the others were 'Nazi' or 'German' camps. They were built in Poland because that's where the majority of Europe's Jews lived, testament to Polish tolerance over the centuries. The *New York Times* has frequently described Auschwitz as a 'Polish death camp.' President Obama has also fallen into the trap. In May 2012, while awarding the Presidential Medal of Freedom posthumously to Jan Karski, a member of the Polish underground who brought news of the exterminations to America and Britain, Obama said: 'When resistance fighters told him that Jews were being massacred on a massive scale he [Karski] smuggled himself into the Warsaw ghetto where Jews were corralled by the Nazis prior to being forced onto the trains and to a Polish death camp…'

It was a massive *faux pas*, one for which Poles are unlikely to forgive him. Karski not only saw for himself what was happening to the Jews in the German death camps in Poland, but also risked his life to bring news of the exterminations to Britain and America. Neither Churchill nor Roosevelt believed him and neither of their countries took any meaningful steps to save Poland's Jews. Perhaps Poles themselves could have done more during World War II to save Jews, but no occupied country did more than Poland to save Jews from the Nazis.

During World War II it was not just Jews who were squeezed into goods and cattle wagons and hauled off by belching steam locomotives. Ethnic Poles were worked and starved to death in

German or Soviet camps, factories and farms, or forced into an exile from which they would never return. More than a million ethnic Poles also heard the clickity-clack of wheels on rails beneath them as they were transported to distant places. The trains never stopped running. When the war ended, millions of displaced persons, Germans included, were moved westwards as the map of Europe was redrawn to please Stalin. Without the clickity-clack of wheels on rails and the piercing whistle of steam engines, Central Europe could not have been reshaped as quickly as it was in the immediate aftermath of the war.

Trains were still reshaping the political landscape nearly half a century later. In the autumn of 1989, as Communist governments were collapsing everywhere in Eastern Europe, I reported on the plight of hundreds of East Germans seeking political asylum in the West German Embassy in Prague. They were eventually dispatched to the west in sealed passenger carriages. As they emerged from the embassy on their way to the train, I heard an old Czech woman proclaim loudly in German how much it cheered her to see Germans locked up and hauled away by rail. I learned that she had listened to the clickity-clack of train wheels on her way to a concentration camp during World War II, so it was difficult to chide her for her lack of charity.

A meeting in 1992 with Zdzisław Nosewicz, the chief forester of the region where we were building our lodge, had put me on the trail of Zbigniew Tarasiewicz and personalised for me the story of Stalin's deportation to Siberia of more than a million Poles in 1940. They had been packed into freight wagons and cattle cars and the trains had taken as long as two months to reach their destinations. Conditions were so appalling that thousands died of hunger and disease along the way. Tens of thousands more died in the Siberian labour camps. In 1941 when Hitler tore up the

Nazi-Soviet pact and launched Operation Barbarossa, the German invasion of the Soviet Union, Stalin 'pardoned' the imprisoned Poles. Most of them made their way by train from Siberia and Uzbekistan to the Caspian Sea. Their journeys took weeks or even months as they were shunted into sidings and often beaten and abused by the Soviet NKVD, the forerunner of the KGB. Again, many died of hunger and disease and only the strongest or luckiest amongst them eventually arrived in Tehran.

I had called on Nosewicz to ask permission to cut down trees on the escarpment where the lodge was to be built. He was an affable man with a ready laugh and he offered Ania and me tea while he talked to us about the trees which, he said, would have to be inspected first. But he didn't see a problem in cutting them out, particularly as I was planting a new forest elsewhere. When he found out that I was a New Zealander, his eyes lit up.

'New Zealand,' he said, almost purring the words. 'I've got a cousin in New Zealand. I haven't heard from Zbigniew since 1941, so I can't be sure that he's still alive. But I think he is.'

He rummaged in the drawer of his desk, pulling out a small, ragged scrap of paper that had been folded several times and in such a way as to make it both letter and envelope. It had been posted from Palestine in 1947 and was from Zbigniew's father, then in the Polish II Corps which had fought in Italy, most famously at Monte Casino. The three boys, Marian, Zbigniew and Edmund, the letter said, had gone to New Zealand from Persia in 1944 and were living in a camp in a place called Pahiatua. He would be joining them soon in New Zealand.

'That's the last we ever heard of them,' said Zdzisław anxiously. 'Do you think you can help me find Zbigniew?'

There were tears in the forester's eyes as he told me of the nightmare journey across Russia in crowded trains, of the cold and hunger in Siberia and of how his aunt, Zbigniew's mother, had been killed by Soviet soldiers. He recalled how he and his cousin had been split up somewhere in Kazakhstan, when his family decided to return to Poland and Zbigniew's father took his three sons south to Persia. The children were placed in a refugee camp near Tehran and their father, Adolf, joined General Anders's Polish II Corps. Few Polish soldiers returned to Poland at the end of the war since they were fearful of reprisals by the Soviets, who never forgave Anders for fighting alongside the British instead of leaving his army at the service of the Soviet Union.

They were right to be fearful. Communists groomed by Moscow had come to power in Warsaw after the failed uprising in 1944 by partisans of the anti-Communist Home Army. The uprising was crushed by the Germans while the Soviet army watched and waited on the eastern bank of the Vistula River. In the early days of World War II the Soviet Union murdered more than twenty thousand of the Polish elite as, according to Soviet documents later released, 'hardened, irremediable enemies of Soviet power'. More than fourteen thousand were shot and buried in mass graves in a forest at Katyń near Smolensk, a massacre that the Soviets did not even admit to having perpetrated until the final days of their empire. The massacre still casts a deep and dark shadow over Polish-Russian relations, especially after the 2010 crash at Smolensk of a Polish Air Force Tupolev 154 carrying President Lech Kaczyński and other Polish officials to a Katyń memorial service. All one hundred people on board the plane were killed instantly, igniting a political row that rumbles on to this day about who, ultimately, was responsible for the crash.

Tarasiewicz obviously isn't a common name in New Zealand, so it wasn't difficult to track down Zbigniew. When I met him in the Porirua Psychiatric Hospital near Wellington his fluffy grey hair was swept back to reveal a nasty scar on his forehead. He was fifty-eight then and had spent most of his life in New Zealand in institutions of one kind or another. Although neither he nor the hospital would confirm it, I believe he suffered from schizophrenia and had done so since his early twenties.

He was in good form the day I drove him north over the Rimutaka mountain range to Pahiatua so he could see the place where he and more than seven hundred other Polish children, most of them orphans, had lived after the troop ship USS *General Randal* brought them from Persia in 1944. Only a roadside monument reminds passers-by of the camp's existence in what are now green fields. Zbigniew looked out over the fields for a long time, lost in thought. He remembered being taken to Pahiatua from Wellington by train and recalled suddenly that it was the first time in his life that he had been in a passenger carriage. 'There were seats and you could stand up and move around. There was even a toilet. We couldn't believe it. We had all travelled thousands of kilometres in trains before. Only in cattle wagons though. They were always crowded and stinking.' Zbigniew's brother Edmund, fourteen at the time, recalled for me the long train journey from Siberia to the Caspian Sea, particularly the moment when their father disappeared for more than a week.

'The train was in a siding at a small station somewhere in Uzbekistan,' he told me in New Zealand. 'We had been there for hours and my father had gone off foraging for food. Suddenly without warning the train steamed off. I thought he was gone forever. But ten days later, he caught up with us at another station. I cried when I saw him.'

Years later Adolf was re-united with his children in New Zealand and the family settled in New Plymouth, the town beneath the volcano on the west coast of the North Island where I had grown up. Edmund

65

married a Polish girl, Władzia, who had also travelled by train from Siberia through Uzbekistan to Tehran. She lost her mother and father on the way and remembered thinking about nothing except food, even in the orphanage in Uzbekistan where she and her three sisters found themselves on their way to Persia. Zbigniew never married, and his only real jobs seem to have been as a tally clerk in the goods yards at New Plymouth railway station and later at the tiny station of Tariki in Taranaki. I wondered how many times at Tariki he had woken in the middle of the night to the piercing whistle of an approaching steam train and for a moment thought he was still on one of his nightmare train journeys in the Soviet Union.

In tracking down Zbigniew and members of his family, I found out that Polish immigrants had arrived in New Plymouth as early as the 1870s and that some of them actually came from the small village of Kokoszki, now an outer suburb of Gdańsk and only twenty kilometres away from where we were building the lodge. One of the group's first jobs after landing in New Plymouth was the clearing, levelling and filling of Pukekura Park, a place written large in my childhood memories. I had stood there with thousands of other children with a tiny flag in my hand as the young Queen Elizabeth drove by waving regally on a post-coronation visit to New Zealand in 1952. I later ran in athletics meetings there and watched the triple Olympic Gold Medallist Peter Snell, a local boy and childhood hero, run a mile at a blistering pace. I'd played cricket there too, grateful as a batsman for the short boundaries.

I brought back news of Zbigniew and a letter he had written in Polish and handed it over to Zdzisław in the forestry department office on the outskirts of Kartuzy. He embraced me and put the letter away in his briefcase to read at home, probably concerned that I'd see the tears in his eyes as he read it. 'Thank you,' he said simply. 'It's been more than fifty years.'

66

My mother-in-law was born and grew up in the oil town of Borysław, south of Lvow in what today is southern Ukraine but was then part of Poland. These eastern borderlands, known as the *Kresy* in Polish, first came under Polish rule in the seventeenth century. In the century leading up to World War I, Borysław was part of the Austro-Hungarian Empire. When it was returned to Poland after World War I, many Ukrainians saw the Poles as settlers. Resentment deepened when Polish veterans of World War I and the 1920 war against the Bolsheviks were given land in the *Kresy* in an attempt to Polonise the region. Most of these settlers were either murdered by the Soviets when they invaded in 1939 or deported to Siberia under the orders of Nikita Khrushchev, later a Soviet leader, then the Communist Party's first secretary in the Ukraine. The Jews, as many as seven thousand in Borysław alone, were murdered by the Germans after they took control of the borderlands and much of western Russia in 1941.

The post-World War II settlement redrew the borders of Ukraine, Poland and Germany. My mother-in-law's family, along with most of the Polish population of Lvov, Borysław and other towns and cities in the east, were packed into goods wagons. In an agonisingly slow journey, they were taken to the former German city of Breslau (now Wrocław) which fell within the new Polish borders. To make way for them, the city's German population made its own slow, uncomfortable and sometimes dangerous journeys westwards to the new Germany. It was a nightmare time during which both victors and the vanquished went hungry and suffered from the cold, lice and overcrowding.

Later my mother-in-law's family moved north to Gdańsk where Ania's parents met and where she was born thirteen years after the war ended. Conditions improved slowly during the 1950s, but life was still difficult and unimaginable to people living in the West.

Ania's family, which soon included a baby brother, lived in a single room in an old, crumbling nineteenth-century apartment building in Wrzeszcz. The only toilet and bathroom were at the end of the corridor and had to be shared with other families. Cooking was done on a single gas ring. They queued every day for staples like bread and milk and had ration cards for meat and sugar. Old newspapers were cut up for toilet paper and nothing was thrown away. They darned socks and stockings many times over, turned the collars of shirts, patched trousers and sewed sequins onto old frocks to make them look different. The war and its aftermath turned a generation of Poles into scrimpers, savers and hoarders, people with cupboards and attics full of things that might just come in handy one day. Fifty years later, my wife has lost none of the imperative to hoard that she learnt as a child.

While I was travelling with Zbigniew in New Zealand we stopped for a quick lunch at McDonald's. As I ordered, Zbigniew set about stuffing his pockets with sachets of sugar, ketchup and mustard, far more than he was ever going to use with lunch. The girl serving me looked at him testily but he avoided eye contact with her and carried on. 'Don't worry,' I said quietly to her, 'I'll pay extra for it.' She was a plump teenager who had probably never missed a meal in her life and she shook her head when Zbigniew moved off to sit at a table near the window. 'Some people are so greedy,' she said. For a moment I felt like telling her about the trains that Zbigniew had been on, surviving for months on end on five to six hundred calories a day. It was fear, not greed, I wanted to tell her, a fear of hunger that he had first experienced as a small child on a train inching itself across the steppes of the Soviet Union.

Most Poles went hungry during World War II and memories of these hard times are etched visibly on the national psyche. During the Communist era when families entertained relatives and friends at home, a groaning table was a sign not just of wealth but of generosity. For the generation that knew starvation during the war, feeding someone was the greatest gift they could give. Even today, many social functions revolve around food in quantities that sometimes seem obscene. At a Polish wedding, a four or five course feast is served after the nuptials. Almost immediately after this sumptuous sit-down meal, a buffet offering dozens of hot and cold foods is set up. Only a fraction of the food will be consumed but a family would lose face if more modest fare was offered. The organisers of family events at Kania Lodge almost always order as least twice as much food as they expect to be consumed. At village weddings, guests return the following day and often the day after as well to finish the food left over from the wedding breakfast.

Of course, the train I heard crawling through the forest near Kania Lodge that night did not carry hungry and frightened passengers. It was a small branch line between Kartuzy and Lębork, a small city of thirty-five thousand people about fifty kilometres away on the main line from Gdańsk to Berlin. But Lębork itself had a gruesome past. There had once been a concentration camp in Lębork (Lauenberg in German), a sub-camp of the notorious Stutthof camp east of Gdańsk. In January 1945, when the Soviets were closing in on Stutthoff, the camp's fifty thousand inmates were marched eastwards in the direction of Lauenberg. More than half died on the senseless death march, either succumbing to hunger or cold or being machine gunned by their German guards as the Soviets closed on the straggling columns.

In the small village of Pomieczyno, a few kilometres from Kania Lodge, there is a mass grave containing the bodies of more than fifty of the hapless Stutthof inmates, both men and women. They were murdered nearby by the Germans in February 1945. Next to the memorial above the mass grave a tombstone commemorates

Jan Mądry, a Warszawian sent to Stutthof in 1944 and killed in February 1945 on the death march from Stutthof. His camp number – 78519 – is consistent with estimates that as many as one hundred thousand people were at one time or another inmates of Stutthof. There are always flowers around the memorial. I once watched an elderly woman, dressed completely in black, light a candle and place the flickering flame on the mass grave, crossing herself before she turned and left.

BIG PHONE, SMALL SUCCESS

The lodge was completed on schedule in late July 1994. Janusz Olkiewicz, the builder, handed us the keys on a day when the temperature reached nearly 30°C and the doors and windows were open to the warm breezes from the east. To celebrate the occasion, Janusz brought a traditional Kaszubian folk band to the lodge. The musicians, four of them, arrived in calf-length black boots, white trousers, long blue frockcoats and jaunty narrow-brimmed black hats, each encircled with a red ribbon. Their frockcoats, reaching almost to their knees and open in the front, were exquisitely embroidered with the looping traditional Kaszubian floral motifs taken from wildflowers, berries and trees of the region. I had seen the embroidery before on white linen tablecloths. Blue was the predominant colour, probably taken from the cornflowers found everywhere in Kaszubia in the summer in ripening fields of rye or oats. The other colours were green, red and yellow, a spectrum that gives the embroidery a cheerful Arcadian character. The musicians carried tobacco snuff in cow horn pouches and tapped out small cones of it on the back of their hands before inhaling, one nostril at a time.

The only recognisable instruments were a double bass and an accordion. The others were what they called a *diabelskie skrzypce*, the devil's violin, and a *burczybas*, which comes from the verb *burczeć* which means to grumble or to groan. The *burczybas* does both. It is a wooden drum over which a cow's hide is stretched. From one end protrudes a long horse's tail which, when pulled vigorously, vibrates the hide and produces an agonised sawing sound that suggests a toothache or torture of some kind. The devil's violin does not look at all like a violin and is in essence a percussion instrument. It consists of a tall pole with the mask of the devil on top. Beneath are loose-fitting bottle tops which rattle tambourine-like when the pole is shaken or stamped into the ground. Lower down on the pole is a flat board which the musician strikes with a long stick while rattling the bottle tops. Another traditional instrument, which the group didn't have on this occasion, is called a *bazuna*. This is a long, tapered pipe made from a single piece of wood which emits a sound a little like the *vuvuzela* which made such a racket during the 2010 World Cup in South Africa.

Kaszubian music is very folksy, with the rollicking gait of the kind of German music that goes with lederhosen and foaming beer tankards. Even my wife had trouble following the words of some of the songs, since they were sung in Kaszubian rather than Polish. Kaszubian vocabulary and grammar has a lot in common with Polish but you need a very good ear to follow a conversation if you are not from the region. It's even harder to understand a folk song, and I needed help to unravel the words of the ever-popular 'My father bought a goat.' It always gets a laugh from Kaszubians even if they have heard it scores of times, as most have, but it's a lot less funny when translated into English. It tells the story of a man who bought a goat and tied it to his wagon as he headed for home. The devil helps the goat escape from the wagon and the man curses and gives chase as the goat heads for the forest. He pulls off his belt to give the goat a beating for escaping and his trousers fall down, causing him to trip up and fall over. He lies there cursing the goat.

After perhaps twenty minutes of listening to songs about goats and lakes, I produced bottles of vodka and shot glasses and the musicians and construction workers cheerfully toasted the new building and our future lives in Kaszubia. '*Na zdrowie*,' [good health], they called out before downing their shots in a single gulp. I quickly refilled their glasses. Kaszubs are regarded as stubborn, hard-bitten people and after a few glasses the musicians began telling jokes. Mothers-in-law featured prominently. 'I was in the yard one day when my neighbour ran in, shouting for me to give him a bucket full of water,' one of them went. 'What for?' I asked my neighbour. 'Because my mother-in-law has just fallen into our well and her nose is still sticking out above the water.'

When Janusz shook hands and left with the musicians and workers, Ania and I surveyed our new domain, aware of how much more work needed to be done. Our contract with Janusz's company had been to build the two buildings, do the brickwork on the internal courtyard and the terraces and smooth out all the bumps and holes that had been made during construction. They had finished the job on schedule despite a harsh winter and Janusz himself had supervised plumbers and electricians in the final stages to make sure that the central heating system worked exactly as it should, that toilets flushed properly and that the lights went on at the flick of a switch. The workmanship everywhere was of a high standard, particularly the carpentry. All the interior doors and architraves, including the large double doors leading to the sitting room, were made from oak. Further west in Europe they would have cost a small fortune but here they had been no more expensive than the mass produced doors then available in Ikea.

Czesław Szwaba had finished the oak table for the kitchen on time and it looked solid enough to last for a century or so. We had employed a stove maker, a *zdun* in Polish, to make an old-fashioned wood-burning stove for the kitchen just in case the power went off. It turned out to be a wise move, even though at the time we sometimes doubted the wisdom of employing the *zdun* from the nearest large village. He was a very precise craftsman but he liked to drink. Once he had taken a few swigs, he quickly became tired. Often he left for the day after placing and grouting-in only a few tiles. But eventually he built us a traditional stove which drew superbly and which proved invaluable when the first serious snowstorm hit us.

We now had a home and rooms to let, but we didn't have any guests. It was probably just as well, since much remained to be done, inside and out. There were no gardens except for two small ones in the courtyard. There was nothing at the front except the brick-tiled terrace, which stopped abruptly at some hastily smoothed-over soil where anaemic looking weeds were growing. There was no way of reaching the lake other than by clambering down the escarpment. When I walked back up the driveway to the birch tree, which had become the place from where I ritually surveyed our progress, the two buildings looked neat and tidy but bare and lonely. They could have been two large dolls' houses left behind by a careless giant. The lodge badly needed walls, fences, gardens and pathways, not to mention lawns, trees, steps and a pathway to access the lake. We hadn't even completely finished part of the upstairs in the main building because we were running short of money.

Our neighbours could not understand why we finished the outside completely when there was work still to be done on the interior. People building houses in Poland in the 1990s generally finished the interior first and often did not get around to the external plaster and painting until years later. That allowed them to live in the house whilst saving money to finish the exterior. Even today houses in the countryside remain unfinished for five to ten years while the owners save the money to plaster and paint the outside walls.

Visitors to Poland sometimes express surprise at the number of unfinished but lived-in houses. Why don't owners borrow the money from a bank to finish the job? And why don't councils insist that houses are properly finished before allowing people to move in? It is only in the last decade or so that mortgages have become available to people of modest incomes. How many people in the West, I ask questioners, would have neatly finished houses if they had to come up with the money themselves? Even now that credit is more readily available in Poland, many people fear getting into debt. They consider an un-rendered, sparsely furnished house without gardens or lawns preferable to living with a bank loan.

That is one reason why Poland was less affected than many other countries by the financial crisis of 2008. Poland had no large national portfolio of sub-prime property loans. Nor did it have banks or financial institutions big enough and unwise enough to have dabbled in sub-prime loans and other dodgy financial instruments of the kind that brought banks elsewhere to their knees and left the banking systems of some countries tottering. But Poland was not totally immune to the global financial turmoil. Polish banks found themselves uncomfortably exposed to mortgages they'd sold to first-time buyers in currencies other than the Polish złoty. Given the low comparative interest rates of some foreign currencies, the Swiss Franc in particular, it seemed sensible to take out a loan for which the monthly repayments would be as little as half those for a loan denominated in higher interest rate Polish złoty. What the banks didn't explain to customers was that there was an exchange rate risk in borrowing in a currency other than the one in which their salary was paid.

Despite the hardship many borrowers have faced, Poland's foreclosure rate remains tiny. People are grateful for incremental improvements in housing. If rapid appreciation of the Swiss Franc against the złoty means that monthly payments go up, people are prepared to tighten their belts in other areas. Losing a house or a flat would mean going to live with parents or in-laws, just as earlier generations did during the Communist era.

Like Communists everywhere, the Polish United Workers Party, *Polska Zjednoczona Partia Robotnicza* or *PZPR* in Polish, was much better at dividing things up than multiplying them. When it came to housing, this generally meant squeezing ever more people into the same space. Even the ugly, low-cost apartment buildings found in most Polish cities could not be built rapidly enough to house a growing population. A couple with two young children who were lucky enough to be allotted a forty-square-metre apartment in the 1960s might, by the 1980s, have been sharing the same apartment with the husband or wife of at least one of their children plus a couple of grandchildren. The other child of the couple who got the flat in the 1960s, now in his or her twenties but unmarried, also had to be accommodated. It was just about possible to create three rooms in a forty-square-metre apartment, which meant that the original parents got one tiny room, the unmarried grown-up child shared a room with the two young children and the second generation married couple had the third room.

In one of these rooms the cooking had to be done and meals taken so, as likely as not, the original parents would sleep on a fold-down couch in what was in effect the kitchen and dining room. The bathroom, so tiny that if you stood in the middle of it you could touch all four walls, was also the laundry room. Tolerance and forbearance were useful qualities in such cramped quarters.

Having a larger apartment was not always a lucky break as you could be forced to share it with another family, people you would never met before and possibly from a different socio-economic background. Larger apartments in older buildings which had survived the war and which were often inhabited by what in other countries might have been termed 'middle-class' people, were often divided in two in the crudest possible fashion – a plywood divider in the middle of a room for example. If there was a kitchen, it was shared. So was the bathroom.

If it was tough in the cities, the chronic housing shortage was probably even harder on people in the villages. Edyta, one of our first employees, brought up three children in one room of her in-laws' farmhouse in the village of Pomieczyńska Huta, just over a kilometre from the lodge. I visited her and her husband just before Christmas one year to find her cooking in one corner on a single electric plate. Her husband and children were sitting on a couch which became the marital bed at night. Under it was a mattress which was pulled out for the children to sleep on. The room was no more than twelve square metres in size. The bathroom down the corridor was tiny and was shared with Edyta's mother-in-law and her brother-in-law's family of four. After scrimping and saving for years, Edyta built a two-storey breeze-block house opposite the village school and slowly, ever so slowly, furnished the rooms one by one. The exterior of the house is still not rendered or painted more than a decade after she moved in. She probably doesn't even notice it now that she can luxuriate in the kind of space that had once been unimaginable.

Divorce during the Communist era played havoc with even the meanest divisions of floor space. One of the parties would almost certainly have to move back in with parents, especially taxing if it was the party with the children. Poland's low divorce rates during the Communist era were possibly due less to religiosity than to the problem of finding places for both parties to live. Sometimes people divorced and continued to share the same apartment until something came up that enabled one of them to move out.

Aware of the disaffection that the housing shortage caused, Poland's Communists loosened up a little in the late sixties and early seventies by allowing those who could afford it to build their own houses. Even if they had the money – generally only those who had dabbled on the black market or who had connections or savings from work abroad – it wasn't easy. First there was a maze of bureaucracy to wade through for planning permission, a maze in which one could always be ambushed by an official looking for a bribe. Then there was the problem of getting materials with which to build. Everything from cement to nails and paint was difficult, and sometimes impossible, to come by. There were no private building companies so most people finished up building their houses themselves with the help of a tradesman working on the sly and a few relatives or friends. Usually it took years to finish a house because of the lack of materials and the fact that people could only work on them in their spare time. Seemingly abandoned houses in all sorts of stages of construction could be seen during the Communist era.

The fact that I hadn't physically taken any part in the building of the lodge was perceived as laziness by many of Ania's friends and relatives, some of whom told me that I would find no satisfaction in moving into a house which I had not myself toiled to construct. It reminded me of New Zealand in the 1950s and 1960s when, if you couldn't build a house with just a few mates to help, or fix a car or tractor on your own with a pair of pliers and a piece of number-eight fencing wire, you weren't much of a man. Trying to explain that it made economic sense for me to earn money at something I was good at in order to pay someone else who was good at building houses, met with a great deal of scepticism.

By paying someone who knew what he was doing, I already had the lodge, stark though it was, and not a building site with a concrete mixer still churning away and stacks of timber lying about a muddy courtyard. True, there were still no paying guests, despite the fact that I had recently spent about three thousand US dollars on a Nokia Talkman mobile phone which weighed three kilograms and was mobile only in the sense that it had a handle with which to carry it. Most of the weight was in the battery which needed to be recharged after a few hours of use. It had a hand piece and curly black cable like a normal stationary phone. It reminded me of the Remington Travel-Writer typewriter I had bought in Australia in the early seventies and carried around the world as a correspondent for the best part of two decades. It weighed nearly seven kilos and it, too, was portable in an earlier definition of what you could reasonably be expected to carry around with you. Even then it didn't always meet the airline definition of carry-on baggage. I found it recently in the cellar with a baggage tag for a flight from Cairo to Beirut still attached. That would have been sometime in the mid-1980s, about the time I got my first 'laptop', a Tandy with an eight-line screen and enough memory to store a story or two. The long-serving Remington had then been retired.

My new cell phone had a built-in aerial which I popped up whenever I needed to use the phone. This worked well in and around Gdańsk, where there was a good signal, but so poorly at the lodge that I had to mount an expensive aerial on the roof. In the early 1990s a three-kilo Nokia Talkman had the same status as a Rolex watch. A cell phone advertisement of the era showed an architect or engineer talking on his Nokia Talkman on a building site. The text read: 'Mały telefon, wielki sukces.' [Small phone, big success]. In my case, big phone, little success, would have been a more accurate tagline. The only thing bigger than the phone itself, were the charges for calls. However, at least I had a phone.

During the Communist era it could take a decade or more for the state telephone company, TPSA, to install a phone. Even then, it was only possible if one lived somewhere near to existing lines.

Having a phone was a privilege and the authorities made sure you knew it. Their eavesdropping was sometimes deliberately clumsy in order to send the message that they were, or might be at any time of day or night, listening to your conversation. Phones, even primitive landlines, could be useful tools in the hands of malcontents. For a long time only local calls could be dialled automatically. Even on the eve of Communism's demise in 1989, overseas calls had to be booked hours, sometimes a whole day or two, in advance. The call could eventually come through at any time of the day or night.

Since it wasn't easy to run a lodge in the middle of the countryside without a phone, I had applied to TPSA the moment we started building. They smiled condescendingly when I lodged the application. 'Not this year for sure,' they told me, 'and probably not next.' In other words, go away and forget about it. When we are ready we'll turn up. None of our neighbours had a phone. The nearest phone was at Czesław Szwaba's house in Pomieczyńska Huta, more than a kilometre away. Before the cellular phone became available, I had even thought, momentarily and whimsically, of using pigeons as a means of communication with the outside world. My in-laws in Gdańsk had a telephone, so why not use their number for bookings and have a pigeon relay the message to us?

I remembered that my friend and colleague Alan Cowell, then with Reuters, had used pigeons to get stories out of a remote guerrilla camp in Rhodesia during the pre-independence elections. While the elections were taking place, nobody was permitted to leave the camp. The camps had no phones or other means of communication with the outside world. Alan enterprisingly borrowed the birds from a pigeon fancier in Bulawayo and winged his stories back to their home loft, from where they were delivered to the Reuters office. The story of his enterprise became a much bigger story than anything he wrote from the camp, harking back as it did to the news agency's start in the nineteenth century, when pigeons were used to deliver financial news.

I was fortunate to have arrived in Kaszubia at the start of the cell phone revolution. I now not only had a number I could give to people so they could make bookings with us, but also the means to carry on making a living as a writer. Since my 'portable' phone could be hooked up to a fax machine, I could send messages and even stories to editors in London, Paris and New York. That's what I did, earning enough during the first winter at the lodge to compensate for the fact that we had only a handful of guests the preceding summer.

If our first summer had been slow, the winter that followed was even worse. It was one of the harshest winters for a decade or two and at times we were completely cut off by heavy snow. Once when I had to fly to Africa on an assignment for an American magazine, the road to the lodge was completely blocked by drifts of snow. I tied my aluminium suitcase to a small sledge and hauled it through the snow for more than a kilometre to the nearest open road, where a driver was waiting to take me to the airport. In February, when I returned from another assignment in the United States, we were still snowed in at the lodge. It was late at night when the driver dropped me off next to the Calvary cross where Ania had left a sledge and gumboots for me. A blizzard was blowing, it was pitch black and my hands and feet were numb with cold before I had climbed the first hill. The suitcase kept falling off the sledge, I sank in patches of wind-blown snow until it was nearly up to my waist and I slipped and fell hard on icy patches of the road the wind had swept clear of snow. My hat blew off and was carried off into a snow-covered field. By the time I reached home I was a pitiful figure. There was snow in my boots and a crust of snow on my hat

81

and scarf which I had wound around my face so that only my eyes peeped out. I couldn't feel my fingers or my toes. Ania had to help me out of my coat and boots.

On one occasion that first winter we had no electricity for almost five days. This meant no lighting or heating because the oil-burning stove wouldn't function. It also meant no water because the pumps which brought up water from the well and moved it around the house weren't working. Fortunately we had plenty of dry wood in the woodshed, a good supply of candles and no shortage of pristine snow just outside the front door to melt on the stove. In fact it was more than a metre deep in the courtyard and two metres deep where the incessant wind from the west had crafted it into dune-shaped drifts. The wood-burning stove in the kitchen that the tipsy *zdun* had finished the previous autumn kept us warm and enabled us to cook. There was even a small bread oven built into the stove so we were able to bake bread, just as Józef Pawłowski, the seventy-year-old farmer living across the lake, had done all his life. The decrepit cottage he lived in on his nine-hectare farm was beyond the reach of the nearest power line and he relied on his wood-burning kitchen stove for warmth and for cooking. A ceramic stove provided some heat to the room where he and his wife slept.

Throughout Kaszubia there were many isolated *chata*, tiny thatched cottages with whitewashed clay walls which had no electrical supply at all. Often these *chata* were inhabited by old people who, like my neighbour across the lake, had grown up without electricity and running water and survived the winters by prudently preparing lots of firewood in the autumn and storing two or three tons of potatoes in cold, dark cellars beneath the cottage, or burying them deep enough in the nearest field to escape frost. Even those with electricity seldom had running water. This they drew from shallow wells with a simple rope winch or, during warmer weather, hauled up from the lake in long cylindrical barrels which fitted neatly onto a farm cart.

In our village I often saw Pani Stromska hauling a bucket of water up from the well in her backyard and her husband carrying two buckets to the house on a wooden yoke which fitted neatly into the contours of his neck and shoulders. On bath days, generally Saturday, there was a lot of traffic from the well to the kitchen where the water was heated on the stove and the family took turns at scrubbing themselves in order to be ready for church the following day.

A snowstorm which blanketed Kaszubia with a metre or more of snow and cut off power for days on end was nothing new for our neighbours. It had been worse when they were young, many older people told me. The winters were colder then and the snow deeper. They could be cut off for a week or two, but they just got on with living in a vastly shrunken world. We found that first big snowstorm exciting rather than threatening. We were warm, we had candles for the evening and warm food, including fresh bread which we baked in the wood stove. By melting snow on the stove we also had water for drinking, cooking and bathing. The pots on the stove needed constant feeding with snow because a full pot yielded only about ten per cent of the snow's mass in water. A great deal of snow was needed to provide enough water to wash half a dozen nappies, but at least they dried quickly next to the stove.

Our cellular phone came in handy while we were snowed in, not just for us but for our neighbours too. Wojciech Szwaba found his way to us on foot because their landline stopped functioning when power and telephone lines snapped under the weight of ice and snow. A young girl from a farmhouse two kilometres away made daily visits to us to call the hospital where her mother had just given birth and was suffering from a post-natal complication. The family couldn't dig their way out to visit the hospital and were anxious for news.

Snow ploughs eventually cleared the public roads and power was restored. Some of the villagers and I shovelled snow from the driveway. The worst part was a section of about twenty-five metres just below the birch tree at the top of the hill. Here the drive dipped and the wind quickly filled the hollow with a metre or more of snow. Clearing it by shovel was hard work, and my back ached for days afterwards. Once out of our driveway, we still had to make a detour through a field to avoid a section of the road filled with snow. A front-end loader was eventually brought in to dig out the snow but it was a long, slow job and one the local council placed very low on its list of snow-clearing priorities that winter.

At least I had a four-wheel drive Jeep, bought in the US and shipped to Poland, and could get out more often than not. The few neighbours with cars drove tiny 500cc Fiats from a factory in southern Poland. It had been by far the most common car on the roads during the Communist era when there were long waiting lists, sometimes of ten years or more, to get a new one. Despite being tiny and sounding more like a lawnmower than a car, owning one offered a whiff of independence. Just a whiff, mind you, because during the Communist era petrol was rationed and long queues snaked their way down roads next to petrol stations. Still, whole families squeezed into the tiny cars and headed to the Baltic coast for a summer holiday or to ski slopes in the southern mountains in the winter. Some brave souls ventured as far as Istanbul where they bought Turkish leather coats to sell back in Warsaw, or to the Black Sea Coast in Bulgaria where everything was still relatively cheap for Comecon Bloc citizens.

Occasionally a *mały* Fiat with Polish number plates could be seen on a highway in Germany, France or even Spain. Every crevice

84

of the interior not occupied by a human limb would be stuffed with food for the journey – hams in tins, long coils of smoked sausage, dark brown rye bread that would keep for weeks and bottles of vodka. No one wanted to waste the little foreign currency they had scraped together for the journey on expensive foreign food. On the roof rack the luggage would invariably include a tent and a bag of tent poles, ropes and horseshoe-shaped metal pegs.

People in the cities discarded their Polish-made Fiats for larger, more comfortable cars as the free market economy opened up in the 1990s. The tiny vehicles found their way into the Polish countryside where most people had been without cars at all during the Communist era. The second-hand 500cc Fiats were now so cheap that even poor farmers could afford them, especially people like Janek Frankowski in our village who could repair and keep them on the road. While my big four-wheel drive Jeep could often power its way through snow that would halt a smaller car in its tracks, it was much more difficult to dig out once it became stuck in a drift. With a Fiat, the driver and a couple of friends could just pick up the front and pull it out. I had to trudge back to the village and ask Janek to bring his tractor, which always had chains on the wheels in winter, to tow my Jeep free. He did it several times that first, harsh winter, when I learnt the limits of even a three-litre, four-wheel drive off-road vehicle in Kaszubia's snow and ice.

BUCKWHEAT SOWERS

By the summer of our second year at the lodge we had done a lot of landscaping, creating a rock garden on the slope in front of the terrace overlooking the lake and a semicircular lawn with a retaining wall below it. Beyond that, we shaped a grassy slope on which we planted two clumps of birch trees. Steps down the slope led on to a flatter but still sloping meadow which finished where the escarpment plunged down to the lake. We also put in lawns on the eastern side of the house and at the front of the apartments in the second building. I worked with the Frankowski family to build steps through the orchard to the lake, wrestling barrows of concrete down the steep slope and taking turns with them on the mixer. Ania was pregnant then and bitterly disappointed that she couldn't do much more than show the Frankowskis where to place the stones for the rock garden. I worked with them to spread the truckloads of rich black earth we brought in for the lawns, mixing it with our own sandy soils before levelling it, raking it into a fine bed and sowing the grass seed. Then we rolled it with a heavy steel roller Janek had made for me in his workshop, garden rollers being unheard of in Poland at that time.

The Frankowski family comprised Janek, his brother Staszek and his brother-in-law Staszek Kiedrowski. Janek and his brother Staszek had married two sisters, Teresa and Basia, who had grown up on a farm near Żukowo, fifteen kilometres away. Staszek Kiedrowski had married Janek and Staszek Frankowski's sister, Małgosia. Leon, the family patriarch, had set Janek and Staszek up on separate farms and was slowly relinquishing control of his own farm to Staszek

Kiedrowski and his daughter, Małgosia. Buying three separate farms was no mean feat during the Communist era, regardless of the fact that they were each just a few hectares in size and only capable of providing enough for the families to survive. Each of the Frankowskis had his own cows, pigs, horses, chickens and geese and grew enough potatoes, wheat and rye to be self-sufficient in food. They had fresh milk and eggs every day.

Bread was baked once a week in special ovens in their wood-burning stoves. The loaves, made from a mix of rye and potato flour, were long, heavy and made to last a week. Every so often the terrified squeals of a pig being slaughtered could be heard. In the autumn, the gaggles of geese in everyone's yard grew smaller and smaller as birds were sold in the local farmers' market, eaten at home or turned into preserves for the winter.

During the Communist era, farmers were officially obliged to sell everything at fixed prices to government agencies or co-operatives such as the milk co-operative in Kartuzy. The Frankowskis and farmers from miles around sent their milk to it in metal milk churns. They were much the same as the ones we had in New Zealand in the 1950s, which I had sometimes help to fill in the milk shed down behind the macrocarpa trees on the farm where we lived. Milk churns had long since disappeared in New Zealand, as the average size of a dairy herd grew to several hundred cows and milk was collected in large stainless tankers the size of petrol trucks. The dozens of tiny co-operative dairy factories that dotted the countryside in dairying districts when I was a child had also disappeared, replaced by a single massive plant which processed as much as fourteen million litres of milk a day and produced everything from butter and cheese to alcohol.

In Poland at that time most private farmers had only three or four cows, which they milked by hand. Janek Frankowski, who had seven, was the only person in our hamlet with an electric milking machine. Each morning he and the other farmers would take their milk churn down to a wooden stand on the corner of the lane leading to the village. The churns, five or six of them, would be carried to a collection point in Prokowo by farmer Gerard Pakura in a cart pulled by a single black horse. Sometimes when Pakura spent too long drinking with friends outside the shop in Prokowo the horse would plod home with the farmer asleep at the reins.

To supplement the meager earnings from their farms, the Frankowski family took jobs with us. The men and their wives arrived early each morning in a cart pulled either by a pair of draught horses or one of their new tractors. They talked loudly amongst themselves as they worked, always ready with advice for one another and sometimes getting agitated when the advice was ignored. The women downed their shovels or rakes at 11.30am and walked home to prepare lunch for the family. Most days it was meat of some kind and potatoes. Vegetables and salads were a rarity. On Fridays, if they could afford it, there was fish with the potatoes. If not, eggs were served because no one ate meat on a Friday.

Lunch was served with French-like precision at noon on the dot and they were all back at work by 1pm. The Frankowskis were good workers, unlike many in the hamlet whose fondness for beer and vodka meant that they worked for a few days and then vanished for a week or more. The Frankowskis were not teetotallers but they only drank from time to time at events like weddings, christenings or birthdays. Sometimes when we finished a job I produced a few beers and they drank with me before heading home to milk the cows or muck out the pigs.

As lawns and gardens took shape that year we began to receive a regular stream of guests, most of them foreigners living in Warsaw. Poles, I quickly realised, either thought Kania Lodge was too expensive or they were busy travelling the world to make up for the decades when it had been difficult and sometimes impossible to venture abroad. I mailed hundreds of letters to foreign companies that spring, singing the praises of this remote but beautiful place in the north of Poland and stressing our fluent English. At that time many foreign companies rated Warsaw a hardship post, and their expatriate employees were entitled to various perks, including company-paid holidays within Poland.

These short-term expatriates spoke no Polish at all but were eager to see something of Poland during their stay, especially since their employers were paying. Kania Lodge was an obvious choice. We were helped by the fact that, at the time, there were few other interesting and comfortable hostelries in the Polish countryside. The only other country retreat about which expatriate visitors spoke warmly was in the mountains in southern Poland. It was owned and run by a Japanese woman, Akiko, who wowed guests with sushi and sake and, most importantly of all, hospitality and good service.

The few Polish guests both Akiko and I received in the early days were generally surprised to find foreigners, one of them Japanese and the other a New Zealander, taking care of guests themselves and moreover doing it casually, easily and with a smile. We cooked, Akiko doubtless much more proficiently than me, and we sometimes served and cleared tables. We even talked to guests, got to know them a little and occasionally became friends. Early Polish guests told me that staying at Kania Lodge was like 'being at home.'

It baffled some of them, though, when I emerged from the kitchen in an apron or cleared their plates away from the table, juggling at least half a dozen in one hand as I had learned to do as a waiter when I was a student. 'Why don't you let your staff do this?' one guest asked me disapprovingly. 'That's what you pay them for isn't it?' It was, but I was teaching my staff customer service by example. I had hired young women from neighbouring villages, none of whom had ever worked in a hotel before or, in most cases, had a job of any kind. I wanted them to be personable and polite with guests. I also wanted them to learn how to cook the eclectic range of food Ania and I were offering our guests. For the first two years one of us had to be in the kitchen most of the time. This and our constant contact with guests would not have been strange in Western Europe, America or Australasia. In Poland it was.

Forty years of Communism had laid waste to the culture of hospitality and service that existed in hotels and restaurants in Poland before World War II. In hotels, service personnel were generally sullen, if not rude and unhelpful, seeing guests as needy supplicants for food and alcohol. Communism had given power to people with aprons, uniforms and the key to the larder. It had also empowered legions of petty bureaucrats who ran the country's offices, sold train tickets and manned libraries and museums. Perpetual shortages of everything from butter to books had enhanced this power and, five years after Communism's official demise, old attitudes and habits were stubbornly hanging on.

I remember complaining around this time to a waiter in a cafe in Kraków about the loudness and unsuitability of the music being played at 11.30 in the morning. It was a mindless, thumping beat more suited to a student disco at 3am, providing everyone was drunk or stoned, than an elegant main street cafe with upholstered chairs and polished wooden tables. 'We all like it,' he said dismissively, waving his hand towards three of his colleagues behind the bar. And that was that. Western hotel chains like the Marriott, which by then had opened in Poland, were investing large amounts of time and money in training staff to be civil and, if possible, helpful, cheerful and enthusiastic. I knew from the managers involved what a tough battle it was. Far from creating equality, Communism had created a hierarchy of bureaucrats and service personnel scornful of the customer and intent on preserving their status and privileges.

Poland had always had a rigid and finely delineated class structure. Status was hugely important. By the end of the fifteenth century, the Polish greater and lesser nobility accounted for as much as twelve per cent of the total population, compared with barely three per cent in other European countries. It had effectively wrested political power from the king and enslaved the peasants who were legally bound to the land on which they were born. Only one son of a peasant family was allowed to leave the village, townsfolk were not allowed to own land and positions in the Church were open only to members of the nobility (*szlachta*). By 1652 the nobility had enshrined the right of *liberum veto* [free veto] in the constitution. This meant that a single member of the *Sejm* [Parliament] could veto legislation. Only the nobility were eligible to contest seats in parliament and to vote for parliamentary candidates. It was a patently ridiculous way to run a country and the squabbling it engendered helped bring about the partition of Poland by Russia, Prussia and the Austro-Hungarian Empire at the end of the eighteenth century and beginning of the nineteenth century, meaning that Poland effectively ceased to exist for the next 123 years.

In theory, all Polish noblemen were equal, with the poorest amongst them enjoying the same legal rights as the wealthiest. In reality there was a clear hierarchy. At the top were the magnates, owners of vast estates almost as big as a small English county with towns, villages and tens of thousands of peasants. They often carried the title 'Prince' or 'Count' after receiving the honorific from a foreign court. Even today Poles associate surnames such as Radziwiłł, Lubomirski, Potocki and Czartoryski, amongst others, with the country's once-powerful aristocracy. They were not useful names to have during the Communist era when private estates of almost any size were taken over by the state. The middle nobility (*średnia szlachta*) owned a village or two, some forest and perhaps a factory or quarry. The majority, of course, belonged to the petty nobility (*drobna szlachta*) and many of them were poor, often without land at all and sometimes no better off than the peasants amongst whom they lived. Those who had to work their fields themselves were sometimes referred to derisively as *hreczkosiej* [buckwheat sowers].

Although they lived in a *chata* with walls of clay and straw and a thatched roof, they were still *szlachta* and a cut above everyone else in the village. The only thing distinguishing them from their neighbours might be a piano they'd inherited or a painting of a very distant relative in the flowing robes of an eighteenth-century nobleman. But they were minor nobility and up to World War II might have expected to be addressed as *panie bracie* [brother] by their fellow *szlachta*, however rich, and as lord or lady by the peasant farmers. Status was often more important than money. Making money through commerce, especially the sort which required you to roll up your sleeves and put on an apron and serve a customer, was not really a respectable way for the minor nobility to earn a living. This was for the Jews and the petty bourgeoisie. Even if they were penniless and hungry, *szlachta* always had their pride to gnaw on.

Some of the early Polish guests at the lodge were descendants of the old aristocracy. They spoke English or French fluently because they had all lived outside Poland during the Communist era and were urbane, sophisticated people. Some had returned to Poland to reclaim family manor houses or palaces confiscated by the state at the end of World War II, others were starting businesses or headed major foreign-owned firms. They no longer had titles, at least not officially, but they still thought of themselves as aristocracy and some had the honorific 'Count' preceding their names on the credit cards with which they settled their accounts at the lodge. I found this indulgence quaint but understandable, and I liked these people a lot more than the newly rich who occasionally turned up to check us out. I spent many a pleasant evening with them. One group still holds the record, albeit narrowly, for the most bottles of wine consumed per person in a single evening.

One summer weekend, when I was working in the garden in shorts, boots and a frayed shirt, I looked up to see a flashily dressed woman in her forties walking down the path towards me. As she got closer I saw she was wearing a lot of gold around her neck and on her wrists, along with a diamond ring that looked as if it had had been bought at Tiffany & Co in New York.

'Where's the owner,' she asked peremptorily, looking through me as if I wasn't really there.

'That's me,' I replied, sensing that this was going to be interesting.

She glanced at my scuffed boots and grubby shorts and snorted, '*nie możliwe*.' ['I don't believe it'].

Wondering whether I had heard her correctly and, deciding that I had, I said, tongue in cheek, 'All right, my wife is really the owner. I just work here.'

'You are not Polish are you,' she stated rather than asked, as if this explained why I was in shorts and working in the garden and not properly dressed and snapping fingers at the staff to order her a glass of champagne. Being a foreigner explained, if not excused, all sorts of social sins in Poland. I was by now well used to being called *nie kulturalny* [uncultured] by petty bureaucrats and shop assistants

I'd crossed by suggesting, for example, that they spend more time serving the public and less time drinking tea with their colleagues.

Having solved the mystery of my shabby appearance, the woman proceeded to tell me what a beautiful place the lodge was and how sorry she was that she wouldn't be able to stay with us. Puzzled, I asked her why.

'Because,' she said, waving the hand with the diamond ring towards the deserted terrace, 'no one would be here to see me spending money like they do on the coast.'

Her crassness was impressive. I knew the hotel on the coast she referred to, and I'd seen its terrace full of people preening themselves and whispering things like, 'Look, isn't that so-and-so, the one who bought the brewery for a song and is now rolling in it?' Or, 'Gosh, you'd think that with all the money they have she'd dress more fashionably.' The lady would certainly be more at home on that terrace than ours.

The collapse of Communism had enabled a small number of people to become rich overnight. Often they were former Communists or friends of the old ruling elite who had swapped Communism for Capitalism with surprising alacrity. They had managed to become owners of former state property, a brewery perhaps, or a cement plant or factory of some kind, at a knock-down price. They may have had a good head for business but they often were not sophisticated or cultured people.

Suddenly showered with riches beyond their dreams, they bought the latest Mercedes or BMW, built flashy houses with columns in front resembling those of old Polish manor houses, and splashed out on designer clothes. The transfer of the means of production from the state to individuals in Poland was, as elsewhere in the old Communist bloc, a messy and often far from transparent business. Bribery and corruption flourished. Courts groaned for a decade or more under the weight of disputes over ownership. The lady with the diamond ring, or perhaps her spouse, was an early winner in the scramble for wealth, money and power in the 1990s.

Also part of the *mêlée* in those days were foreign companies, some of which conducted business in ways that would not have been acceptable at home. One company paid me in advance for an all-inclusive weekend stay for someone they described as an 'important business partner.' He arrived on a Friday evening in a shiny new car and immediately jumped out of the driver's seat and ran around to open the passenger door. Out stepped an expensively dressed woman whom he introduced as his wife. The pair didn't behave like a married couple and spent much of the weekend in their suite where they consumed prodigious amounts of alcohol. They drank so much that I found myself telling Ania that the bloke was either wasting good wine or a good mistress. I had no idea who he was and the man wasn't giving anything away in the brief conversations I had with him. I later found out from the manager of the company paying for the weekend that he was the chief tax officer for the region in which the company was located. 'We had a tax inspection during which a few problems came up,' the manager said. 'I think everything has been resolved now.'

Our growing popularity with the expatriate community in Warsaw meant that it was time to finish the upstairs of the main building, turning it into a three-bedroom apartment in which we would live and freeing up the rooms downstairs we were occupying. My forays abroad during the first two winters to write for American magazines meant that we had some spare cash. I had also just received a legacy from my grandfather's wife, his third, who had died recently in the Lake District in England. My grandfather, James Borrell, had himself died a decade or so earlier after spending most of his life in India.

The legacy wasn't a huge sum but it paid for the finishing work, some new furnishings for the family suite upstairs in the main building and the tennis court we put in the following year. I think my grandfather would have been pleased that money he had earned in India during the Raj had found its way into a building overlooking a lake in northern Poland. He had gone to India in the 1920s and returned to Britain more than forty years later.

The new family suite we built with grandfather Borrell's legacy gave us another couple of rooms downstairs for guests. We filled the lodge easily most weekends during the spring, summer and autumn, but winter was still difficult, mainly because the road was sometimes impassable. However, guests did start coming in greater numbers the second and third winter after we had started. Sometimes they had to leave their cars in the village of Pomieczyńska Huta, and we'd bring them and their suitcases to the lodge in a sleigh pulled by two of Janek's massive horses. On one occasion the guest was a diplomat from the Canadian Embassy in Warsaw. When he called to make his reservation he gave his name as Jim Visutskie, not a Polish name the way it was spelt but sounding like one when spoken. He arrived late on a Friday evening and I went with Janek to meet the Visutskie family in nearby Pomieczyńska Huta. Chatting to him on the way back to the lodge, I asked him if he spoke Polish.

'No,' he replied, 'but I speak Kaszubian.'

I was astonished. The Kaszubian dialect, perhaps best if crudely described as a hotchpotch of Polish and German, is spoken by as few as one hundred thousand people in the world. They don't even understand it in Gdańsk, let alone in Warsaw or Ottawa. It certainly wasn't a language one would learn in the Canadian Foreign Service.

'Kaszubian?' I said disbelievingly to him and then to Janek in Polish: 'The gentleman speaks Kaszubian.'

96

And he did, chatting to Janek on the way back to the lodge. Janek told me later his Kaszubian was good but old fashioned.

'It was like talking to my grandfather or to an old person who has lived all his life in a remote village,' Janek told me in Polish. 'Some of the words he used you no longer hear in everyday speech.'

Jim's forebears were Kaszubians who had emigrated to Canada in the nineteenth century, the first few families having gone there in 1858. They settled in the Ottawa Valley in a place they named Wilno after the then Polish city which is now Vilnius, capital of Lithuania. With its lakes, forests and harsh winters, the Ottawa Valley must have reminded them of home. Even better, there were no Germans around to boss them about, dispossess them of their land or force their children to learn German at school. Jim's great-grandfather had gone to Canada from the village of Leszno, not far from the lodge, in 1883. His surname was Wysocki, which Canadians found difficult to pronounce until it was changed to Visutskie, a phonetically close transcription into English. The family had spoken Kaszubian at home and passed on the language from generation to generation, right up to Jim's generation, those born immediately after World War II. Jim's wife was British and Jim was a career diplomat who moved from post to post around the world. They had not carried on the tradition of speaking Kaszubian at home with their children, sadly breaking the link.

Over the following years we were to have many Canadians of Kaszubian origin stay with us as they sought out relatives, towns or villages, sometimes even an individual farm, from which their forebears had originated. One of them, Shirley Connelly, later produced an exhaustively researched history of Kaszubians in Canada running to more than three hundred and fifty pages.

Others with distant links were also drawn back to Poland. One of our earliest guests was Nicholas Rey, the US Ambassador to

Poland from 1993 to 1997. Nicholas was a descendent of Mikolaj Rey, Poland's best known poet of the renaissance period. He was also related to Andrzej Rej, the nobleman in Rembrandt's painting which hangs in the National Gallery of Art in Washington. Nicholas was born in Warsaw and was two years old when his family fled just four days after the Nazi invasion in 1939. Nicholas and his family visited us several times and the ambassador and I would go cross-country skiing together and chat about politics over a glass of wine in the evenings. The Russian Ambassador to Poland, Nikolai Afanasjevski, was also a visitor to the lodge but never at the same time as the Rej family.

Some of the other guests in the early days of the lodge came, not because of their Polish roots, but because they had known me in my earlier life as a correspondent. Adrien Brody, who played the Polish-Jewish pianist Władysław Szpilman in the Roman Polański film *The Pianist*, visited us with his parents after filming in Warsaw was finished. He had dieted fiercely to lose weight for his role and I'd like to be able to write that he visited Kania Lodge because he knew how good our food was and was keen to put on some weight. The reality was that he came with his parents. His mother is the photographer Sylvia Plachy, whose irreverent, wry pictures for a long time graced the pages of New York's alternative weekly, *The Village Voice*. Sylvia and I had worked on the same stories in different parts of the world and remained in touch after I ceased to be a foreign correspondent. Sylvia had been smuggled out of Hungary in 1956 when she was thirteen, ending up in New York like so many other twentieth-century European refugees. The lodge was already full the weekend Sylvia and her family visited and Adrien had to sleep on a fold-down bed in the office. The bed collapsed in the middle of the night and he slept on the floor.

Probably the most tentative and uneasy of the people looking for their roots in Poland were the Germans whose families had lived in

Pomerania and East and West Prussia for generations, sometimes centuries, before being expelled at the end of World War II. Their deep affection for Prussian forests and lakes or the once huge farming estates of Pomerania existed uneasily alongside residual guilt for the horrors of the Nazi era. They were tip-toeing back, anxious not to offend but keen to get a glimpse of the past that had been theirs or their family's. Many stayed with us on their way to Mazuria, further to the east, which had once been part of East Prussia. It stretched all the way from just east of the Vistula River to the present-day Russian enclave of Kaliningrad, also the name of the enclave's main city. For centuries Kaliningrad was Königsberg, a thriving German city where the eighteenth-century German philosopher Emmanuel Kant was born and where he wrote his major works, amongst them *Critique of Pure Reason*. East Prussia also was the home of the *Junkers*, the militaristic landed gentry who owned vast estates and imposing palaces and sometimes saw themselves as successors to the Teutonic Knights, the Germanic order which had conquered the region in the thirteenth century. The knights had been defeated by a Polish/Lithuanian army at Grunwald in the fifteenth century. But Germany's sense of manifest destiny in the region was rekindled when it routed the Russians at the battle of Tannenberg, not far from Grunwald, during World War I. A decade later work began on a giant brick monument redolent of the castles of the Teutonic Knights. Martial and bombastic, the monument laid down a marker in the east and expressed Germany's growing contempt for the Treaty of Versailles. Adolf Hitler gave a speech there in 1934 at the funeral of Paul von Hindenburg, the hero of Tannenberg and Germany's president during the Nazi leader's rise to power. Hitler announced the abolition of the presidency and his assumption of total power as 'Fuhrer'. In 1945 as the Russians advanced westwards, Hindenburg's remains were removed and several of the eight massive towers were blown up. In the 1950s the Polish Government levelled it completely, using bricks and other buildings materials from the site in the restoration of Warsaw. The Germans had destroyed much of the Polish capital in 1944 and the symbolism was blunt and politically charged. Germany's Baltic borders now stopped at the Oder River, not on the Memel, some six hundred kilometres to the east.

While nothing remains of the monument at Tannenberg, there is a statue of Kant in Kaliningrad and red-brick architectural reminders of the German era in most cities and towns of what was once East Prussia. Our German visitors heading eastwards had maps with place names in German and they poured over them before setting out, asking me how long it would take to get to particular places and what sort of accommodation they could expect. Some of our visitors were searching for places much closer to us in what was once West Prussia, centred on Gdańsk (*Danzig* in German) and spreading south and westwards to include Kaszubia. Before World War II, Kartuzy (*Karthaus* in German) was a German administrative centre. Had Kania Lodge existed then, we would have paid our taxes in *Karthaus*, spoken German on a daily basis outside the home and perhaps even voted for a representative in the Bundestag. Our children would have had to serve in the German army.

There are many reminders of this recent Germanic past. The main Catholic church in Kartuzy was originally a Lutheran church, its origins obvious in the austere, practical architecture. There is an equally austere red-brick school near the now-closed railway station, it too of German origin. Squat, red-brick Prussian houses, some with dates on their facades, can be found in most small towns. In the countryside a few Tudor-like half-timbered cottages are still standing. An overgrown cemetery in the nearby village of Kolonia

100

is littered with crumbling headstones weathered to anonymity. The cemetery was opened in 1802 by Prussian settlers who had been encouraged to move east by Friedrich Wilhelm III, the king of Prussia. In his honour they called the village Wilhelmshuld. It remained a predominately German village until the end of World War II. Three giant lime trees, which were probably planted at the time the cemetery was established, still stand in its north-eastern corner.

Some of our guests had family histories traceable back to small villages like Kolonia, and they would set out in the morning with maps, flasks of coffee and sandwiches. They often returned delighted that they had found the name of an ancestor in a cemetery or come across a village priest who spoke German and who had helped them locate a house or a street where their family had once lived or that they themselves could remember from childhood. Considering how murderous the Nazis had been during World War II, it was surprising to me how little animosity Poles showed towards the returning Germans.

There were scare stories occasionally in the popular press about Germans returning to take back property they had once owned. The xenophobic far Right expressed fears that rich Germans would circumvent restrictive land ownership laws by getting poor Poles to buy property for them. Common sense suggested that Germans in their sixties and seventies were not going to return to a country they only vaguely remembered and which was now under new management. They would much prefer to keep the little house in Bremen or Cologne and their generous German state pension and health benefits. Still, I sensed a little wistfulness in some of our German visitors and knew myself that there was something special about the place where one had been born or from which one's family originated. It would always tug at the heart. *Tęsknota* they called it in Polish, homesickness, but more powerful in its sense of loss, yearning and melancholy than the translation would suggest. Perhaps this was because Poles understood better than most what loss and yearning were all about. They'd lost their whole country for more than a century and had regularly been dispossessed of homes, farms and sense of place.

I was beginning to the feel the weight and texture of the word *tęsknota* myself, but not in regard to New Zealand or to my family's England. I did sometimes miss New Zealand but I felt no strong, compelling tug to go back. England had no appeal at all. Kania Lodge wasn't a place my family had owned for centuries or even somewhere that evoked warm childhood memories of swimming in the lake in summer or picking forest mushrooms in the autumn. Neither was I linked to it by memories of a first romance when the snow was deep and thick and smoothly contoured and everything was silent except for the beating of two youthful hearts. My children would one day have that kind of memory. But I felt a deep attachment to what we were creating and to the land itself, and I could imagine how I'd feel if some foreign army swept through and I lost it, as Poles had done over the centuries. My feeling for the word *tęsknota* was therefore largely in the future conditional tense as in '*If I were to be dispossessed sometime in the future, I know how I would feel*'. But I also had some practical experience of dispossession. It wasn't at the hands of some foreign army or the result of an ideological shift in domestic politics. It came from within the family itself and was to have repercussions I could then have hardly imagined.

THE MEADOW

One of the first pieces of land I had bought after the collapse of Communism in 1989 was a tiny meadow and a small stand of one-hundred-year-old trees, most of them beech but one a venerable oak. The meadow bordered the lake and there was a path from the hamlet to a rickety wooden jetty which was used by fishermen and the village children for a few weeks each year in summer. The meadow had been owned by one of the villagers, Eugeniusz Plichta, who had been glad to sell it because it was too small to be of much use, even for a farmer with just three cows. When we signed the deal, he said he was also willing to sell an adjoining piece of land which was a continuation of the escarpment we already owned.

This was a missing piece in the jigsaw of land we were buying to create a small but contiguous estate around the lodge that we planned to build. I was keen to buy it immediately, but Gienek (the diminutive of Eugeniusz) now had dollars in his pocket from the sale of the meadow and trees and felt he could wait a year or two before selling the adjoining piece. Like most small farmers in those days, Gienek didn't have a bank account. When farmers came into money they always kept it in cash, hiding it under the floor boards or a secret place in the attic. Cash could always be lost or stolen, but no one could run off with a piece of land. It was better to keep the land until you needed the money.

When we tried to register the purchase of the meadow in the land ownership books maintained by the council in Kartuzy, we found we had a problem. In the books the meadow we were buying

103

carried the same survey number as the adjacent piece of escarpment. Because there were trees there it was considered a forest and as such could not be divided. We could only legally buy the whole piece, so we couldn't register the sale to us of the meadow. This meant that although I had paid Gienek, the meadow was officially not ours but his. At the time this didn't seem much of a problem to me. Gienek had signed an agreement with us for the purchase of the meadow, a formal-looking typewritten document that had been witnessed by Ania's mother, her uncle and a neighbour. We could register the sale the following year when Gienek sold us the remainder of the forest. We would even save money on notary fees by doing it all at once.

In the spring of 1992, while waiting for planning permission for the lodge, we towed our caravan down to the meadow which everyone now regarded as ours. We already owned the meadow next to it, a sloping piece of ground of about half a hectare which descended to the water's edge. We had bought it from the Pakura family, who lived in a traditional wooden *chata* about one hundred and fifty metres away and used the green and yellow tractor they had bought with proceeds of the sale to plough the remainder of their land. The part of the meadow nearest the lake was level enough for me to organise pick-up games of football for children from the village and from the summer houses nearby. Sometimes there were as many as twelve players ranging in age from eight to twenty and games often became hotly competitive. I played and refereed at the same time, not to everyone's satisfaction in either role.

When the ball found its way into the lake, the game stopped while two boys jumped into a canoe and paddled after it. I was always pleased for the break since it got hot during the summer, occasionally more than 30°C. At the end of the game everyone stripped down to their shorts and dived into the lake to cool down.

I changed into a swimming costume in the caravan and dived in as well, often leaving them splashing about near the jetty to swim across to the other side of the lake where reeds grew in the shallow water. Sometimes I stopped in the middle of the lake and floated on my back, letting the sun warm me and thinking how lucky I was to be in the middle of a lake in Kaszubia rather than the middle of a war in Bosnia like many of my correspondent friends.

During the summer, people wandered down the path to our meadow throughout the day. The path was actually the property of the owners of the six summer houses, amongst them Ania's parents, her uncle Leszek and Zbyszek Wojnowski, the neighbour who had also signed the agreement I had with Plichta for the sale of the land. Families from Sytna Góra also used the path to access the lake and at weekends, if the weather was good, there were sometimes as many as thirty people lying about in our two meadows and using the jetty. I didn't mind the villagers and the people from the summer houses using our land. It was important to develop good relations with our neighbours. Local people had used our new meadow and the jetty for decades and since it was a good distance from the lodge there was no reason to stop them continuing to swim and picnic there. We regularly gave the village children sweets or ice cream and sometimes I shared a beer with the farmers while they watched their children splashing about in the water. Everyone was very friendly, my Polish was improving little by little and I felt at home in our caravan beneath the oak tree.

The oak tree had assumed a special importance for me because one day that spring Ania's uncle jogged down the path to tell me that my father had died. Leszek had received a phone call from Ania in Gdańsk who in turn had been called by my mother from their house in Corbridge, the pretty village on the Tyne in Northumberland where they lived. It was early evening and I was sitting outside beneath the oak tree. I had just noticed that my watch had stopped a couple of hours earlier and was wondering where I would find a new battery for it. The previous year, at the age of seventy, my father had undergone a heart bypass operation, and when I visited him a few months later he told me it didn't seem to have improved things. He was still suffering from angina. The morning I had to drive back to London he was still in bed when I went to say goodbye. Propped up against the pillows with his blue-striped pyjamas open at the neck, he looked old and tired. But his face lit up when I came in, and we talked for a few minutes. I promised I'd be back to see him and Mum in the autumn. Then I left.

I got as far as the bridge over the Tyne before I started crying, sensing that I might not see him again. I wished I'd hugged him and told him what a good father he'd been before I walked out of the bedroom. But that would have been admitting that his life was all but over, and I didn't want to acknowledge that. I couldn't have told him without tears and he would probably have cried too. We would both have been embarrassed and lost for words. He probably shed his own tears in the bedroom after I left. He had been a wonderful father, and I may have turned out to be a much better son than he could have hoped for when I left home at the age of sixteen and later dropped out of university.

Since I was travelling the world, much of our adult relationship had been built line by line on blue aerogrammes, those lightweight, single-sheet letter forms that were the cheapest and fastest way of corresponding in the pre-internet era. My father's tiny, meticulous handwriting told of family affairs, commented on events of the day and contained low-key advice and encouragement. Each letter was constructed with the same painstaking attention to detail and style as the fine pen and ink drawings he did as an architect to show clients what their new building would look like. World War II had helped hone his skills as a letter writer, letters being the only way he had of staying in touch with his fiancée, my mother, during the five years they were apart during the war while my father was serving in the Indian Army. Dad's letters were always eagerly devoured after I picked them up from a post office box or *poste restante* somewhere in Asia, Africa, the Middle East or Latin America. He always signed off 'favver,' reminding me how difficult I had found pronouncing 'th' as a child. I would write back more or less immediately, telling him and my mother what I was up to and where I had been, and engaging my father in discussions about world events.

Later, when I was enjoying some success as a correspondent, I flew to England at least once a year to spend time with my parents. Dad and I would sit up long after my mother had gone to bed and talk about everything from the local council's misdeeds to the geo-politics of the Middle East. My father had spent World War II in India and the Middle East as a lieutenant in the Indian Army and he loved it when I was posted to Beirut and later Cairo, sharing my views on the folly of much of American policy in the region and even becoming a subscriber to the magazine I worked for. He was thrilled to be able to visit me in Cairo, where I had a penthouse apartment in Zamalek. When he came back from the river cruise from Aswan to Luxor I had organised for him and Mum, he would sit in the shade on the apartment's terrace and work on watercolours of the rooftops of Zamalek.

A few years earlier, after he'd given up architecture and was making a precarious living painting landscapes of Northumberland and the English Lake District, the two parts of Britain he most loved, I was able to help my parents' finances by buying the house they were living in and giving them a lease in perpetuity. This freed up a lot of their cash, which they invested in interest-earning accounts and funds. I also bought two shops and gave them the income from the leases. It was to this house in Corbridge that I flew the following day to be with my mother and brothers and to say goodbye to my father. He was lying on a slab in an undertaker's in nearby Hexham, his body wrapped in a shroud with just his face showing. He looked younger and less wrinkled than when I had last seen him, as if death had released him from worry. I kissed him on the forehead while the undertaker looked on and then I left, fighting back tears. The following day I stood in a field of yellow buttercups and watched the black hearse take him off to the crematorium. He had told Mum that he didn't want any of us to go there, so we held a wake in the house at which the local vicar spoke of grief and the healing that time brought and urged us to 'let him go.'

Dad had died of a heart attack while on a ladder trimming a vine on a wall of the house. He'd fallen and banged his head, leaving blood on his glasses. He died at the exact hour, 1.30pm, as my watch had stopped in Poland, a good two hours before I heard the news of his death. Curiously, the watch started ticking again after Leszek had delivered the news. I know that it can be nothing more than coincidence, but I like to think sometimes that this was his way of telling me that his heart had stopped ticking and he was gone forever.

Gienek did not sell us the remaining piece of land the following year because he had yet to spend the money from the sale of the meadow. I was not particularly concerned. We had a contract and by now everyone recognised it as our piece of land. Anyway, there were other things on my mind. We had waited more than a year for planning permission for the lodge. Everyone told me that it was probably being held up because officials in the councils were waiting for an 'envelope' from me. Bribes had become part of the system during the Communist era and it was easy to see why.

Nothing was transparent and perpetual shortages of everything from cement to apartments and hospital places meant that people controlling access to these scarce commodities, they themselves poorly paid and scrabbling for something else not readily available, were almost expected to make something on the side. In his book *Mad Dreams, Saving Graces*, my friend and fellow correspondent Michael Kaufman, who was in Poland for the *New York Times* just before the collapse of the Communism, cited a wonderful example of just how corruption worked in small towns.

A peasant farmer from eastern Poland called Stanisław Kułaczkowski decided in the late 1980s to take advantage of a change in the law which allowed peasant farmers to become small-time entrepreneurs as well. This was at a time of falling farm incomes when the government feared that peasant farmers might join shipyard and factory workers in strikes and protests. Kułaczkowski was unable to eke out much of an existence on the few acres he owned so he wanted to make cinder blocks for building. Since this was a government-backed initiative, he had no problem getting a loan from the local farmers' co-operative bank. The bank director, a woman whom Kaufman describes in his book as 'stylish' with gold jewellery around her neck and wrists and an imported car parked outside the bank, was helpful in arranging the two-instalment loan. After Kułaczkowski received the first instalment and bought himself a truck, the bank manager instructed him to deliver a load of cinder blocks to a house she was building. He did, knowing that this was the 'pay off' for getting the loan. A few weeks later, she asked him to make another delivery to a house she was building for her son. He refused, saying that one was enough. She told him he was making a costly mistake.

Within days, police visited him saying that they would find something to fine him for if he caused trouble. The local tax office called him too and said, regardless of a regulation exempting farm businesses from taxes, he had to pay. He appealed to the Ministry in Warsaw, which sided with him. When he brought the decision to the notice of the local tax office he was arrested and held for several days. Police told his employees not to turn up for work and the bank manager refused to authorise the second part of the loan. He returned to Warsaw and obtained a written judgement that the bank manager had acted improperly. She then had him charged with slander in a Lublin court, which found him guilty.

His son's school principal called him in and warned that the boy's grades could be affected by his conflict with local officials. 'It was all one cabal,' Kułaczkowski told Kaufman. 'The banker, the police, the tax authorities and the courts were all tied together. At first they were after me just for the bribes. But later, as more and more people saw me fighting back, they realised they had to crush me to save face and power.' Kułaczkowski eventually triumphed in the courts but the story illustrates the power of the *nomenklatura* during the Communist era. It didn't miraculously disappear when the Communists were voted out of office. Local *układy* (cabals of local officials who scratch one another's backs) clung on like leeches, especially in small towns like Kartuzy near where I wanted to build the lodge.

One of the reasons why I did not have planning permission for the lodge a full year after applying, was probably because I didn't yet understand how the local *układ* functioned, or indeed who was who in local politics. If I had known that Elżbieta Wilkowska, the mayor's wife, had formerly been the town architect and now had a private business which specialised in preparing planning applications, I might usefully have made my submission through her. Had I known that the brother of the electrician who had done work for us was a good friend, town councillor and political ally of the deputy mayor, I might profitably have had a man-to-man conversation (*męska rozmowa*, they call it in Polish) with him over a bottle of vodka. A small envelope with a few crisp one hundred dollar bills given to the right person in the right circumstances might also have speeded the planning application through the system.

The mayor, Marian Wilkowski, had written to us that there was no provision in overall planning for the region for a hotel or lodge to be built where we proposed to build Kania Lodge. Yet the mayor had just built a huge house on a hilltop overlooking another lake. His deputy, Mieczysław Gołuński, whom I was to get to know well in the coming years after he became mayor, talked loftily of 'environmental concerns' at a time when untreated sewage from Kartuzy found its way into a lake near the town and most villages in the region had no sewage system at all. It was then that I first learnt the Polish word *załatwić*. It means to 'sort out', but in certain circumstances carries the understanding, readily understood, that the sorting out will be done in return for a bribe.

Bribes were not part of my culture. I knew too that, if I started bribing people, they and their friends would expect envelopes forever. For the local council, my project was a big one. In the immediate aftermath of the collapse of Communism, most Poles, especially those in small towns like Kartuzy, believed that all foreigners were rich. The burden of Polish history also made foreigners, even those from a country like New Zealand which had never invaded or enslaved Poles at any time in their history, popular targets for a shakedown.

Many foreign companies discovered this to their cost during the transition from a command to a free market economy. Foreign companies also found that history had given Poles cohesiveness in the face of enemies, real or imagined, and that it was extremely difficult to prise apart the overlapping layers of deceit beneath which some operated. One of my friends was involved in the building of one of the first big office blocks to go up in Warsaw in the early 1990s. Everything was going well in the planning stages until an important city official told him that local residents might hold up planning permission for the building.

'Has someone complained?' he asked. 'No, not yet,' he was told 'But they might. I could probably help you head off any protests.' A sum of money was mentioned. My friend declined the official's offer of help and, sure enough, there were protests which delayed construction, much to the annoyance of his principals in the United States. My friend employed a private detective to look into the local residents' association that had filed the complaint. The association had only just been set up, he established, and residents had been encouraged to band together by a lawyer who was a relative of the city official. The lawyer had even drafted their complaint for them on the understanding that, if they won damages, he would be entitled to a fee which, my friend assumed, would be shared with the lawyer's ally in city hall. In the end the company paid rather than fought.

Another friend, Zdzisław, a successful American lawyer of Polish descent, received a shock when he discovered that a garnishee order had been placed on his salary by a Warsaw court. The court had made the order in connection with a case a former landlady had brought against him over disputed rent. But Zdzisław had never been advised of the case, nor had he received notification of the court session. It turned out that notification had been sent to an address completely unknown to him. The registered letter had been signed for, by whom he was not able to find out, then returned to the court, which proceeded with the case in his absence. When the judge was told this, she did not rescind the garnishee order and set a new date for the case to be heard properly, but simply told Zdzisław he would have to appeal. In the meantime her judgement stood.

Since I was not prepared to bribe anyone for planning permission, my only option was to keep responding to the endless queries written in opaque bureaucratic language and hope the authorities would tire. Fortunately, I was busy writing and also had an income from investments. I also had no banks or partners chasing me for results or a quick return on borrowed capital. In 1993 the bureaucratic logjam suddenly freed itself up in a way that convinced me I had been right in thinking the lack of a bribe had been holding things up. At that time, mayors in Poland were not elected by popular vote but by their fellow councillors, themselves popularly elected. There were essentially two groups jostling for power in the Kartuzy council, and the opposition managed to rustle up the numbers and engineer a vote which ousted Mayor Wilkowski and his friends. The victor was Maria Koska-Kowalewska, a businesswoman in her thirties, who promised to clean up the murkier aspects of the conduct of local government business in Kartuzy. I quickly brought my longstanding application to Maria's attention and within weeks we had planning permission to build Kania Lodge. In my several meetings with her, there was never any suggestion that I should pay under the table or that I 'owed her' for the decision.

Maria, who had visited the site of the lodge, believed that my investment would be good for the region and that it was the kind of development her council should encourage. 'I don't know why the previous office holders held up your application for so long,' she told me. 'We desperately need investment of all kinds if we are to move ahead.' Maria was to be deposed as mayor two years later by the same cabal she herself had ousted, but by then the lodge was up and running.

When building work started, I was too busy to give much thought to the meadow we had bought and paid for, but still didn't officially own. Gienek had assured me that next year he would sell us the small piece of forest on the escarpment which would enable us to register our ownership. I had no reason to doubt him. The forest was of no use to him, and it was not a piece of land anyone else would have a reason to buy. We spent the winter in my parents' house in England, which my mother had vacated after Dad's death because it was too big and held too many memories for her. In January, I flew to Poland to check on progress and make payments to the architect and builders.

Ania's uncle Leszek drove from Gdańsk to Kaszubia to accompany me as I toured the building site with Marek, our architect. 'It's huge,' said Leszek at one stage, 'How are you going to use all this space?' I explained that most of the space would be for guests and that our own family quarters would take up only a small part of the space. 'Still too big,' he said, 'you'll never get enough people to come out here to make it worthwhile.' He became so gruff and short with me I wondered whether seeing the buildings had made him envious.

The two buildings were big by local standards. Leszek was my age and had spent the best years of his life scrabbling to make ends meet in a system that discouraged anyone or anything from standing out. During the Communist era, Poland had developed its own ideologically-sound version of envy. It wasn't about coveting something your neighbour had or seeing a fancy car drive past and wishing you had one. It was about dispossessing others of anything that incited your envy. Poles even made jokes about the negative connotations of their envy. A common one, taken from the original crabs in a bucket tale and with all sorts of variations when it comes to nationalities, goes like this: There are three pots of boiling oil, one full of Germans, the second full of French and the third full of Poles. The Germans and French are seen clambering up the sides and escaping. No one is getting out of the Polish pot. As soon as someone gets near the rim, his countrymen pull him back down. Another joke is about an old farmer who is told by God that he can have anything he wants. However, whatever he chooses, his neighbour will get twice as much. He thinks for a while and replies: 'Okay, then gouge out one of my eyes.'

Since envy is the sibling of pride, I imagine that the Polish version, if indeed one can attach a flag to something so nebulous, has a lineage which can be traced back at least to medieval times when status and honour meant everything to the ruling classes. The Polish Nobel Prize winner Czesław Miłosz once wrote that envy in English was not nearly as true to the Latin *invidia* as *zadrość* is in Polish. Like the Latin *invidia*, he suggested in his essay *Saligia*, Polish *zadrość* has the meaning, not just of envy in the English sense, but also of hatred and slander. He felt that the twentieth century in Europe ought to be called the age of *invidia*, arguing that the huge social mobility it spawned was at the root of envy. When the rigid caste systems throughout Europe collapsed, people no longer knew their place in the hierarchy. The collapse of Communism in Poland had again shaken up the social order. The egalitarianism of poverty that had marked that era was giving way to a world in which risk-takers were often rewarded, sometimes conspicuously. There was plenty to be envious about, especially if one was too old or unskilled to share in the new opportunities and rewards.

Envy is not the exclusive preserve of Poles. The Anglophone world, most particularly Australia and New Zealand, has its Tall Poppy Syndrome (TPS), the etymology of which can be traced to Greek and Roman mythology. The Oxford Dictionary of

New Zealand English describes a Tall Poppy as 'a person who is conspicuously successful and whose distinctions frequently attract envious notice or hostility,' and TPS itself as 'the New Zealand habit of denigrating or cutting down those who are successful or are high achievers.' The Australian golfer Greg Norman describes the difference between American and Australian envy thus: 'If someone in the US bought a sports car Americans would say 'nice car.' If someone in Australia bought a sports car, Australians would say 'scratch it'.' When I was growing up in New Zealand in the 1950s, a time when the country's cradle-to-the-grave welfare culture was probably at its zenith, my father frequently railed against TPS and its cult of mediocrity. Recent visits have confirmed to me that New Zealand still does not like winners very much, unless they happen to be fifteen strapping men in black shirts playing rugby. That could be one reason why New Zealand continues to suffer a brain drain.

I went back to England puzzled by the souring of Leszek's attitude towards me, but still not imagining what was to unfold when we returned to Poland in the spring. The day we disembarked from the *Inowrocław* a few months later, Leszek and his wife Hanna joined us at Ania's parents' home for supper. Halfway through the meal, my father-in-law, Marian, cleared his throat and said he had something to tell us. He spoke good English and chose his words carefully as he proceeded to explain that the law regarding the sale and purchase of rural land had changed in our absence. It was now possible to divide land like the meadow we had purchased from Plichta.

'In fact,' he said, 'we have already officially registered our ownership of the land at the *notariusz* [public notary].'

'Our ownership?' I asked, not quite sure what was going on. 'What do you mean by 'our'?'

'We divided the ownership into three parts,' he said, 'Alicja and I have a half, Leszek and Hanna a quarter, and you and Ania a quarter. We'll give half of ours to Peter [Ania's brother] when he comes from America next month.'

'But why?' I asked, astonished by what I was hearing. 'Ania and I paid for the land. It's ours. We didn't ask you to divide it up.'

My father-in-law reminded me that in the autumn of the previous year I had removed the rickety wooden jetty on the lake without consulting them. They were worried that I was going to deny them access to the lake.

'But that's ridiculous,' I spluttered, getting angry now and raising my voice. 'I told you we'd build a new jetty in the spring. The old one was falling to bits and dangerous, you know that. I have already ordered the timber for the new one. As for access, you own part of the path down to the lake. I couldn't stop you even if I wanted to – and why would I, you're Ania's parents.'

'*Mało masz?*' [Do you have too little?] interjected Leszek, while his wife berated Ania for siding with me. 'We're your family,' she hissed.

The '*mało masz*' did it for me. Gathering up our things and waking Harley who was asleep upstairs, I loaded up the car and headed for a hotel in Gdynia.

'How could they do this to us?' I kept asking Ania well into the night as I paced the room. 'It doesn't make sense.'

'*Zazdrość*,' [envy] she said. 'That's all I can think of.'

'But why would they be envious of their own daughter and niece?' I asked, still not comprehending.

'They just want to put us in our place,' Ania replied.

Over the next few days I berated Gienek for signing the land over to them and talked to lawyers about what I could do. Nothing, they told me, it's already in the land registry and that's that. The family tried to placate us with gifts of honey and offers to babysit Harley. Periodically I went over to Ania's parents' summer house to try to persuade them to give back the land which now had Iwona, Ania's sister-in-law, as a fourth owner. This further complicated matters. It was also senseless because Iwona and Peter, Ania's brother, lived in the US. They were unlikely to return to Poland for anything but fleeting visits. Marian tried to pay me in US dollars for the share he had taken in the land but I handed the envelope straight back. This wasn't about money, I told him, it was about not doing things behind our backs.

'It is madness,' I railed over and over again at Ania. 'Here I am investing everything I've got in a venture in a foreign country, and the first people who stab me in the back are my in-laws. Think what sort of message that sends out to everyone we have to deal with around here. If his own family can cheat him, so can we.'

Families anywhere are an inherently unstable social group – you can, after all, *choose* your friends. Balance and functionality in a family can be disturbed or destroyed by a single member or single incident. Polish families are probably no more prone to dysfunctionality than families elsewhere, but Polish culture shapes the form of the structural failure. In recent times Catholicism and Communism had colluded unwittingly in strengthening the hand of the older generation in family life. To the 'honour thy mother and father' teachings of the Church, the Communists had added the tyranny of overcrowding and lack of private space. Because it was almost impossible to get an apartment, young people lived with their parents well into their twenties, often into their thirties or forties, and very often long after they were married and had children of their own. Two generations of grown-ups can only survive together in a fifty-square-metre apartment if there is a fairly rigid pecking order, with the parents still parents and the children, even in their thirties, still children. The land grab was the family's way of telling Ania that she was still the child, regardless of being married and having a son of her own, and that they still had the final say on anything. Having a foreign husband complicated matters because he didn't respect them as the ultimate decision makers.

In his book *The Last Mazurka*, Andrew Tarnowski, a fellow journalist and scion of one of Poland's most aristocratic families, recalled a visit he made in 1999 to the family's recently recovered mansion at Rudnik in southern Poland. Four generations of the family, some thirty people, were gathered to celebrate the return and partial restoration of the imposing manor house which once stood at the centre of several thousand hectares of farm land and forest. The family gathering ended in argument and recrimination after Andrew asked about the renovation of several Tarnowski family properties. 'It was my first real view of the depths of the family's wretchedness,' he wrote in the final chapter. 'But I realised later that I was part of the problem. While the family seemed impossibly dysfunctional to me, to most of them I was an intruder committing the unpardonable offence of questioning the dispositions of Staś, [Andrew's father] and Sophie [his aunt].' They were both in their eighties and joint owners of the inheritance. 'The legacy of the past, with its archaic ways that excluded common sense and rational discussion, was as cruel as it had been sixty years earlier,' Tarnowski wrote.

Eventually Ania's parents gave us back their quarter share. Leszek said he would too. Then Ania's father died suddenly of a heart attack, collapsing at his summer house on a day when we were expecting him for lunch. We brought his body to the lodge and laid it on a carpet in the lounge, a pillow under his head, while we waited for a doctor to sign the death certificate. I felt wretched as I crouched next to him, trying to console Ania and her mother. Until the business with the land I had never had a cross word with him and had genuinely liked him. I admired the fact that he had built two houses with his own hands and that everything he did was completed with detailed precision. I knew that Ania and her brother had had wonderful childhoods growing up in Africa when he worked as an architect in Ghana. I knew, too, that I would never understand what it had been like to grow up during German and Russian reigns of terror or to live through, even prosper, during forty years of Communism.

Perhaps I had been too precipitate in dismantling the jetty. I wondered whether I shouldn't have turned a blind eye to the loss of the meadow and been a bit more humble. I could be stubborn when I felt wronged or cheated. Sometimes I didn't see the larger picture. But if they had concerns, why had they not raised them with me rather than sneaking off to the *notariusz* when they found the law had changed? I think Marian knew that what had happened hadn't been right and regretted it. I believe he was talked into it by Leszek and my mother-in-law, Alicja, who was Leszek's sister.

The following year, when Leszek had still not made good on his earlier promise to return his share of the land, I went with Ania and Harley to visit him at his summer house.

'So when are you returning the land Leszek?' I asked after having greeted him.

'What land?' he demanded, his eyes narrowing.

'You know what I'm talking about, the meadow.'

'Oh, that,' he said, feigning surprise. 'I'm not returning that.'

Ania remonstrated with him, reminding him of his earlier promise.

'You killed your father with all your nonsense. What are you trying to do now?' he asked, 'Kill me too?'

Ania confirmed what I thought Leszek had said and, furious, I hit him. It was a single, right-handed hook to the head and it brought him to his knees.

'You're a coward Leszek,' I said to him in English, knowing that he wouldn't understand but feeling more comfortable berating him in English.

Within the hour the police were knocking on my door. A month later, a registered letter informed me that a local court had found me guilty of assault.

WORKING CLASS, *INTELIGENCJA* OR ARISTOCRACY?

The court's decision came by registered letter in the form of a *nakaz karny* [notification of a fine] from the Regional Court in Kartuzy. I was shocked when I opened and read the three-page decision with the purple stamp of a crowned Polish eagle on the last page. I had never been informed that the case was going to court, let alone been given a time and date for the hearing. Worst of all, I had been charged not just with hitting Leszek, but with threatening to burn down his house and kill him. I was flabbergasted. Not only had I not made any threats but my Polish was not up to making them. 'I'll burn your house down,' or 'I'll kill you,' were not the sort of phrases picked up from Polish textbooks. Arson and death threats were not in my lexicon. Leszek spoke no English so could hardly be claiming that I had made them in my mother tongue.

It seemed like rough justice, the sort one expected during the Communist era when police, prosecutors and judges worked hand in hand. Why had I not been informed of the charges and the date of the trial and been given the opportunity to defend myself? The court secretary just shrugged when I asked, offering no explanation but telling me I had the right to appeal if I wasn't happy with the judgement. I was very unhappy. It was not so much that the penalty was a fine of one thousand złoty (about two hundred and forty dollars at the then rate of exchange) or twenty days in jail, but that I would also finish up with a criminal record.

I appealed to the County Court, which sat in Gdańsk in a grey nineteenth-century building with massive pillars and wide echoing corridors leading to high-ceilinged court rooms with heavy wooden furniture. Not only was the architecture oppressive, but county courts were still burdened with many of the trappings and procedures of the Communist era. At the trial I was first asked to provide my parents' Christian names and my mother's maiden surname. Every bureaucrat seemed to ask you these questions, the relevance of which only those who have lived in a police state would fully understand. They wanted to know exactly who you were and be able to trace your antecedents in case any were class enemies. Your father might well be a Kowalski [Smith], but perhaps he had married a countess and that would change everything.

The next question the judge asked me was my social class. I wondered why this was relevant. Coming from a relatively egalitarian and classless society like New Zealand, I had no answer. No one had ever posed the question before. Seeing me struggle, the judge helped me: 'Working class, *inteligencja* or aristocracy?' he asked. I imagine that during the Communist era you wouldn't have done yourself any favours by admitting that you were part of the dispossessed and despised aristocracy, at best an exploiter and class enemy in socialist parlance. The *inteligencja* were suspect while the Polish United Workers Party held sway from 1948 until 1989, not so much because of the actual work they did as doctors, university professors or actors, but because they could think, reason and spread subversion. Both Stalin and Hitler had also feared Poland's *inteligencja* and had executed them in large numbers during World War II.

Towards the end of the Communist era in Poland, even the workers themselves were disloyal and could not be relied upon to support the party. At the very end they teamed up with the *inteligencja* to give the last rites to the Communist system. The shipyard where Lech Walesa and his *inteligencja* allies in Solidarity had brought down the system was just a kilometre or so from the courtroom where I now found myself wondering whether I should declare myself a worker or part of the *inteligencja*. The Judge solved the dilemma for me. 'What's your profession?' he asked. 'Journalist, writer,' I answered. '*Inteligencja*,' he said.

The next question was harder to answer and even less relevant, or at least should have been, to the case before the court. 'How much do you earn?' the judge asked, peering at me with his pen poised to record my answer. 'That's difficult to say,' I responded, 'because I don't actually have a job right now. My earnings at the moment depend on what I earn from articles I write for magazines.' The judge frowned. 'So how much did you earn last month?' 'Nothing,' I said. 'I didn't write anything last month.' I could see he was getting irritated and thought it best not to antagonise him, so I gave him a figure that I had recently earned from a US magazine for an article. When he raised his eyebrows at what doubtless would seem quite a lot of money to a public servant in Poland, I quickly assured him that I had written only three such pieces in the whole of the previous year.

I hoped that would get me off a massive fine if the case went against me. It seemed strange to me that, in this new democratic age, my salary was of any relevance in a court case. But I knew it was not uncommon to be asked this question in relation to a potential penalty one faced. A police officer in Kartuzy had once asked my wife how much she earned as he started to write out a parking ticket. 'What does it matter?' she asked. 'The richer you are, the more you pay,' he replied, oblivious to how farcical and silly his explanation sounded. 'Then I'm poor, out of work and have children to support,' Ania replied.

Leszek had brought four witnesses to the court, three of them friends who had been at his summer house and the fourth, Gienek

Plichta, the farmer who had sold the disputed piece of land. Leszek took the stand to tell the court that I had punched him in the face and then threatened to kill him and burn down his summer house. 'In what language were the threats made?' the judge asked him. 'Polish,' he replied. The first witness told the court that I had been shouting in English and Polish and threatened to kill Leszek in such a way that 'it looked as if the threat might be carried out.' She said she had seen me hit Leszek but, when I cross-examined her, she couldn't remember whether my threat had been in English or Polish. The judge raised his eyebrows. 'There's quite a big difference, surely you can remember.' She shifted uneasily. 'I am not sure.'

The third witness, the husband of the woman who had appeared on the stand before him, could not recall hearing any threats. Neither could the fourth, our neighbour Plichta, who had been working in a garden next to Leszek's house at the time. But he did admit that I had been talking loudly and that if I had made the threats, he would certainly have heard them. My only witness was Ania, who told the court that I had not made threats of any kind. The judge found the evidence contradictory and unreliable and dismissed the charges, fining me a small sum for the scuffle with Leszek because I admitted striking him.

That should have been the end of matters. But it wasn't. First of all, the police turned up at the lodge looking for me because they had received a complaint that I had locked up my wife in the house and was restricting her 'personal liberty.' I was in Africa at the time, and Ania was both amused and angry at the police visit. 'Look, this is absurd,' she told them. 'My husband is in Africa right now, so how could he lock me up even if he wanted to? And why would he? We have a happy marriage. Who has told you such nonsense?' They sheepishly admitted that the complaint had come from a member of her family but insisted I report to the police station when I returned to make a statement. Two weeks later, I shoved my airline ticket and passport across the desk to the investigating officer. 'There, check for yourself that I wasn't even in Poland at the time.' I signed a statement and stormed out, still angry because I knew the police would do nothing about the false and malicious report. They were enjoying the little drama.

Plichta and his family had by now thrown in their lot with Leszek and set about harassing us at every opportunity. They occupied the jetty down at the lake and made it difficult and unpleasant, through constant use of expletives and obscenities, for guests at the lodge to use it. I built another jetty two hundred metres away and out of sight of the old one. When I anchored an old shipyard pontoon belonging to Ania's brother at the end of it, Plichta's family kept moving it to the old jetty for their own use. One day, just after retrieving the pontoon and anchoring it again near our new jetty, I found Plichta's eighteen-year-old daughter, Magda, standing on the jetty directing some youths in a boat to move it. I told her to get off our property and not come back. She went slowly, swearing at me as she went. The youths, meanwhile, jeered and swore before rowing off. The following morning the pontoon had gone again. The police, of course, took no action.

That same week, Plichta waved down my car on the narrow village lane and proceeded to kick at the passenger-side door. When I opened the door to protest, he hit me three times across the arms and back with a long piece of willow used for herding cows. 'You leave my daughter alone,' he swore, suggesting I had done something more than just order her off my property. The assault was witnessed by Emilia Pobłocka, one of our lodge employees, from the window of the house opposite. When the police arrived, they tried to discourage her from making a statement. When she insisted, her witness statement and the police report were forwarded to the public prosecutor. He decided that, as my injuries were not serious, it was not in the public interest to charge Plichta with assault and malicious damage to my car.

On another occasion, when I had stopped in the lane to take photographs, Plichta emerged from his house and removed my car keys through the open window. The police responded to my call about an hour later. By this time Plichta had thrown the keys back through the window. 'So what's your problem?' they asked me. 'Your keys are there and you are blocking a public road. We could charge you for that.' The police were similarly unhelpful when Gienek chopped down recently-planted trees on our property and when one of his dogs attacked and badly injured one of our sheep. Some of our workers witnessed the attack and told the police what they had seen.

It was clear that, not only could I not expect any help from the authorities in Kartuzy, but Plichta was probably being encouraged to make problems for us. Some people didn't like the fact that there was a foreigner in their midst. Kartuzy is a small town and the police, public prosecutor, courts and local council were not used to people standing up to them. One was supposed to be meek and subservient and I was neither. They saw me as arrogant, not only for challenging decisions but for asking questions. The old guard were back in power in the council and I was beginning to learn just how interrelated people in Kaszubia were and how important it was to know who was who.

Plichta's next move was to demand payment for access to Kania Lodge. He owned the land through which the road leading from the hamlet to the lodge passed. But he'd given us written authorisation to use it without payment, authorisation which was an essential part of the planning application for the lodge. Without documented right of access, there would have been no planning permission. Years earlier, before what we now referred to as 'the troubles', Plichta had happily exchanged use of the road for permission from us to access one of his meadows through our land. Now he wanted to be paid, not in cash, but in fuel for his tractor. He could have run two or three tractors on the amount of fuel he wanted.

I wasn't planning to reward him for breaking the agreement. I knew that an official valuation of the land would be low and that we could ultimately get a court order confirming the access. So we applied to the civil court in Kartuzy for what in Polish is a *droga konieczna*, probably best translated as a 'necessary' or 'obligatory' road. The court awarded us the *droga konieczna* and, basing its valuation of the land on a report from an agronomist on the quantity of rye that could be grown there, ordered us to pay Plichta the sum of two hundred złoty, then about fifty euros, per annum in rent.

Plichta appealed the decision and set about making it extremely difficult to negotiate the turn from the lane into the access road leading to the lodge. He did this by using large rocks and earth to block the easy turn at the corner beneath the old pear tree. This made the turn an acute right angle that was extremely difficult to execute given the confines and contour of the lane. We could do it in our cars, but trucks had real difficulties. When the tanker that emptied our septic tank got through one day, Plichta responded by rolling a large stone into the middle of the road. Other trucks delivering supplies refused to drive to us as they had before. Guests, too, had problems, and I had to keep explaining what was going on. Had there been a fire at the lodge, the fire brigade would not have been able to reach us. I tried enlisting the fire chief's help but quickly realised that he was a close ally of the mayor's. I tried to solve the problem by gathering together most of the other villagers and having them remove the stones and dirt to restore the turn to its original condition. They helped, albeit reluctantly, telling me a week or two later that the priest had remonstrated with them after mass for helping me.

Plichta then put up a wooden fence that again made access a difficult ninety degree turn. The fence was built illegally without the planning permission which is required for fences adjoining public roads but, far from ordering him to remove it, the council gave it retrospective authorisation. When I changed the contour of the road and built up the far side of the turn to make access much easier, Plichta erected a barrier on the access road. He dug in heavy posts on either side of it and suspended a long pole between them. A hand-painted sign said 'Private property. No Access.' Ania and I removed the pole every time we drove in and out of the lodge. In our rear view mirrors we would see Gienek or one of the other Plichtas rushing out to replace it.

The Frankowski family began to be harangued by Plichta's wife, Janka, who demanded that they pay to use the road. Other lodge employees were also harassed by the Plichtas, who used crude language in their attempts to intimidate them. Fortunately, there was no love lost between most villagers and the Plichtas and they responded contemptuously. Most sympathised with us. We were by then employing nearly a dozen local people; we paid well and were regarded as good neighbours and fair employers.

One night I received a call from Roger, an ex-Rhodesian farmer who worked for a tobacco company based in a city two hundred kilometres away. I had been expecting him because I thought I might grow tobacco on some of our land. He was stuck at the barrier where someone was yelling at him. 'What's the problem?' he called to ask me. I told him I was on my way to sort things out. When I reached the barrier, Plichta was there and Roger was sitting in his car looking bewildered. Without speaking to Plichta, I removed the pole from the barrier and waved Roger through. Suddenly I felt a blow to the back of my head. I turned around to see Plichta with a thick fence pole in his hand. I put my hand up to my head, and it came away bloodied. I could feel blood trickling onto my neck. I ran to the car and reversed quickly down the drive. Roger followed. When we reached the house, I asked Ania to call the police and then look at the wound. 'There's quite a lot of blood,' she said, 'but it doesn't seem to be very deep.'

This time the police and public prosecutor would not be able to turn a blind eye. Clubbing someone over the head could never be considered a trivial matter. The blow could have killed me and I had a witness to everything. When the police arrived the bleeding had stopped but my hair was matted with blood and my collar still soaked. They gave everything a cursory glance and one of them said: 'That doesn't look very serious. I'd forget about it if I were you.' They had already stopped at Plichta's house and told me that he was complaining that I had run over him. Roger said this was nonsense, that he'd seen everything and was happy to make a statement. The police reluctantly scribbled a few notes on a pad and left. 'Bastards,' I swore as I heard their car starting. 'You can be sure that if I had hit Plichta on the head with a fence pole they'd have taken me away in handcuffs and thrown me into a police cell. Then they would have charged me with attempted murder.'

The next morning I visited the hospital in Kartuzy and got a doctor to examine the wound and to write a report saying that the injury was consistent with being hit on the head from behind with a fence pole. I knew that I needed as much evidence as possible to force the public prosecutor's hand. Then I went to the police station to make a statement. The police were again unhelpful, telling me that the injury did not seem very serious and that perhaps it would be easier if I just paid Plichta what he wanted for use of the access road. 'So if Plichta had shot at me and the bullet had just grazed my temple you would be saying the injury wasn't serious and therefore he had no case to answer?' I asked. The two officers looked at each other, mumbled something I couldn't hear and then, with unconcealed reluctance, took my statement.

Three weeks later I received notification from the public prosecutor that since I hadn't been hospitalised or forced to take sick leave, it was not in the public interest to prosecute Plichta. During those three weeks, I noticed police cars parked outside Plichta's house on several occasions. I also noticed that after each visit there were fewer geese in his yard.

Ania and I were dismayed at the decision not to prosecute. It portended further, perhaps even worse, violence. It encouraged Plichta to take the law into his own hands, and it threatened our business and the jobs of all the people who worked for us. We talked well into the night, wondering whether the sensible thing to do wouldn't be to sell up and go somewhere else. But where? And what would we do? Harley was now five and attending pre-school in Kartuzy. Alexander was three and would shortly be joining him there. They loved it at the lodge, as any child would. There were soft, closely cut lawns to play on in summer and snowy slopes to sled down in the winter. They had a lake on their doorstep and forests and ponds to explore as they got older. It was the same sort of outdoor children's paradise in which I had grown up in New Zealand.

We loved the lodge too. We had lived in some of the world's biggest cities, London, New York, Cairo and Mexico City amongst them, and knew how lucky we were to wake up each morning in such natural beauty. We enjoyed the challenge of making things work. It is one thing to build a fancy lodge in the middle

131

of nowhere, another to persuade people to patronise it. But we were succeeding. Our guests now included ambassadors and the presidents of some of Poland's largest companies. Articles about us were appearing in national newspapers and magazines. Polish friends were sympathetic and supported our fight against the local *układ*. '*Zazdrość*,' they'd say, 'It's all about envy.' We had the comfort, too, of knowing that most of the village was on our side. But it was immensely frustrating and stressful to be living in the midst of a conspiracy, to know that we couldn't trust any branch of local administration to be rational, reasonable or, most of all, fair.

'Of course, you know that's what they want us to do – sell up and move on,' Ania pointed out. 'They'd rub their hands with glee if we did that. It would be a big victory for them.'

She was right and I knew we couldn't give up without putting up a fight. I found a lawyer and we filed a private prosecution against Plichta for assault. I didn't expect to win this in the regional court in Kartuzy, but reckoned we might succeed on appeal to the County Court in Gdańsk. My earlier experience there suggested that the tentacles of the local *układ* did not reach that far.

The case meandered for more than a year, as court cases often do in Poland, until one day I found myself sitting in a tiny, bare room in the run-down courthouse waiting for the judge's verdict. During the trial, Plichta had produced a witness who claimed to have seen the incident and swore that Plichta had not hit me. We proved the witness was at his home three kilometres away at the time of the incident. The police produced a report that said Plichta was an upright, honest citizen and highly thought of by his neighbours. We showed that at no stage had the police canvassed the opinions of any of his neighbours. The clincher, of course, was evidence given by Roger. He had witnessed the assault and drove to Kartuzy especially for the court session. But I still worried about the verdict

132

and it was a relief to hear the judge pronounce Plichta guilty. She imposed a fine of 2,870 złoty, nearly one thousand dollars, a lot of money for a subsistence farmer. She also gave Plichta a suspended jail sentence. 'Yes,' I said to Ania outside the courthouse, clenching my fist and emphasising the word with a hiss. 'We got the bastard. Now he's going to have to watch his step.'

Plichta did not appeal against this decision. He had already appealed not once but twice against the earlier court decision regarding the road which valued our usage of it at fifty dollars a year. The original decision had been validated by the County Court in Gdańsk and now he had appealed to the Supreme Court in Warsaw. Ania took the train to Warsaw on the day of the judgement and called me in the afternoon. 'We won,' she said breathlessly, 'The court upheld the earlier decisions. And that's the end of it. No more appeals are possible.'

Ania was right about no more appeals being possible, but that still wasn't the end of our harassment. Soon afterwards we learnt that the state-owned television company, *TV Polska*, was planning to screen a documentary about a poor but plucky Kaszubian farmer whose life had been ruined following the arrival in his neighbourhood of a rich and rapacious foreigner. You can guess who the farmer was and who the rapacious outsider. A formal, printed invitation to a press preview screening which had come my way via a friend, said the film's title was: '*A shocking story of greed and helplessness*.' It concerned, the invitation went on, a Kaszubian village which had changed from 'paradise to hell' [*Kaszubska wioska która zamienia się z raju w piekło*] following the arrival of a foreigner. The main characters, the press invitation said, were Kaszubian villagers (plural) and a New Zealander. I had run into the cameraman and script writer the previous year while they were filming Plichta manning his barrier across our access road. The cameraman displayed a complete lack of professionalism by trying to stop Janek Frankowski from driving a two-horse buggy down to the lodge. 'Don't you know that this is private road?' he shouted at Janek. 'There's no access here.'

Janek ignored him just as he ignored the abuse hurled at him from time to time by the Plichtas. I also knew that the cameraman and the scriptwriter, a woman in her late fifties who had obviously learnt her trade during the Communist era, had not filmed or talked to any of the other villagers. But she had visited the priest in Prokowo. Had he, I wondered, been a source for the narrative about Sytna Góra changing from paradise to hell since my arrival a few years ago? I doubted it. He knew I had provided people with jobs, paid for language lessons for my staff, supported the local school and funded road improvements. He also knew I was invited to weddings, dances and other social events by most of the villagers. He had even seen me in his church for the funerals of two of his parishioners. I got on with everyone in Sytna Góra except Gienek Plichta. Why had Sytna Góra suddenly become hell and what had I to do with the sudden transition?

Curious to find out, I sought a meeting with the director of *Telewizja Polska* in Gdańsk, Bogumił Osiński. He refused to meet me. He informed me through an assistant that I would be unwelcome at the press screening of the film the following week. But I was a journalist, I responded, why the discrimination? The aide came back to me a couple of days later. He had checked with the Foreign Ministry and I wasn't registered with them as a journalist. 'But this is 1999, not 1949,' I told him. 'This is not the Communist era when journalists were corralled and told what they could do and where they could travel to. Poland is now a democracy, a member of NATO and about to join the European Union. Foreign journalists don't have to check in with a ministry anymore. Only people afraid of being scrutinised try to keep journalists at bay.'

He would not relent. I sat down and penned a three-page letter to Director Osiński pointing out that no less than the Supreme Court had upheld our right to use the access road, that Plichta had been convicted of assault and given a suspended jail sentence and that no one else in the village had been canvassed for their opinion.

'Although I have not yet seen the film, both the title and the manner in which your team has conducted itself in and around Sytna Góra suggest that it contains material that is deliberately inaccurate, untruthful and consequently libellous. I am horrified at the lack of professionalism shown by your reporter and cameraman and need not point out that in Poland there are several laws concerning accuracy, fairness and intent and that ultimately the documentary will be judged on these grounds.'

Osiński, himself a journalist, albeit one who had learnt his trade under the Communists, was not giving any ground. Bureaucrats in Poland are generally reluctant to admit a mistake or climb down from a silly or even dangerous position. This is partly misplaced pride and partly the fact that, throughout the Communist era, functionaries were never wrong. Their decisions might be ridiculous, pathetic, dangerous, unfair or even self-defeating, but they were never wrong. To admit that would bring into question the omnipotence of the system itself. One could not be at the vanguard of a socialist revolution and admit to getting things wrong.

The gist of Osiński's response was that he found the documentary fair and balanced. He warned me that if I continued to question the professionalism of his team, he might take me to court.

'Please do Mr Osiński,' I wrote back. 'I'd love to meet you and your very unprofessional employees in a court of law.'

While he wasn't backing down, my complaints were probably forwarded to *Telewizja Polska*'s lawyers. Extensive changes to the documentary were ordered. The title '*A shocking story about greed and helplessness*' disappeared, as did the line about Sytna Góra changing from paradise to hell following my arrival. When the documentary was eventually screened it was so disembowelled that I found it impossible to work out what they were trying to say. I was amused by a shot of Plichta in his kitchen with a pile of legal papers and court documents. 'Look,' he bleated plaintively, 'I'm being harassed all the time.'

GOOD NOSE, NICE FRUIT

My decision to stay on and fight the local *układ* and the bureaucratic legacies of the Communist era was influenced by the fact that I had stumbled haphazardly into a new business which was complementary to the lodge and which was beginning to grow. For the first two years after the opening of the lodge, I had been happy to make it work well enough to provide us with a modest income. This it quickly did. Building the lodge had not been an investment in the sense that I sat down with a calculator and crunched numbers to calculate profit margins, the return on investment and an exit strategy. If the primary purpose had been to make money, I would have done a lot better buying a McDonald's franchise. We'd built the lodge primarily as a place to live, taking in guests to provide me with the means to escape being constantly on the road as a foreign correspondent.

Success in journalism had come at a price and I was seldom at home, living most of the time in hotels somewhere near conflicts in the Middle East, Africa or Latin America. And while I saw myself as cool under the pressure of news gathering in dangerous places and of meeting New York's deadlines, I suffered from cluster migraines which occasionally almost disabled me. I had seen specialists in London, Vienna and New York who offered palliatives but no cure. Cluster migraines are excruciating and the best bonus I got when I finally resigned from *Time*, better even than the company stock I received, was that since that day I have never had so much as a hint of a migraine. It was as simple as that. Had I known that curing

137

the cluster migraines required nothing more than a change of job, I would have done it earlier.

The shares I received were also welcome. I had resisted the temptation to cash them in years earlier and by the mid-1990s they had reached their highest ever price levels on the New York Stock Exchange. The timing was propitious because I was launching a mail order wine company, the first in Poland as far as I could establish, and I needed capital. I had always been interested in wine, having consumed a fair amount of it, starting with the cheap port-like wines sold in half-gallon jars in New Zealand during my youth and working my way up over the years to Grand Cru Classes from Bordeaux, Super Tuscans from Italy and standout wines from Australia, South Africa and South America.

I had even learnt a thing or two about wine, mostly by reading magazines but occasionally by visiting wineries and hearing the argot of winemaking and tasting. I could therefore hold forth fairly fluently, if not especially knowledgeably, about wine and did so with guests at Kania Lodge, where the wine list started out short and eclectic. This was because it was difficult to source interesting wine in Poland in the early 1990s. Under the Communists, the only wines readily available came from fellow Comecon countries like Hungary, Romania and Bulgaria. Like most things produced in the Communist bloc they were not very good, sometimes sweet and sickly and sometimes tannic enough to leave one's tongue fuzzy. Standards varied enormously, not only from vintage to vintage, but from batch to batch.

Vodka was the drink of choice. At official functions and private dinners there were always bottles of vodka on the table. It was served in tiny shot glasses and downed in a single gulp following a toast. 'Na zdrowie,' [To your health], the host would call out and glasses would be raised. Then the glasses were refilled ready for the next toast.

In 1994, when we opened the lodge, Poland had only a couple of serious importers of European and New World wines. They tended to favour big names rather than search for interesting producers. At the other end of the scale there were cheap wines, mostly French and Bulgarian, some of the former so tight, mean of spirit and tannic that to this day many Poles will simply not drink French wine. What was lacking, especially for customers like mine at the lodge, were wines better than could be found in supermarkets but not so expensive that one would grimace and move on when seeing them on a wine list.

Before I set up the wine company I had imported mixed pallets, more than one thousand bottles in total, from a wine merchant in England. This was just for the lodge and included Sauvignon Blanc from New Zealand, Shiraz from Australia, Malbec from Argentina and various French wines including Chablis. I had found a small company in nearby Gdynia which was already importing Italian wines, including some interesting Barolo and Brunello. Together, these wines formed the basis of my wine list. Since it included the first New Zealand Sauvignon Blanc available anywhere in Poland, it was much appreciated by guests at the lodge. Many were soon taking a case home with them when they left the lodge.

Within weeks I was getting calls from Warsaw and other cities from people saying they had finished the case. Could I send them another one? Then there were calls from people I had never met, asking for a case of the same wine that their friends had bought at Kania Lodge. Some people were so keen to have my wine that they waited at the railway station in Warsaw to collect the case from the conductor of a passenger train. We also started using Servisco, a courier company which had just been launched by some enterprising Polish-Americans and which was later sold to the global giant, DHL. Credit cards were starting to take off in

Poland, so it was possible to collect payment before shipping. In the autumn of 1996, convinced there was a market waiting to be tapped, I launched Wine Express Ltd, the name reflecting the speedy delivery which I was offering clients.

I filled the large gaps in my wine knowledge with the help of the *World Atlas of Wine* by Hugh Johnson and Jancis Robinson and a subscription to *Decanter*, the British wine magazine. I had looked carefully at how mail order wine businesses were run in other countries, particularly Britain, and realised that I had a couple of things going for me. First, there wasn't much competition. Existing wine companies would ship to private customers but did not specialise in doing so. Even those at all interested in private customers largely ignored the expatriate community, then quite large and more accustomed to drinking wine on a daily basis than their Polish counterparts. Speaking English was an advantage, as was our extensive list of English-speakers who had stayed at Kania Lodge over the years. Other wine companies were headquartered in Warsaw or other major cities, where storage facilities and labour costs were high in comparison to those in rural Kaszubia. I could compete on delivery costs because Servisco charged the same to deliver a case of wine to an address in Warsaw from a warehouse on the outskirts of the city as from my warehouse in rural Kaszubia, three hundred and sixty kilometres away.

But first I was going to have to jump through some bureaucratic hoops, many of them legacies of the Communist era. The law required licensed importers of alcohol to have at least two hundred square metres of warehouse space, not much for an established business but more than I needed at the time and, moreover, more than I had available in Sytna Góra. I thought of building more space but abandoned that idea because I was sure the council in Kartuzy would do everything it could to obstruct me. I looked at renting more space locally but, again, there were bureaucratic barriers. In the end, I addressed the problem by asking an already existing wine company in Gdynia to act as agents for us. They had the statutory amount of warehouse space and could deal with customs, the public health inspectorate (*Sanepid*) and the County Quality Inspectorate for Wholesale Farm and Grocery Products. (*Wojewódzki Inspektorat Jakości Handlowej Artykułów Rolno-Spożywczych*).

Getting another company to act as our agent in clearing the wine seemed a straightforward solution. But it wasn't. Nothing in Poland that requires an official stamp or someone's signature is straightforward or easily complied with, a legacy perhaps of the ponderous bureaucracies set up by the Russian, Austrian and German occupiers during the nineteenth century. From the end of World War II the Communists grew bureaucracy into a monster. As late as the 1980s there were still ration cards for meat, sugar and petrol, amongst other things, and endless forms to fill out in order to buy a car, find a flat or obtain a passport. Supplicants queued for hours in overheated or draughty corridors of government buildings, shuffling slowly towards the door where the haughty and condescending bureaucrats waited to turn them down. The bureaucrats saw nothing strange in requiring people to queue outside two or three different doors to complete a single transaction. Offices were run for their convenience, not that of the public. Service was particularly slow whenever a member of staff had a birthday or a name day and cakes, coffee and presents made their appearance in an office. There was seldom anything as helpful as an information desk.

Most of the order in the system came from the supplicants themselves, who formed queues and waited patiently. Some queues were so long and slow-moving that it was better to pay someone to stand in line for you. Having experienced the maddening unhelpfulness of the Communist-era bureaucracy myself, I was constantly surprised that more Government officials were not simply strangled at their desks or whole corridors of them wiped out by angry supplicants running amok. I also felt that anyone who believed that the world would be a gentler, kinder place if it was run by women, should have been made to spend a day or two navigating the corridors of Polish officialdom. 'Biurwa,' some supplicants muttered as they came out of an office. Biuro is the word for office in Polish. Biurwa is a scatological play on words since it rhymes with the Polish word kurwa, or prostitute. It can only be used pejoratively in the sense of 'office whore' so it was best whispered.

The dawning of democracy saw few changes in either personnel or the way the bureaucracy functioned. Wine importers, for example, were still burdened with the Communist-era requirement of affixing excise labels to each bottle of wine sold in Poland. All countries collect excise, but most have devised simpler ways of doing it. Polish excise labels, thin strips of paper with detailed designs and a hologram, had to be glued to the neck of the bottle. They had to be put on outside Poland, which meant sending them by courier to wineries throughout the world. Since they were not self-adhesive they had to be affixed by hand, a tedious and costly process. But before all this could be done, the importer had to get his hands on the excise banderolas.

The first requirement was a certificate from the tax department stating that the company's tax payments were up to date. This could take weeks. Then an application was made to customs for the number of banderolas required for each specific winery. Another wait ensued. When excise labels were finally ready, the importer had to collect them in person from an office in Warsaw. A courier service could not do it. A company in Warsaw did not have far to go, but one headquartered three hundred and sixty kilometres away faced many long journeys. Needless to say, the banderolas could not be issued to anyone without at least two hundred square metres of warehouse space. We had to outsource this as well, which meant that when the wine arrived it was not technically ours. Since payment to first-time suppliers was normally up-front and a single container-load of wine from New Zealand or Australia could cost thirty thousand dollars, this was not an ideal way to do business. In fact it was downright risky.

Fortunately, there were no fiscal mishaps. Even more fortunately, the law was changed and it was no longer mandatory for an importer to have at least two hundred square metres of warehouse space. I employed Teresa Łepkowska to negotiate the bureaucratic labyrinth on my behalf. Teresa lived in nearby Kartuzy, had a commerce degree from Gdańsk University and, more importantly, she had practical experience in imports and exports. This included dealing with customs and other agencies, something that required stoicism and patience of a magnitude that only someone who had come of age during the Communist era could possess.

We sent out our first catalogue in the spring of 1997. It ran to twenty-four pages and was printed in a single burgundy colour on cheap paper and boasted on the cover 'Great wines delivered to your door.' It was in English only and included short descriptions and serving suggestions for all the wines listed. The catalogue promised same-week delivery to all customers and next-day delivery to most. Purchasers could pay by bank transfer, credit card or cash on delivery. In addition to working from the list of Kania Lodge clients, we scoured chambers of commerce membership rolls, diplomatic lists and trade journals for the addresses of anyone who spoke English, however badly, and might be interested in wine. We printed two-thousand copies of the first catalogue. Women from the village addressed and stuffed the envelopes. They also applied stamps by hand because there was no franking machine for bulk mails at the Kartuzy post office. Later we packed thousands of envelopes into cardboard boxes and took them to the main post office in Gdynia, where grumpy women operated a franking machine.

The response was astonishingly good. By the time we sent out the next thirty-two-page catalogue in the autumn of 1997 we had had a nearly twenty per cent response to our first mailing. In the direct mail business, one to three per cent is generally considered a good response. As ours was so outstanding, I persuaded several advertisers to pay me for space in the autumn 1997 catalogue. They included American Express, Scandinavian Airlines and Volvo and their ads effectively covered the entire cost of printing and mailing the catalogue.

I wrote many of the advertisements myself and made sure that pats on the back from clients were well publicised. In addition to the list of wines with descriptions and pairing recommendations, I ran several articles on wine in the second catalogue. I featured the executive chef at Warsaw's most prestigious hotel and his recipe for salt crust fillet of salmon. He paired it with one of our New Zealand Sauvignon Blancs. I also launched a wine club in the catalogue that was to develop into one of the mainstays of our business. For three hundred and forty-five złoty a month, then about one hundred dollars, members signed up to six separate monthly deliveries of a mixed case of wine.

My first wine column appeared under the headline: 'How to impress the boss and cower fiendish waiters.' 'The first rule in dealing with wine-waiters is never be bullied.' I wrote. 'You are paying; they are bringing. If you want to drink red wine with fish or a bottle of Chardonnay with your pepper steak, go ahead and do it. If eyebrows are raised a mite too high or there is any tut-tutting, don't bother to tip. And make it obvious why.' At the time, wine drinking in Poland tended to be a snobby and pretentious business, especially in restaurants. A self-important waiter handed guests a leather-bound wine list. At least half the wines on the list were not available. 'Why don't you just tell me what's available?' I always asked in the 1980s. 'It will be a lot quicker and easier.' Waiters glowered at me as if I had profaned an ancient gastronomic rite.

As for impressing the boss at lunch, I suggested that corporate climbers forget about German wines because the names were often unpronounceable and the labelling too complicated. 'When the wine you have chosen arrives,' I wrote, 'swirl the tasting portion around in the glass for a moment or two then bury your nose in the glass. Then taste a generous portion, sucking in air noisily as you slosh it around your mouth. Look pensive for a moment and then pronounce clearly for your boss to hear: *Yes, good nose, nice fruit and a very pleasant finish. I think this will be a good match.*' What was good about this, I told readers, was not that it was insightful or learned, but rather that it was universal. You could use it with any wine, red or white. It sounded good.

The cover of the Christmas 1997 catalogue was in colour and had a paid-for colour insert from Diagio, the world's largest liquor company, advertising a range of whisky, cognac, vodka and port. Since we had such a responsive mailing list, Wine Express didn't need to own and possess everything it sold. We could charge others for access to our clients and 'drop ship' purchases of liquors advertised in our catalogue. This is a great way to preserve capital and improve cash flow and is used by many successful mail order businesses worldwide.

The Wine Express catalogues advertised weekends and special events at Kania Lodge and promoted the increasing number of wine dinners and other events we were doing at restaurants in Warsaw. These were important in reaching private clients and also for making contact with potential corporate clients. We were careful in our dealings with restaurants because owners generally lacked cash in the 1990s and saw wine suppliers as a ready source of working capital, delaying payments until they stretched out over several months and amounted to thousands of dollars. Even waiters in restaurants expected to earn something from the wine supplier, many of which offered small under-the-table commissions which they calculated at the end of the month by counting corks.

Since most expatriates lived in Warsaw and most of the country's biggest companies were headquartered there, I went to the capital frequently, generally by train and often lugging along a case of wine samples. I was lucky to be able to stay with my friends Karolina and Krzysztof Niedenthal, who had a lovely villa in Mokotów not far from the American Ambassador's residence. Krzysztof, or Chris as Anglo-Saxons like me called him, had grown up in Britain but had returned to Poland during the Communist era where he made a name for himself as a photographer, first for *Newsweek* and later for *Time*. His most famous photograph captured the essence of martial law, imposed in 1981, when the Solidarity movement was banned and many of its leaders arrested, Wałesa included. It showed an armoured car from the Polish army near a cinema called *Kino Moskwa* [Moscow Cinema], whose marquee advertised the Francis Ford Coppola film *Apocalypse Now*. The image was printed worldwide and is frequently reprinted in Poland, so often in fact that it has become the defining image of martial law and made Chris a celebrity.

The wine company grew fast, and we soon topped one million dollars in annual sales, a decent turnover for a wine company in Poland in those days. We expanded our range of wines, shipping full containers of wine from the southern hemisphere and full truckloads from across Europe. I was pleased with myself for selling fourteen thousand bottles with a special label to one corporate client, especially since we trucked the wine to them directly from Italy without it even passing through our warehouse. We also did well out of a wine club which I proposed, set up and ran for Citibank, which was then aggressively expanding its retail banking sector in Poland. We did other wine clubs too, and worked closely with American Express as it grew in Poland.

It was a busy time, very different from the measured, slow-paced life I had when we started Kania Lodge and which I had enjoyed after so many years of last minute flights and deadlines. It had been wonderful to have the time to wander down to the lake in summer with the children, grill sausages with them over an open fire at lunchtime on a Tuesday or take them ice skating in winter. It was nice, too, to be around for memorable moments like the time they danced naked on the terrace in a thunder storm or set up a shop in the tree house. I loved getting my hands dirty and wheeling barrows of concrete as we built paths, steps and walls in the garden, digging holes to plant trees or chopping firewood in the autumn. It was satisfying to rise early in autumn and walk for miles through the surrounding forests in search of mushrooms that Ania had taught me to identify. For Poles, mushrooming is a rite of passage. Ania has seldom been as delighted as when she once found ceps, the most prized of all mushrooms, while we were on holiday in the Eastern Highlands of Zimbabwe. Local people weren't interested in them, and Ania was in paradise for days, bringing back basket after basket to our rented cottage. We dried them and took them back to Europe. In Kaszubia I also had time for long, leisurely bike rides exploring the countryside, and I quickly learnt where the least trafficked lanes and paths were so that I could travel forty kilometres without seeing a car.

All around us were extensive mixed forests where spruce, pine, beech, oak, birch and ash grew haphazardly, one next to the other rather than in the neat, regimented rows of a plantation. When small sections of mature trees were logged, the land was replanted to maintain the original diversity. Not only was this a sound and sustainable form of forestry, but it also produced vistas of stunning beauty. I would round a corner on my bike and find a crystal clear stream tinkling across stones in a glade of beech and oak. From somewhere nearby a raptor's strident cry would break the silence and I'd stop, mesmerised by the stillness and beauty of it all. Occasionally I would come across loggers using pairs of draught horses to haul logs to the road from deep in the forest where a chainsaw was bringing down more trees. Often I spotted deer grazing at the far end of a water meadow. Hares would spring up unexpectedly, making twisting, angular runs for cover. I watched fox cubs wrestling in a sunny glade, unaware of my presence. Occasionally I came across a viper wriggling its way across the road, and two or three times a year I would disturb a *kania*, the indigenous red kite. It would flap off ponderously and querulously from a branch high above me.

In winter the lake froze and fresh falls of snow produced perfect conditions for cross-country skiing. I would click my shoes into the skis, pull a woollen cap over my ears and head off around the lake. Apart from the occasional angler huddled over an augured ice hole, the lake was deserted. It was silent too, but for the sonar ping of shifting ice. The lake was mine at such moments, all of it, including the forest beyond and snow-covered hills even further away. The local *uktad* couldn't get at me here and at that moment I had no neighbours, good or bad.

I had, however, become bored with the freedom to take a swim whenever I wanted, drink half a bottle of wine at lunch or spend a morning picking mushrooms. I was happy to be building a wine company from scratch, structuring my days and putting in long hours. I had always liked challenges and risk and felt I had an eye for niches like the one Wine Express was filling.

When I was a freelance journalist covering the war in Rhodesia from Lusaka in neighbouring Zambia, where one of the guerrilla armies was based, I had once made a lot more money out of catering to the needs of journalists than I could ever have done writing. In 1979, when the Commonwealth Conference was scheduled for Lusaka with Rhodesia as the central issue, I had already been in the Zambian capital for three years reporting for the BBC, *Guardian*, *Economist* and other news organisations. I knew my way around, I was on top of the story and I had good relations with all the main players, from Kenneth Kaunda, the President of Zambia, to the Zimbabwean guerrilla leaders Robert Mugabe and Joshua Nkomo.

I also knew that the conference, one which Queen Elizabeth would open and which would be attended by the British prime minister, Margaret Thatcher, would attract hordes of journalists and photographers. The war in Rhodesia, with Prime Minister Ian Smith's continued resistance to black rule was one of major world news at the time. The news organisations I represented would all be sending staff reporters to cover the Commonwealth Conference, meaning that I would become a journalistic caddy rather than the main man on the story. It was always frustrating to be sidelined at big events and have one's brains picked by a staffer from outside but that was, and doubtless still is, the life of a freelance journalist. I was to pick other people's brains myself when I became a staff correspondent. I also knew from covering Organisation of African Unity summits and other conferences in Africa that events like this were badly organised, particularly from the point of view of the press. We were always allocated the worst hotels, facilities for filing stories were poor and there was seldom any logistical help to cover events away from the conference centre itself.

I knew that Queen Elizabeth and her entourage would be flying from Lusaka to both Victoria Falls in the south and the Luangwa Game Park in the north of Zambia. There would be no easy way for the press to get to either place, so I chartered a Boeing-737 and two Hawker-Siddley turbo-prop planes from Zambia Airways. I got the British Embassy and the Zambian Government to allow my planes to fly ahead of the royal flight so that everyone could be in place for the photo opportunity when she arrived. Since it would be difficult to reach either place any other way, I could charge high prices. I even offered first-class seats and free champagne on the Boeing-737. Many of the major American publications and some of the British tabloids happily paid to sit up front.

It was a gamble because I had to pay Zambia Airways in advance for chartering the planes. In the end, I filled nearly all the seats and made a handsome profit. I also leased a hire car company's whole fleet of cars and rented them out to journalists. Since accommodation was in short supply, I let houses to journalists as well, sharing the rent with the owners. My office was turned into a press communications hub and the garden into a restaurant, where we did as many as eighty meals a night for more than a week. In the pre-internet, pre-cell phone age, communications were not always easy for journalists in the field, especially in places like Africa. Stories were sent to head office by telex, a typewriter-like machine on which the text to be sent was first punched out on a paper tape. Then the number of the recipient was dialled and the tape was fed through a slot which decoded the tiny holes in the tape and printed out the story in an office on the other side of the world.

Public telexes at post offices were often unavailable after 5pm and those at conference halls were not very reliable. So owning a working telex in a place like Lusaka during a big story was almost a licence to print money. By the time the conference started I had three telex machines, as well as operators with lightning-fast fingers to punch the copy. Journalists could hand in their copy and wander out to the terrace or garden to our 'pop-up' restaurant. Our cook grilled steak, chicken and fish to order on a charcoal fire and guests could choose from a range of dishes prepared in the kitchen of our house next door and kept warm on hot plates. There were salads, cheeses and desserts on a buffet and we offered Roodeberg and other wines from the KWV co-operative in South Africa, locally produced beer and spirits of all kinds.

As they ate, journalists would be given copies of their already transmitted stories and get confirmation that everything had been received in London, New York, Paris or wherever their offices were. The food was good enough to attract diplomats as well as journalists, making our 'restaurant' on the lawn a meeting place where information was traded over a cold beer or glass of wine. A journalist could have covered the whole Commonwealth Conference without ever leaving the terrace of my office. Some did just that, even counting on me to change their dollars or pounds into the local currency.

The success of the Commonwealth Conference in Lusaka paved the way for the Lancaster House talks in London which led to Zimbabwe's independence. I had written not a word about the history-changing diplomacy undertaken on my beat in the heart of Africa. But I had not caddied for anyone from head office, had enjoyed myself immensely and made more money in two weeks than I usually made in a year. Business could be fun and rewarding, I had discovered.

With Wine Express I worked hard on the supply chain, logistics and, above all, service. That was sorely lacking in Poland in the immediate post-Communist era, and standing out in regard to service propelled us forward. Many Poles found it hard to believe that we guaranteed a refund, not only on corked or spoilt wine, but on any bottle a customer didn't like. 'People here will cheat you,' they told me. 'They will drink half a bottle and then tell you they don't like it so that you have to send them another one.' We might have lost a few bottles to such sharp practices but we were customer friendly when little in Poland was customer friendly. My staff were also shocked that I didn't demand payment in advance from many of our customers, predicting massive bad debts. But I knew how annoyed I became when firms demanded money before they delivered the goods. I was right. Our bad debts were a few hundred dollars a year, a small price to pay to win and retain the business of hundreds of other clients. We soon added Polish customers to our expatriate client base and double digit growth continued year after year.

LIGHT MY FIRE

By the turn of the century we were ready to expand at Kania Lodge. I wanted to put in a spa, wine cellar and tasting room, and we also required more office space for both Kania Lodge and the rapidly growing wine business. Even more pressing was the need for a second lounge. Guests who wanted to carouse until the early hours of the morning had to use the lounge in the main building. This was not a problem when everyone at the lodge was from the same group, but was unfair to other guests who wanted to sleep. No one knew this better than me. Our family still had a three-bedroom suite upstairs in the main building and while almost nothing disturbed Ania and the children, a single loud guffaw or peal of high-pitched laughter from a guest in the lounge below woke me up.

There was always a direct correlation between the amount of alcohol consumed and the volume of the music. I might have left the guests listening happily to a four-handed piano suite by Gabriel Fauré or the laid-back tinkling of the Norwegian jazz pianist Tord Gustavsen but by 2am they would switch to Tina Turner asking what love had to do with it at a decibel level suited to Wembley Stadium. Sometimes they found music to rumba to ('Light my Fire') or jive to ('Rock Around the Clock.') From time to time I went down in the early hours to ask boisterous guests if they could make a little less noise. Such pleas to people already on their second bottle of single malt or vodka tended to fall on deaf ears. If I declined their invitation to join in, I was left tossing and turning upstairs to the same guffaws and peals of laughter, now punctuated with loud admonitions of 'Shsh, shsh, John's sleeping.'

I was keen to build a house for ourselves about one hundred metres away from the lodge on land I had recently bought from Adaś Pobłocki who, years earlier, had sold us the field where the lodge now stood. Adaś disliked farming and had already sold the tractor he had bought with our payment for the first piece of land. The site I had chosen for the house had a splendid, uninterrupted view across the lake to marshy meadows and state-owned forest a few hundred metres away. The view also had depth to it because a few kilometres beyond the forest rose a ridge of green fields and more forest. The nearby meadows were leased to Janek Frankowski by the Forestry Department. This meant they were state land and could not be built on, even in the unlikely event that someone might decide a soggy, north-facing meadow was a good place to build. Janek took two cuts of hay off the meadows in summer each year and grazed his cows there after the second cut. The rest of the year they were too wet for anything but the storks and cranes which visited in large numbers in spring and early autumn to stalk frogs, mice and insects. We already owned all the land between the building site and the lake so no one could compromise the view. In many ways it was an even better place to build than the place where we had constructed the lodge.

Three things stood in the way. The first was that I didn't have the money. To get it I needed to sell the house I had in England, something that was proving more difficult than I had anticipated. This turned out to be a blessing because it gave me the idea of demolishing the house and building a small luxury apartment house with underground parking on the one-acre, tree-lined property. A ten-apartment building could be constructed without disturbing any trees, neighbours' views or protected fauna. The local council had already indicated that it would look favourably on a planning application. Planning permission alone would be very valuable, so I was working on raising the capital for the development and consulting with the architect on the design. Once this all came to fruition I'd have more than enough money to build our house. But it was going to take time.

Of greater concern was the on-going conflict with our neighbour, Gienek Plichta. Since his conviction for assault, he had set about harassing us in non-violent ways. Next to the site where I wanted to build our house was a field of about half a hectare owned by our neighbour. It overlooked us, rising to a crown near the old birch beneath which I had watched the first day's work on the lodge. Sensing that we didn't want to be overlooked, Plichta had sub-divided the field into a dozen plots and was selling them as building land. We knew this because the council in Kartuzy had been obliged to send us, as neighbours, plans of the development. We had protested and I had made several visits to the council offices to talk to the town architect, Mr Grodzki. As had happened before with the fence on the access road which hindered the turn onto the village lane, Grodzki threw up his hands and said there was nothing that he could do. People had a right to sell their land for whatever purpose they wanted and it didn't matter to the council that we had created a lodge which was known nationally and which attracted hundreds, if not thousands, of well-heeled visitors every year. The fact that we provided full-time employment and good wages to at least a dozen local people provoked no more than a shrug of the shoulders and an expression which said 'So what?' He was not being candid. The council could easily have rejected Plichta's application to sub-divide the land for housing on the grounds that it was inappropriate for the area.

155

In my lowest moments I had visions of the field overlooking the lodge being full of badly built and poorly maintained summer houses with scruffy yards. The owners would invite friends for barbeques in summer and there would be loud music, drunken singing and smoky bonfires. During the day there would be squabbling children and fractious parents, not to mention barking dogs and a quad-bike or two. We would have endless arguments with people who believed they had a right to access the lake through our property, use our jetty or pick mushrooms in our forest. Our second-floor windows would be level with most of their terraces and the houses at the top of the hill would look straight through our attic windows. There was such a residential development on a lake not far from us. It looked awful and it seemed a tragedy that councils allowed people to build one on top of another in beautiful rural areas. The owners paid virtually nothing in local taxes, created no local employment and often dumped their rubbish in the forest on their way home from a weekend at their *działka* [summer house]. I could not build a home for my family cheek by jowl with such a development.

The third concern I had was about planning permission for the house. The city architect had already made it clear that I would have problems getting permission for the building that would contain the spa, wine cellar and offices. The first problem was that the plans had first to be forwarded to our neighbour. His inevitable objections meant the application would go into a sclerotic bureaucratic pipeline of site visits, hearings, appeals, counter-appeals and perhaps even a court appearance or two. Neighbours had a right to oppose any building on property adjacent to theirs, and they almost always did. Objecting was an easy way of extorting money from a neighbour.

Paying up was almost always cheaper and quicker than letting an objection wend its way through the system. If you didn't pay, you could spend five years or more in the bureaucratic maze. Another problem, the city architect explained, nodding his head in the direction of the mayor's office, was that I wasn't very popular with Mr Gołuński. 'So what?' I asked, bristling. 'Whether the mayor likes me or not has nothing to do with a planning application.' Grodzki looked at me, plainly puzzled. We obviously were not talking the same language.

By now I was sure that one or more people in local government were helping Plichta. Objections written by him and forwarded to me by the council were word perfect and quoted sections of planning acts and regulations that no lay person would be familiar with. They could only have been written by someone working for the council or a person with very good contacts in the planning department of the council. Our house could wait, but a new building at the lodge was urgently needed. To delay building would cost us money. One day, when I was bemoaning the lack of transparency in the process to Marek, our architect, he came up with an idea: 'If you build a garage half the size of the building you are planning to put up then you don't need planning permission,' he advised me. 'But that would be far too small,' I said. 'Then build two garages side by side and join them together,' proposed Marek. He had grown up and qualified as an architect during the Communist era and was well versed in ferreting out loopholes in planning law. 'But I don't want it to look like two garages stuck together,' I protested. 'It won't,' said Marek, 'because we'll build it as one building and then tell the council that we knocked two garages together and built a new facade. If the measurements are correct, we should get away with it.'

I was sceptical that the council would rubber stamp such an obvious ploy to circumvent the regulations, but I was willing to take a gamble. What could they do to me once the building was up? Order me to take it down, fine me, put me in jail? I knew that none of these things were likely to happen because Poland was a country of compromise, of drawing back from the brink just in time, of preserving honour with lots of mealy-mouthed words, a little bluster and the promise that next time there would be all hell to pay. So we started building without planning permission. We had just poured the concrete for the first floor when I received a call from Grodzki. 'Your neighbour has complained that you are building illegally,' he said. 'Is that true?' I muttered something about that depending on your interpretation of the law and asked him what the council planned to do about the complaint. 'We could order you to take it down. The mayor's not very happy about this.' I laughed. 'Then I hope the mayor will be on site when the bulldozers come in to demolish the building in front of lots of journalists. He can tell the national press why a much needed investment in your area is being torn down.'

I was taunting him, because I already knew that neither the mayor nor the town architect had the power to order the demolition of our new building. This rested with the building inspector from the *powiat* [county], the next tier up of local government from the *gmina* [council] of which the mayor was the leader. I also knew that the leader of the *powiat* (called the *starosta* in Polish), Janina Kwiecień, was at loggerheads with Mayor Gołuński on many issues. There were overlapping areas of administrative responsibility between the *gmina* and *powiat* and turf wars were going on all the time. I knew too that the local fire chief, Edmund Kwidzinski, was a close friend and political ally of Mayor Gołuński. He was also the leader of the elected members of the *powiat* and was said to harbour ambitions to take over Janina Kwiecień's job at some stage. So I reasoned that the *powiat* had no reason to do the mayor's bidding and might even go out of its way to frustrate him.

When we finished construction, the building inspector from the *powiat*, Krzysztof Nowak, made a site visit during which he scribbled furiously for twenty minutes on a clipboard. He made no comment, but a week or two later we received his report in the mail. He noted that we had already 'joined' the two supposed 'garages' together, built a cellar underneath the whole building, changed the position of windows and replaced the 'garage' doors with large windows. That was a very generous interpretation of what we had done. We had totally ignored the original sketches for two adjacent garages of a size that didn't require planning approval and had gone ahead with the building we wanted, one that required prior planning consent. Despite this, the building inspector approved the 'changes,' effectively giving us retrospective planning permission. Copies of the decision, I could see from a circulation note at the bottom of the letter, had already been sent to both Plichta and the council. I could imagine their consternation. They had been outflanked. We had what we wanted: a new building with a tasting room and wine cellar, spa room and offices. No bribes or inducements had been paid to anyone.

During the spring of 2001 we finished the interior of our now legal building. Instead of buying a plastic, ready-made jacuzzi, we made our own on site. First we poured concrete into a curved form with steel reinforcing bars, leaving holes for water circulation, lights and the pressure outlets that would enable users to have their backs massaged while in the water. Before applying the tiny three-square-centimetre tiles in patterns I had drawn out, we sealed the concrete so that even if some water escaped through holes in the tiles it would not seep into the cellar below. We bought a pump, filters and a temperature gauge and installed everything ourselves. In the end we had a large, elegant jacuzzi. Wojtek Szwaba, the village carpenter, built and installed a sauna next to it and we moved on to tiling the floors and walls of the spa and adjacent shower room.

159

When I say 'we,' I don't mean that I rolled up my sleeves and set to work with wet grout and a trowel. The tiling was all done by Zbyszek Lejkowski, a tradesman from the village. Zbyszek had a problem with drink but also an amazing ability to work while slightly, sometimes visibly, sozzled. Providing someone was there to supervise in the sense of seeing that the overall design was being adhered to, Zbyszek was careful and meticulous in his work. Sometimes I felt he worked even better after lunch, part of it liquid, than in the mornings when he could be grumpy and out of sorts. My part of the 'we' in all of this was to make sure the overall design worked and make on-the-spot adjustments when it didn't.

My inspiration came from the tiling on the Lisbon metro, where each station has different designs, all of them big, bold and expressive. I bought green, gold and white ten-square-centimetre tiles for the job. In the shower room I made the basic colour green, and in the spa itself, yellow tiles predominated. Large diamond-shaped inserts in reverse colours went into the walls of the shower room and spa. We had to get each of the inserts in exactly the right place and my back-of-the-envelope sketch hadn't taken into account curves in the wall or what the visual impact would be from different angles. So I was in and out of the new building several times a day as Zbyszek worked, sometimes changing part of the design in the insert or reworking a design on a curved part of the wall. It was painstaking work, but the result was spectacular.

In the cellar we had a fireplace with sofas and chairs around it and a bar made from oak. Behind it were shelves for wine and a rack for storing wine glasses. There was also a sink for washing glasses. We added a good sound system, television and video player and by the summer that year had a space where people could party until the early hours of the morning and not disturb other guests – or me. 'You can even sing here or dance on the table at 5am,'

I told guests as I showed them the new space. It quickly became popular and some people did indeed sing, amongst other things, at five o'clock in the morning. In one corner of the basement I built a wine cellar, taking care to insulate the walls and door in such a way that, even when a fire was burning in the hearth, the wine cellar maintained a temperature of 14°C and humidity of around seventy per cent. I put a curved ceiling in the cellar to give it the right feel and simulated age with one-hundred-year-old bricks from an old manor house which was being demolished.

Into it went quality wines from the nineties I had collected, some Bordeaux and Burgundies together with highly regarded wines from Australia, New Zealand, South Africa and California. One of the first New World wines I put down was the 2000-vintage Coleraine, a Bordeaux blend, from Te Mata Estate in New Zealand. A few years later at Vinexpo, the biennial wine trade fair in Bordeaux, a jury of top French oenologists chose the 2000-vintage Coleraine as one of the top five wines in the world. It was in august company, sharing the accolade with such heavyweights as the Bordeaux first-growth Chateau Lafite-Rothschild and Opus One from California. I patted myself on the back for having made the purchase long before the French oenologists made their choice.

The idea of the cellar was to be able to offer guests a selection of quality wines that had been properly aged. There was nothing wildly expensive, just interesting wines whose provenance I could vouch for. Most of the Bordeaux that went into the cellar I bought *en primeur* and included several top Cru Bourgeois, the fifth-growth Chateau Lynch-Bages and Pavillon Rouge from Chateau Margaux. I had also just discovered the wines of Jonathan Maltus from St Emilion, in particular his cult wine, *Le Dome*. From the New World my selection was eclectic, comprising wines like Hardy's Jack Mann from Western Australia, Kanonkop Pinotage from

161

South Africa and Duckhorn Pinot Noir from the Anderson Valley in California, a wine that was later served at President Obama's inauguration lunch. Within a few years the US wine magazine *Wine Spectator* described the Kania Lodge wine list as 'one of the most outstanding restaurant wine lists in the world.'

While I busied myself with the wine and felt pleased with myself for having got the building up and legalised, things were not standing still up the hill on Plichta's sub-division. First, I heard that someone had bought the two plots with direct access to the village lane. Then the buyer sold them both to a Daniel Jabłoński. I quickly established that he was a driving instructor from Gdynia who also bought all the other plots in the sub-division. I knew for sure that the land had been sold when the new owner planted a row of conifers down the northern boundary. A few months later we received notification from the council that Jabłoński had applied for planning permission for the property on the basis that he was a farmer. Under a law dating back to the Communist era, to qualify as a farmer one needed at least one hectare of land. This was an absurdly small amount of land for qualification but someone recognised as a farmer had certain privileges. Amongst them was a much easier route to obtaining planning permission for a building. The land Jabłoński had bought from Plichta totalled less than one hectare so I was sure the council had made a mistake and that I would be able fight the application on grounds that gave me every chance of winning. I sent off an objection to the council assuming that would be the end of the matter, at least for some time.

It was not. Not long afterwards a letter from the city architect said that Jabłoński owned another piece of land in a different *gmina*. His total landholdings, therefore, amounted to more than one hectare. This meant he met the legal requirements for classification as a farmer and his planning application would be treated accordingly. I was furious. The law allowing someone to become a farmer with just one hectare of land was stupid enough. Allowing someone to qualify by owning two small parcels of land at least ten kilometres apart was clearly absurd. I wrote to the Local Government Appeal Court in Gdańsk complaining about this interpretation of the law and copying the council. The council responded with a letter to the court backing Mr Jabłoński's claim to be a farmer on the basis of owning more than a hectare in two separate pieces of land in different *gminas*. To my consternation, the Appeal Court supported the council's position, ruling that there was nothing in the law that required a hectare of land to be contiguous or even in the same county. In fact one could qualify as a farmer by having four or five separate pieces of land totalling a hectare, even if the pieces were each two hundred and fifty kilometres apart. This meant that Jabłoński could proceed with his application for planning permission and that before too long we might have a house on the hill overlooking the very spot where I wanted to build a home for ourselves.

There was no other court to which I could appeal, so we resigned ourselves to waking up one day and finding bulldozers on the hill above us and to staying on in the apartment in the lodge. Maybe, just maybe, Jabłoński might change his mind, become bankrupt or get run over by a tram in Gdańsk. For several months, I heard nothing from either the council or Jabłoński. Then one day a young man parked his BMW outside the front door of the lodge and asked to see me. 'I'm Paweł,' he said, 'and I'm a friend of Mr Jabłoński who is your neighbour up the hill.' I said nothing and waited for him to continue. 'Mr Jabłoński is prepared to sell the land to you,' he said, naming a price that was roughly twice the going rate for such land. Long experience in negotiating with villagers had taught me to show no emotion and to express no real interest in any offer. When I told him I wasn't interested, he became agitated. 'Mr Jabłoński will build a hotel on the hill and take your customers away,' he said, waving an arm in the direction of the hill and telling me that his friend was on good terms with the mayor of Kartuzy. 'Getting permission won't be any problem,' I laughed. 'Wish Jabłoński good luck with his hotel,' I said, ushering him to the door.

It seemed strange that a driving instructor like Jabłoński could afford a relatively expensive piece of rural land and plan to build a fancy house or hotel. Perhaps that had never been his intention. Perhaps this was a scam involving several players. It was not in the council's interests to compromise the businesses of the biggest employer for miles around, someone who brought large numbers of visitors to the region each year. And yet the *gmina* had actively helped Jabłoński establish his right to be classified a farmer. Although I had no direct evidence of collusion, no explanation other than that it was a 'sting' made any sense of the way events were unfolding. When I talked about it with Polish friends, they agreed there was no other rational explanation. 'That's why they are using this Paweł, as the go-between,' said one lawyer friend. 'They can always deny any connection to him.'

It was clear, too, that any collusion between officialdom and Jabłoński would be buried in reams of documents showing that the proper procedures had been followed. If there was something fishy going on there would be no paper trail of private conversations between officials and Plichta or Jabłoński. Any money that changed hands would be in cash. They had me where they wanted me, but I wasn't going to make it easy for them. Now that it seemed Jabłoński had no real intention of building on the hill, I had room for negotiation. If my suspicions were correct, he needed to sell the land to turn a profit and pay off any loans or accomplices. The hill he had bought didn't have uninterrupted views over the lake, because the lodge was in the way. It was doubtful that people with the kind of money Jabłoński was asking for the land would build their dream house overlooking other buildings. Also, they would have no direct access to the lake because I owned all the surrounding land. Why build a fancy house on a lake if you couldn't reach the water? Sit tight, intuition told me. You are the person they have to sell this land to.

Within a month, Paweł was back. 'Mr Jabłoński is prepared to discuss the price,' he told me, less self-important this time but still peddling the story about the option of building a hotel and going into competition with me. 'But I'm not really interested in that piece of land,' I told him. 'Nobody's going to build there because they have no access to the lake.' That seemed to stun him but he went away saying that Mr Jabłoński had friends who could sort that out. 'Wish Jabłoński good luck,' were my final words again. Within a few weeks, I had a call from Jabłoński himself, asking if he could come to see me. When I repeated what I had told Paweł, he said he would take twenty per cent less than the original asking price. Eventually, after two more meetings and with lots of feigned indifference and reluctance on my part, I agreed to buy the land at a price not too much higher than what I knew to be a fair price for rural land. A month later, we met in the notary's office in Kartuzy and then walked across the street to my bank where the manager counted out the money in cash in a back office and pushed it across the desk. Jabłoński stuffed it into a bag and that was the last I saw of him.

The way was now open for us to build our new house, since we would have a grassy field next door instead of a collection of pokey summer houses or a large residence. But first I wanted to build a proper wine warehouse with direct access to the lane that ran through the village. The wine business was growing rapidly, and I was storing wine both in a garage at the lodge and in a larger garage I had built in the village. Both were overflowing, and in winter heavy vehicles and even small delivery vans sometimes had trouble reaching us. The land I had just bought from Jabłoński bordered the village lane, so I asked our architect to submit plans to the council for a warehouse, offices and a large tasting room. Since the building would occupy more or less the same site as that for which Jabłoński had submitted plans when he owned the land, I didn't envisage problems. However, I soon received a copy of a letter from Plichta to the Local Government Appeal Court in Gdańsk asking it for a ruling that, because I was not a farmer, I should not be allowed to build on the land in question. The neatly typed and carefully laid out letter quoted from earlier decisions of the Ministry of Infrastructure relating to similar land use applications and was couched in language that no one but a bureaucrat, and then only one with an intimate knowledge of planning law, could have written. A week later Grodzki, the town architect, paid me a visit at the lodge.

I asked Teresa, my office manager, to join us in the conference room, telling the town architect that she would help me with anything I didn't quite understand in Polish. She was really there as a witness. I had always found Grodzki a Uriah Heep figure and what he had to say did nothing to change my mind. He wanted to help me, he said, with the problems I was having with getting planning permission for the building in the field I had bought from Jabłoński. *'Ale wie pan, jest bardzo trudno,'* ['But you know sir, it's very difficult,'] he said, a classic bureaucratic first step on the way to saying that, difficult though the problem is, it can perhaps be resolved with extracurricular help from the person in front of you. To reinforce how difficult it would be, Grodzki told us that Mayor

Gołuński was determined to stop me building in that field. 'Why?' I asked. 'He doesn't like you,' Grodzki said. 'But maybe I can help change his mind.'

I was angry, seeing this as a shakedown. The council had written to the Local Government Appeal Court in support of Mr Jabłoński. Now that we wanted to build on the same piece of land, it was refusing to write a similar letter. This was as Kafkaesque as my long-running battle with the old guard *układ* had become. I was momentarily speechless. When I recovered I told Grodzki that unless he or Gołuński wrote to the Appeal Court supporting my application, as he had done for Jabłoński, I would consider taking legal action against the council.

UNFORESEEN NECESSITIES

At the time of Grodzki's visit, Poland had a poor reputation regarding the transparency and integrity of its public institutions. Almost every day newspapers published stories about one public figure or another in court on charges of corruption, embezzlement or cronyism. Poland's top film producer, Lew Rywin, had just been found guilty of soliciting a thirteen-million-euro bribe from the country's biggest newspaper in return for helping to push through legislation that would enable the newspaper to buy a national television station. Rywin, who co-produced Steven Spielberg's *Schindler's List* and Roman Polański's *The Pianist*, told the newspaper's founder and editor-in-chief, Adam Michnik, that he was acting as an intermediary on behalf of the left-wing SLD party. This was the successor to the old Communist Party and it was then in power. Michnik, imprisoned as a Solidarity activist in the early 1980s, was well known for his stubborn integrity, once turning down a chance to be released in return for agreeing to go into exile. Unknown to the film producer, Michnik had taped the conversation. Rywin was sentenced to thirty months in jail. While the scandal brought down the SLD-led government, a parliamentary commission failed by a narrow margin to link Rywin to the governing party. Nonetheless, his repeated claim that he was acting as an intermediary for 'the group holding power' entered the language as shorthand for a corrupt government elite.

Transparency International, the Berlin-based NGO which monitors corruption around the world, at that time ranked Poland

168

in sixty-first place in its corruption table. This put Poland beneath Bulgaria, Tunisia and Botswana and only a few rungs higher than Cuba, Egypt and Ghana. This was not exactly exalted company for a country that had just joined the European Union and prided itself on its Christian heritage. Even worse, in regard to my situation, Transparency International's annual reports consistently identified local government in Poland as having high levels of corruption.

It was tempting to think that corruption was a transitional product of the collapse of Communism and the privatisation of tens of thousands of state-owned companies, large and small. There had been no wholesale clearing out of the Communist-era bureaucracy when Poland shrugged off its Soviet shackles and became a democracy in 1989. This meant that the old *nomenklatura*, at the higher levels consisting of once card-carrying members of the party itself and closely linked to the old order's politicians, played a big part in the privatisation process. As in Russia, they often helped their friends get started in business. Some of today's richest and most influential businessmen were doubtless helped by well-placed friends in government.

Their help would not have been forgotten by the beneficiary of the nod, wink or quickly-scrawled signature on the piece of paper that helped him take over a brewery or construction company at a favourable price. It would be interesting to chart the private sector careers of many senior members of the old *nomenklatura* who quickly found that getting rich was a lot more fun than wielding power behind a padded door off the long corridor of a grey Soviet-era building in central Warsaw. Such a large-scale transfer of ownership and wealth from the state to private individuals would have spawned corruption anywhere in the world, even in places like New Zealand and the Scandinavian countries which consistently top Transparency International's list of the world's least corrupt countries.

Corruption in Poland did not just suddenly occur when Communism collapsed, triggering a race to convert publicly-owned assets into private ones. The Communist era itself was so permeated with corruption, much of it petty, that it became institutionalised and part of the fabric of everyday life. Doctors were so poorly paid, most earning less than coal miners, that they expected and received small payments or presents from patients for whom, officially at least, health care was free. A bottle of whisky would help persuade the storeman at a state-owned company put aside five bags of hard-to-find cement. Chocolates or stockings were the currency used to thank female bureaucrats for stamping a form or making sure that your papers were handled with alacrity rather than left languishing at the bottom of an in-basket. Since many life-changing possibilities depended on the whims of officials, larger bribes were common too. Getting on a list for an apartment or a new car, or persuading an official to issue a passport so that you could go abroad to work, were hugely valuable and worth paying for. There was no point in shouting at someone that you were entitled to a passport and they had better hurry up and issue it. Those who wielded the stamps and seals had power. They could only be dealt with on their terms.

It would be comforting to say that corruption started with the Communists. But the *nomenklatura* were only occupying government offices where corruption of one kind or another had been endemic since the Russian, Austrian and German occupations of the nineteenth century. The carving up of Poland by its three neighbours could itself be blamed at least partly on the corruption of some of its parliamentarians, who were all too willing to sell their souls to a foreign power. Nothing, after all, could be more corrupting than the *liberum veto* that allowed a single parliamentarian to veto legislation by shouting '*nie pozwalam*' [I don't allow] on the floor of the Royal Castle in Warsaw. How little it must have cost Catherine

170

the Great in Moscow or the Habsburgs in Vienna to prevent or overturn any legislation inimical to their interests. All they needed was to identify a single Polish aristocrat with large gambling debts or huge ambition and bribe him.

Delve into Polish literature and the corrupt and venal public official is almost a caricature. One of my favourites is Mr Skrofułowski, the town clerk of Woollyhead in Nobel Prize-winning novelist Hendryk Sienkiewicz's *Charcoal Sketches*. Mr Skrofułowski is young, arrogant and ambitious and is putting in time in a rural council before moving on to what he hopes will be a more distinguished post. He regularly creams off money from fines and permits levied against the peasantry, putting as much as half aside for what he describes as 'unforeseen necessities.' Any nobleman requiring some bureaucratic problem to be sorted out would summon Mr Skrofułowski, give him dinner and then palm crisp banknotes into his hand. 'Oh, sir,' the town clerk would ritually intone as he transferred the notes from his hand to his pocket, 'Between us this isn't necessary. As for your problem, you need not worry.'

When he is rebuffed by a peasant farmer's buxom wife to whom he has taken a fancy, Mr Skrofułowski tricks the farmer into signing papers that will have the poor man conscripted into the army in place of the son of a village councillor. He then persuades the distraught wife that this decision can be reversed in return for sex, reneging on his part of the bargain once he has had his way with the wife. Skrofułowski also pockets a handsome bribe from the councillor for keeping his son out of the army.

Placing crisp banknotes in the palm of a local official might have helped me in my dealings with the *układ*. Even if I had been willing, I wouldn't have known how to go about it. It was not part of my culture, and I would rather have given in, sold up and moved on than bribe a Skrofułowski-type character for anything. In any case, one bribe would not end all my problems and in fact was likely to make me vulnerable to an endless number of future shakedowns. The *układ*'s sense of entitlement and frequent displays of arrogance reminded me of government ministers in dirt-poor African countries stalked by famine, high infant mortality and crumbling education and health systems. Amidst that disintegration I had watched them stretch out comfortably in the back of their chauffeur-driven Mercedes Benz, vain, smug, venal and parasitic. In the one-party states in which they lived, there was no opposition or free press to take issue with them.

There was opposition to our local *układ*, and it was active and at times energetic. But it was seriously handicapped by the fact that the local press was at best sycophantic and, at worst, craven. There were three local weekly newspapers, plus the Gdańsk daily, *Dziennik Bałtycki*, which published a local Kaszubian insert twice a week. It circulated widely in the region and had a local staff of two or three journalists. One of the weekly newspapers, *Głos Kaszub*, listed Mieczysław Gołuński, the mayor of Kartuzy, as one of its shareholders and, like its competitor *Gazeta Kartuska*, it ran dull, repetitive stories with pictures of the mayor or fire chief or some other functionary opening a new school classroom or handing over a fire engine to a sub-station. An adulatory tone infused every story about local officials. There were few controversies and even these were reported in a partisan fashion. Regular fare included competitions to find the most popular nurse or school teacher in the region. There were also long, torpid pieces on the history of Kaszubia. Sport was covered in a desultory fashion. Even *Dziennik Bałtycki*, part of a chain of big-city Polish newspapers owned by a Swiss investor, did little to foster any debate or discussion that might upset the existing order.

Dziennik Bałtycki often seemed to be unprofessionally close to those in power in Kartuzy and the other town and rural councils throughout Kaszubia. Each year in the summer it ran what it called a plebiscite to find the most popular public official in the region. To vote, readers had to clip a coupon from the newspaper, fill it in and post it to the newspaper's offices in Gdańsk. Given that public opinion polls at the time showed that some ninety per cent of the population distrusted politicians of all persuasions, it seemed unlikely to me that people would rush to vote for anyone in this plebiscite. Only fifty-five per cent, after all, had bothered to vote in the most recent local and national elections.

Yet the incumbents throughout Kaszubia, the mayor of Kartuzy included, regularly received a surprisingly large number of votes in *Dziennik Bałtycki*'s plebiscites. The winner one year, the *wójt* or head of the parish council in Sulęczyno, population 2,500, received ten thousand votes. The same year, the president of the city of Gdynia, population 250,000, received just twelve votes. It would have to be a pretty dim or dishonest editor who did not ask how, in a parish of some 2,500 souls, more than 10,000 people supposedly cast votes, while in a city of 250,000 almost no one voted. Our mayor, Mr Gołuński, always did considerably better than any opposition leader, even those like Andrzej Pryczkowski, who had lost the 2002 election to Gołuński by just a handful of votes. In one of the *Dziennik Bałtycki*'s plebiscites, Gołuński received five hundred and seventy votes and Pryczkowski just six.

The plebiscite seemed to me to be a joint scam undertaken by the newspaper and old guard incumbents. I believe the votes were calculated on the number of extra newspapers sold in each official's area during the period of the plebiscite. By buying large numbers of extra newspapers the incumbents boosted the newspaper's circulation at a time of the year when sales traditionally sagged, enabling it to maintain its circulation figures and therefore its advertising rates. For the old guard incumbents, schooled in all the tricks of vote rigging during the Communist era, this was a convenient way of hoodwinking gullible voters about their popularity. The next time an undecided voter looked at a ballot paper and wondered for whom to vote, he might remember the story of an incumbent being so popular that hundreds, if not thousands, of people had voted for him or her in a plebiscite.

With such a pliant and at times grossly partisan and unprofessional press, it was difficult for opposing voices to be heard. Members of the *układ* were as smug and secure in their posts as a government minister in a one-party African state. What Kartuzy needed was a real newspaper, one that was independent of any political party or faction and which saw good stories as a way of boosting circulation and guaranteeing a commercial future. It would have to be bold enough to tackle corruption and cronyism in local government and big enough to stand up to bullying officials. Anyone publishing a truly independent newspaper would get no local government advertising – that all went to *Dziennik Bałtycki* and other friendly newspapers – and would find other potential advertisers leant on heavily by the *układ*. Deep pockets would be helpful, if not vital.

The idea of becoming a Kaszubian Citizen Kane appealed to my vanity. Having been a war correspondent for much of my life, I was probably much more suited to the role of the bumbling William Boot from Lord Copper's *Daily Beast* in *Scoop*, Evelyn Waugh's classic. But who else had both the journalistic background and the independence and cash necessary to start and run a crusading newspaper in a small town in Kaszubia? Moreover, however well qualified, who would want to? Owning a newspaper has always been a good way of generating lots of red ink in ledgers. 'You're right,' says Orson Welles of the crusading newspaper *The Inquirer*

174

in his 1941 masterpiece, *Citizen Kane*. 'I did lose a million dollars this year. I expect to lose a million dollars next year. At the rate of a million dollars a year, I'll have to close this place … in sixty years.' You could knock a row of zeros off those numbers for the losses I could expect, but a start-up local weekly still wouldn't be cheap. I calculated that it would take two years at least to start to break even – if I was lucky and everything fell into place.

Stoking my Citizen Kane fantasy was the fact that both the lodge and the wine business were doing well, generating enough revenue for a foray into foolishness. Common sense told me that it would be better to invest my spare cash in the existing businesses and to ignore the local *układ*. But my life had seldom marched to the measured beat of common sense. Impulsive risk-taking and a quixotic, almost Polish, disdain for practicality had always ruled both my personal and professional lives, not always leaving me the winner. The French novelist and playwright Honoré de Balzac once wrote of Poles that, shown a precipice, they were bound to jump over it: 'They have the very spirit of cavalry; they fancy they can ride down any obstacle and come out victorious.' I share their rash streak, which made a charge against the opaqueness of the local *układ* all the more appealing. So what if I lost money and the newspaper eventually failed? The journey itself would be fun, perhaps even exhilarating. And there was just a chance that I might do some good and see the newspaper flourish.

While impulse battled with common sense, the council decided to change the name of our village from Sytna Góra to Sitna Góra. The name change was part of a nationwide harmonisation of place names, and the Ministry of the Interior's guidelines for change required that local residents be consulted on all changes. Our council had not consulted us or anyone else in the village. The name change was imposed as a fait accompli on the basis of demonstrably dubious research by an academic at the University of Gdańsk. Changing a 'y' for and 'i' might seem too trivial a change to raise hackles. But in Polish it changes the sound and meaning of the word. *Sitna* in Polish is pronounced *sheetna* and sounds, to the untutored Anglo-Saxon ear, something like a bowel movement. *Sytna* is actually pronounced *sitna* and is much more melodious. Its etymological pedigree is also more refined, coming from the Polish word *sytość*, meaning sated, or from *syta*, an old Polish word for the wort that was fermented to make beer. The Gdańsk academic argued that the name of the village was derived from the word *sitowie*, or reeds, and claimed that German maps from the nineteenth century showed the name of the village as Sitna Góra. Since 'y' is rarely used in German and certainly not in this instance, that hardly proved anything. Had I been allowed to, I could have produced any number of eminent Polish and German philologists who would have poured scorn on the Gdańsk academic's reasoning.

Apart from not being consulted and the fact that we now lived in a place that sounded like a bowel movement, I was annoyed because this was not the first time the council had changed the name of our village. When we first arrived it had been Sytna Góra. Then it was changed to Prokowo Wybudowanie, perhaps best translated as a built-up extension of Prokowo, a larger village nearby. Then it reverted to Sytna Góra. With each name change the law required new documents to be issued, everything from the identity card [dowód] which every Pole has to carry, to driving licences and company documents. Obtaining them meant traipsing around lots of different government offices, standing in queues and licking revenue stamps.

Half the village had given up trying to keep up with the name-changers in the council and, in several families, siblings and parents officially lived at an entirely different address. Everyone in the village signed a petition to the council asking for the name to be changed back to Sytna Góra or, failing that, for the council to carry out a consultation with residents, as required by the Ministry of the Interior.

Within a month the mayor had written back saying there would be no consultation and that the name Sitna Góra would remain. He enclosed a copy of an opinion from two academics at the University of Gdańsk which purported to provide etymological and historical reasons for the new name. Amongst them was the fact that in 1951 the regional council in Gdańsk had used that name. It seemed like rough justice to be trumped by a Stalinist-era council which would have rubber stamped any piece of paper pushed in front of them. It also seemed outrageous that, more than a decade after Poland became a democracy, a whole village was being denied even a say in the name of the place where they lived. I had read the Ministry of the Interior's guidelines for name changes and they clearly called for consultation with residents before any decision was taken. That the mayor had not bothered in the first instance and wasn't going to allow any consultation even now, demonstrated an arrogance that raised my hackles.

'That's it,' I told Ania as I paced the kitchen with Mayor Gołuński's letter in my hand, 'I don't care how much it costs but I'm going to start a newspaper and stand up to these people.'

TELLING IT LIKE IT IS

As I pursued my plans to start a newspaper, I thought nostalgically of my first job as a cub reporter on the *Daily News*, a newspaper in my home town of New Plymouth, New Zealand. In those days, sub-editors wore green eye shades, teletype machines clattered constantly and a much-feared spike on the chief reporter's desk was where stories that didn't pass muster finished up. Cub reporters made tea, sharpened pencils, drew isobars on the daily weather map and noted the comings and goings of ships in the port. In the evenings we went off to shorthand lessons to learn how to turn spoken words into dashes, dots and squiggles. We wrote our stories on clunky old Remington typewriters on desks with the initials of previous occupants etched into them. Sometimes we got to accompany sub-editors down to the composing stone to watch them work with printers putting pages together from one-line slugs of text from the hot metal typesetting machines. Since pubs closed at 6pm in those days, there was a dash across the road to the bar of the Imperial Hotel just after 5pm and we were initiated into the ritual of 'shouting' a round of drinks for the group.

I quickly came to like the camaraderie of newspaper life, the smell of printers' ink and the sound of the presses rumbling into action in the early hours of the morning. I enjoyed racing off with a photographer to follow a fire engine or ambulance, or sitting through a court session where miscreants were dealt with and you looked for something salacious or shocking with which to start your story. Being a reporter enabled you to be a free spirit, a voyeur corralled only by deadlines and the need to get your facts right. Even on just nine pounds ten pence per week, and subject to periodic verbal lashings from the chief reporter, Denis Garcia, I was happy.

Most of my early strife came over leads, the first paragraph of a story. They were examined forensically by the chief reporter and were rejected if they weren't short, to the point and interesting enough to lead the reader on. 'Twenty-one words,' Denis would shout. 'If you can't tell the bloody story in twenty-one words you shouldn't be here.' To reinforce his message that leads had to be short, sharp and pithy, balding Denis waved his arms theatrically in the direction of a sign on the building across the street. 'Fresh fish for sale here today,' it read. 'So what's wrong with that sign?' he asked. I shrugged and muttered something about the letters being too small or something. 'No, you twit,' Denis replied and proceeded to dismantle it word by word 'What's the point of the word 'fresh'? Would they be selling rotten fish?' No. 'What's the point of saying that it's for sale? Would they be buying fish here in the middle of town?' No. 'Why the word 'here'? It stands to reason they are selling the fish where the sign is.' Yes. 'And 'today'? They are obviously selling it today and not tomorrow or next week.' Yes. 'So that leaves you with one word – FISH. That's all you need. Remember that when you write your next lead. Make it short, sharp and pithy.'

In Anglo-Saxon journalism, stories are built in the shape of a pyramid, with the most pertinent, attention-grabbing details at the pinnacle. People reading the lead are supposed to know exactly what the story is about and have their interest piqued enough to want to read more. Then one works downwards, with layers of new information and background in descending degrees of importance. This is the kind of introduction and second paragraph that would probably have escaped impalement on the spike on Denis Garcia's desk:

A $3.5 million Olympic-size swimming pool with a gym and restaurant is to be built on the site of the city's old brewery.

The City Council last night voted in favour of the swimming pool complex despite strong resistance from several councillors who argued that the money would be better spent on improving the city's sewers.

After an at times heated debate, the swimming pool plan was passed by eight votes to four.

The Polish approach to structuring a newspaper story is more haphazard and whimsical. Sometimes it is necessary to read halfway through a story before one can be certain what it is about, and few Polish journalists I know would have passed muster with Denis Garcia. The story above might easily start something like this in a Polish newspaper:

The City Council spent four hours yesterday discussing the respective merits of a new swimming pool and extensive repairs to the city's sewage system. One councillor described the sewage system as antiquated and outdated and a public health threat. Another claimed it had not been upgraded since the nineteenth century. In the end the swimming pool plan was approved. An Olympic-size pool will be built on the site of the old brewery. Plans call for it to include a gym and a restaurant.

Actually that's not bad. Some lead paragraphs in Polish newspapers are even more convoluted than this and I have frequently imagined the reporter shuffling the information randomly like a pack of cards before scattering it across the page. Sometimes when I wade through a front page political story in *Gazeta Wyborcza*, the country's biggest daily, I get to the end without being certain who is doing what to whom – or why. When I ask my wife or a Polish friend to tell me what they think is going on, they are at best uncertain, at worst as baffled as me. Some stories in Polish newspapers would not be salvageable by the best sub-editor in the world. Others need restructuring to bring the most interesting or salient facts to the top in order to capture the reader's attention.

Even if I had been planning to publish a national daily in Poland, it wouldn't have been easy finding reporters to produce stories which not only pulled no punches but were short, sharp and pithy. In Kartuzy, anyone who had ever worked on a local newspaper knew all about pulling punches and about editorial self-censorship. They knew almost nothing about being concise or how to make a story interesting to readers. I would have to train my future staff, starting with the basics of who, what, why, when and where.

First, I needed to find an office and a company with a newspaper printing press. I also needed to register the name of the paper, which I had decided to call *Express Kaszubski*, spelling *Express* the English way rather than *Ekspress* as in Polish. Using the area name Kaszubia rather than Kartuzy, the name of our town, gave it a regional remit which, I hoped, would improve our chances of getting advertising. But it would complicate distribution because Kaszubia is a region of scattered villages and occasional small towns. The local municipal council or *gmina* comprised both the city of Kartuzy and the surrounding district, with roughly a fifty-fifty spread of voters. If we were to have any impact on the council we needed to reach potential voters throughout the region. My friend Mariusz Kasprzak, himself a councillor and one of those unhappy about the way the council was run, became our circulation director and general fixer. A grocer who promised to support the paper with advertising recommended an office manager/receptionist, a young woman with a background in bookkeeping. My wife found us an advertising company to do our page layouts, bring in advertisers and deliver the finished pages to the printer in time. They, too, were looking for offices and we soon shared a large four-room suite not far from the railway station. Poland's leading daily, *Gazeta*

Wyborcza, had a modern, state-of-the-art contract printing press in Pila, a small city about one hundred kilometres away. They agreed to print *Express Kaszubski* for what seemed a reasonable price.

Advances in technology over the past few decades have simplified the day-to-day business of publishing a newspaper. Original copy produced on a laptop in the corridor of a courthouse or the press box at a football ground can speed its way electronically to the printing press via editors and page make-up. Not a single piece of paper needs to be used and the typewriters, paste pots, razor blades, scissors and red pencils of the news room of old have been banished to museums. So have the green eye shades and the spike embedded in lead on which the painstaking efforts of so many young reporters were brusquely impaled for all to see. Gone too are the clanking linotype machines churning out one-line slugs from hot metal, as well as the compositor's stone and the workshop making concave zinc metal plates for the drums on the printing press. There is no longer any need for the darkrooms where films were developed, the images emerging slowly on special paper dunked with tweezers into trays of developing fluid and hung up to dry on nylon lines. Now, a photograph can be taken and readied for publication in minutes.

When I moved on from the *Daily News* and became a reporter on Rupert Murdoch's *The Australian*, technology helped the then fledgling press baron create Australia's first viable national newspaper. Before *The Australian*, the country's newspapers were all regional, vast distances making same-day intra-state distribution virtually impossible. When I joined the paper it was edited in Sydney and the printing plates were flown by light aircraft to waiting presses in Melbourne, Adelaide and Brisbane. Before I left the newspaper, the pages were being transferred in minutes by facsimile from Sydney and Murdoch was able to start printing in distant Perth as well.

Later, as a correspondent with *Time*, I took possession of my first laptop, an eight-line Tandy-100 with a built-in modem and an 8k memory. I sent my first Tandy story through what was to become known as the internet in 1987. Using crocodile clips and tape, I connected the Tandy to phone wires in the wall box of my hotel room in Managua, Nicaragua. Within minutes my whole file was in New York. It was magic. That was the end for the heavy portable typewriter that I had first used when travelling for Murdoch's *The Australian*. It was also the end of the telex.

Without the changes that had taken place during my working life it would have been difficult – and much more expensive – to launch *Express Kaszubski*. However, some things hadn't changed at all. Sales people were needed to sell advertising space. Journalists were required to write stories. Having staff meant paying payroll taxes for medical cover, pensions and other benefits. That added another fifty to sixty per cent to salaries which, along with rent and the cost of printing and distributing the newspaper, would be my major costs. I calculated that I might just get by on fifty thousand złoty (about 12,500 euros) a month but needed to allow for costs of up to twenty thousand euros.

My first choice of an editor proved to be a mistake and finding a replacement delayed the launch by several weeks. Eventually Janusz Świątkowski, a former *Dziennik Bałtycki* reporter, became the first editor-in-chief. It was a grandiose title for someone on such a small newspaper but Polish law required all newspapers to have an editor-in-chief. I could be the publisher but only a Polish citizen could be the editor-in-chief, one of those quirky, inexplicable laws one comes across from time to time in Poland. Another former *Dziennik Bałtycki* reporter, Wojtek Drewka, also joined the staff. Świątkowski and Drewka had both had political stories spiked during their time at *Dziennik Bałtycki*. Both men were young, Janusz

183

in his early thirties and Wojtek just twenty-four. Both seemed excited by my vision of a completely independent newspaper with a mission to make public officials accountable and to dig deeper for stories than any local publication had ever done. The third member of the editorial team was Ewelina Karczewska, a young woman just back from working in Ireland, who wanted to be a journalist. Two students joined as part-time reporters and another student, Marcin Meyer, agreed to do our cartoons and other artwork.

Once we had furniture and computers in our new offices we made mock-ups of *Express Kaszubski*. It would be a twenty-four page tabloid size paper and would come out each Thursday in order to give it a little weekend shelf life. We would start with a print run of five thousand and see how it went. The cover price would be 1.90 złoty (about forty-five cents) and a year's subscription would work out at about one złoty (twenty-five cents) a copy. We would cover only local news but that meant both hard investigative journalism and soft, human-interest stories. We'd have a women's page, another for gardeners and foodies and one with pictures of newlyweds. Our competitors ran pages full of pictures of newborn children, but I thought day-old babies in swaddling clothes all looked much the same. A local photographer would provide the pictures of newlyweds each week, and all we needed to do was contact the bride and groom for permission to publish and get a few details on how they met or where they went on honeymoon.

We set aside two pages for sport. Kartuzy had a team in the third division of the national football league, as did Koscierzyna, a city some twenty-five kilometres from Kartuzy. We would also distinguish ourselves from other Polish newspapers by having an editorial page. I would write the main leader each week until my staff settled in and learnt to ask big questions, take a stand on an issue or simply write tongue-in-cheek about local celebrities. Under a byline with their picture, they would write short opinion pieces on whatever topic they chose. The rest of the page would be taken up with letters to the editor, five questions asked each week of a public official or a business or cultural leader, and opinion pieces by anyone from outside with an axe to grind or something interesting to say. I wanted to encourage both my staff and outsiders to discuss and debate in our paper. I wanted the discussions to be lively and spirited. There would also be an editorial cartoon in which Marcin could make his own comment on the topic of the week.

To make our crusading intentions clear, we devised a motto along the lines of the *New York Times*'s 'All the news that's fit to print.' After an in-house debate about what sounded good in Polish, we decided on '*Nie boimy się pisać ... serio.*' This might best be translated into English as 'We are not afraid to tell it as it is.' It was displayed prominently beneath the title *Express Kaszubski*. The word *Express* was printed in red 72-point italic type and *Kaszubski* in black 36-point italic. It looked as good as anything Charles Foster Kane might have done. At one of our pre-launch editorial meetings around the large table we used for conferences, I told everyone that we had the beginnings of a real newspaper.

It is hard to sell advertising in a newspaper before it exists. We persuaded a few local advertisers to sign up for the launch edition and I used my contacts in Warsaw and Gdańsk to obtain ads from big companies like Nestlé, Amplico and Mercedes Benz, some of them impressive looking half and full-page advertisements. I published them for free at the beginning, knowing they would help us look like a serious newspaper and encourage local advertisers to spend their money with us. These advertisements would also annoy our competitors, none of which ran national advertisements. We wanted to take their readers and their advertisers and the better we looked as a paper, the more likely we were to succeed.

On the twenty-seventh of September, 2005, the first edition of *Express Kaszubski* hit the streets of Kartuzy and we rushed it around news kiosks and shops throughout the region. We had a good story for the lead. '*Trujące domy*' [Deadly homes] the banner headline screamed. Above it was a strap which read '*Połowa populacji może bić zagrożona*' ['Half the population may be at risk']. The story disclosed how a dioxin called Xylamit had been used in the floors of most Communist-era housing blocks. Doctors told our reporters it was cancer inducing and deadly. People who believed their health had been affected by the dioxin gave us quotes and we got a public health official to say that the dangers should not be underestimated. To illustrate the piece we ran a picture of a drum of Xylamit with a skull and cross bones on it. Janusz produced a lead of just fifteen words, a lead which probably would have passed muster with my old chief reporter.

Half the population of Kaszubia may be living in homes contaminated by the deadly toxin xylamit.

Inside, my first editorial stated that *Express Kaszubski* would be the eyes and ears of the local community and that we intended to stand up to arrogant civil servants, expose corruption and guarantee that ordinary people were properly and fairly treated by those in power. 'We will do our job of informing and entertaining you without fear or favour, because good newspapers like *Express Kaszubski* are independent and not connected with any political party or interest group. Our logo *nie boimy się pisać ... serio* [we are not afraid to tell it as it is] sums up what we are about. The only interests we represent are those of our readers. That means the interests of the community at large. As the eyes and ears of the community we believe you should know what all sorts of people are up to.' It could have been Citizen Kane speaking out as he launched *The Inquirer*.

Yet while I basked in the beauty of the words and a time-honoured crusading proprietor's vow, I was all too aware that Citizen Kane's *Inquirer* had gone bust.

NEXT YEAR WILL BE BETTER

By the time I launched *Express Kaszubski*, we had finished the new house at Kania Lodge, enabling us to escape our upstairs suite in the main building and the late-night revelry that kept me awake. Surprisingly, we had obtained planning permission without a lengthy fight with the council or spending time in court with our neighbour. I think the council realised how stubbornly I would fight them if they refused planning permission. They also knew I had outfoxed them with the auxiliary building at the lodge and might do so again. With the council quiescent, Plichta seemed to have run out of steam. Having purchased the field overlooking the site where we wanted to build, we had ensured that the family home wouldn't have any immediate neighbours. A flock of more than thirty sheep bred from two ewes and a ram I had bought years earlier, were grazing in the new pasture. It was a much more pleasant sight than a collection of summer houses.

We built our house with the southern end overlooking the lake. The front door was on the side of the house overlooking the lodge. Between the house and the lodge was a paved courtyard with a large parking area, curved brick walls, gardens, hedges and trees. Aesthetically, it worked better than if we had turned things around, as our architect proposed, and had the front door facing the lake. It joined the house visually to the rest of the buildings, but left it far enough away to be completely independent. On the ground floor at the southern end was a large lounge with high ceilings and French doors leading out onto a semicircular paved terrace from which steps led down to the lawn.

Crowning the building was a clock tower. The clock lit up at night and was large enough to be seen from the tennis court on the far side of the lodge. Whimsically, I decided to put a longer view of time on the western side of the turret opposite the clock. I had always liked the Father Time figure on the weather vane at Lord's Cricket Ground in London, the one in which the skeletal figure with the scythe is removing the bails for the end of the day's play. I had a replica painted in white on a black sheet of metal about a metre high. That was the easy part. Trying to explain the symbolism to the Frankowski family as they put it up was much more difficult. They looked at me uncomprehendingly as I drew an analogy between the removal of the bails at the end of a day's play in a cricket match and death itself. They probably still think it is some strange pagan symbol from the Antipodes.

The basement housed the oil storage tanks and boiler, as well as a laundry and two other large rooms which filled up with all sorts of things I didn't know we had. On the ground floor at the northern end of the building we had made a large garage and storage area for outdoor tables, boats and other equipment that needed to be put away during the winter. It was a big, spacious and comfortable home. The five-hundred-square-metre house was built by Janek Frankowski and his family, the bathroom tiling was the work of Zbyszek Lejkowski, the elaborate wrought-iron balustrades and light fittings were forged and hammered into shape by blacksmith Geruś Pakura, and the doors and floors were installed by Wojtek Szwaba, the carpenter from nearby Pomieczyńska Huta. A French cabinet maker who had settled nearby produced elegant furniture, some of it with glass doors made to measure by an artisan glassmaker who was a friend of Ania's.

Not only did we now have a home of our own but also wall space on which to hang the paintings and other artwork I had col-

189

lected on my travels. Most of it was naive painting from Africa and Latin America, some of which I had commissioned well-known local artists to paint. There was also a big oil painting of Mount Taranaki, the almost perfect 2,518-metre volcanic cone beneath which I had grown up in New Zealand. On one of my trips back to New Plymouth, I had commissioned artist Margaret Scott to paint it for me. Upstairs I hung architectural and other drawings by my father, including an intricate black and white pen-and-ink drawing of Saint Mary's Church in New Plymouth where I had been a choir boy.

Our first-floor bedroom had a panoramic view of the lake and the hills beyond. It also looked out onto a south-facing field which sloped down to the lakeside escarpment. Standing at the bedroom window shortly after we moved in, I remembered a chateau I had stayed at in Bordeaux which overlooked vineyards leading down to the Gironde estuary. Without the vines, the view would not have been half as spectacular and I wondered how the field below our house would look planted in vines. At fifty-four degrees north we were considerably further north than the major wine producing regions in Germany. But there were small vineyards in Denmark and Sweden and, closer to home, a small vineyard just seventy kilometres from Kania Lodge. So why not try? A vineyard would complete the view, and I could envisage guests lunching on the terrace in summer and imagining they were in Tuscany or the south of France.

We were too far north to plant the European *Vitis vinifera* grape varieties like Chardonnay, Sauvignon Blanc, Riesling, Cabernet Sauvignon or Merlot. *Vitis labrusca* grape varieties, native to the eastern United States, are much hardier and can survive winter temperatures of more than minus 30°C. They are not as popular as *Vitis vinifera* because they produce wines with a foxy taste, hence

190

the name, and they are only planted where it is too cold for *Vitis vinifera*. A winemaker from southern Poland, Roman Myśliwiec, who had first planted *Vitis labrusca* varieties like Rondo and Seyval during the Communist era, came to Kania Lodge with several wines for me to taste. None of them was soft on the palate, exhibiting the tart, green characteristics that come from grapes that have not ripened fully. They also lacked the body that the average wine drinker today is used to. But they were drinkable. I was not thinking of a vineyard as a business proposition; we were too far north for that. If I could make even a small quantity of wine it would be a good advertisement for Kania Lodge and improve the view from the lodge and our house.

I ordered more than one thousand vines of six different varieties, two white and four red, from Myśliwiec. No one had grown vines in Kaszubia before and I wanted to see which varieties did best in our climate. I had already had soil tests done and added magnesium, potash and some other trace elements to the soil. The Frankowskis dug one thousand small holes, one metre apart, in eighteen rows running north to south. We planted the vines in a day, watering each one with lake water to help them get started. Next to each vine we drove a two-metre-long stake into the ground for them to climb. When we'd finished we had half a hectare planted and the field already looked good. Each row was planted in a cultivated strip about a metre wide and there were two metres of cut grass between each row.

Almost every vine took and there was soon a splash of green in the vineyard as they reached a metre in height. After the first winter, during which temperatures fell below minus 20°C, I waited anxiously to see if the vines had survived. They had and needed to be tied higher and higher up the stake as they grew vigorously during spring and summer. By the third year, each vine bore bunches of grapes. It had been a cold wet summer that year and in the autumn, when I checked the sugar levels with a refractometer, the Brix readings were between eleven and fifteen. A Brix of at least twenty is needed to make a decent wine, so we left the grapes for the birds.

Things looked more promising the following year. I was getting Brix readings of sixteen and more by mid-September and the weather was still good. Another two to three weeks and perhaps it would hit twenty. I hoped to harvest the grapes in early October when I returned from a wine-buying trip, but a family of badgers had also been waiting for the sugar levels in the grapes to rise. When I returned I found they had devastated the vineyard, digging up large patches of the cut grass in search of worms and devouring all the best bunches of grapes. Since badgers forage at night, no one had seen them. I knew the raiders were badgers because I found tufts of their coarse hair caught in wire fences beneath which they had burrowed. Later, I found their sett in a forest we had planted more than a decade earlier. Badgers, I had learned, were slowly moving north in Poland as temperatures rose and they were now to be found in Kaszubia.

The answer was to erect a wire-mesh fence around the vineyard after *veraison* in late summer, when sugar levels rose and the grapes turned colour. But the following year disaster struck long before summer. In May, when the vines had budded after two weeks of balmy weather, we had three nights of devastating frost. There were hardly any grapes for either us or the badgers that year. I kept hoping that the following year would be better, but it wasn't. We had three cold, wet summers in a row and sugar levels were too low to make wine without adding raw sugar during fermentation to raise alcohol levels to at least twelve per cent. I decided not to do this but to wait for a long, hot summer that would ripen the grapes sufficiently. The vineyard was not a business but a hobby. It was also a way of landscaping the lodge grounds to create the special atmosphere I wanted.

HOIST WITH HIS OWN PETARD

When the first edition of *Express Kaszubski* hit the streets of Kartuzy at the end of November 2005, Poland had just elected its most right-wing government since before World War II. *Prawo i Sprawiedliwość* (PIS), Law and Justice, was the creation of twin brothers, Lech and Jarosław Kaczyński. As cherub-faced children they had starred in the film '*O dwóch takich, co ukradli księżyc*' [*The two who stole the moon*] and had later been active in underground anti-Communist politics. Lech, a lawyer, advised Lech Wałęsa and Solidarity during the Round Table talks in 1999 that effectively brought the Communist era to a close. He was later an advisor to Wałęsa as the first post-Communist president of Poland. While mayor of Warsaw from 2002 to 2005, Lech gained a national profile thanks to his war on corruption within the city administration and for his right-wing views on abortion and gay rights. During his term as mayor he twice banned a gay rights march in Warsaw, calling homosexuals perverts and claiming the marches encouraged a homosexual lifestyle. He was later found guilty by the European Court of Human Rights of violating the principle of freedom of assembly.

PIS won 155 of the 460 parliamentary seats in the 2005 election and formed a minority government with Lech's brother, Jarosław Kaczyński, as prime minister. In 2006 it became a majority government in coalition with two even more right-wing parties, *Samoobrona* [Self Defence] and the *Liga Polskich Rodzin* [League of Polish Families]. In the presidential elections, also held in 2005, Lech Kaczyński narrowly beat the centrist Donald Tusk, later a long-serving Prime Minister, to become President of Poland. Lech Kaczyński remained in office until his death in 2010 when his plane crashed on approach to the airport of Smolensk in Russia. He was on an official visit for a commemorative service for victims of the Katyń massacre. One of the most prominent members of Jarosław Kaczyński's first cabinet was justice minister and prosecutor general, Zbigniew Ziobro. Campaigning on an anti-corruption ticket in his Kraków constituency, Ziobro had won his seat with the biggest majority in the country. Corruption, clearly, was an issue that concerned many Poles. They were troubled, not only by the newly rich and their displays of wealth, but also by a suspicion that the *nomenklatura* of the old order still pulled the strings in many areas of the economy. There was plenty of evidence to suggest they were right. During its recent term in office the SLD (The Socialist Democratic Alliance), the successor to the old Communist Party, had been mired in corruption scandals linking senior government officials with shady deals.

I was no fan of the Kaczyński brothers and their prickly, abrasive and often boorish behaviour, or their links to the conservative, xenophobic wing of the Catholic Church. Like many of my Polish friends, I saw the Kaczyńskis as the bumbling Tweedledum and Tweedledee of Polish politics, *Alice in Wonderland* figures of fun abroad and unnecessarily divisive at home. When compared by a German satirist to a potato, Lech called off a planned French-German-Polish summit, drawing even more attention to the satirist's jibe. As embarrassing and petty as they were, they had struck a rich vein of discontent over corruption. Although most of their votes came from the poor, rural areas of eastern Poland, PIS also did well in the 2005 election in conservative, deeply religious Kaszubia. Many priests openly supported PIS candidates from the pulpit, and the party did considerably better than the more liberal, business orientated *Platforma Obywatelska* [Civic Platform] led by Donald Tusk. While I suspected that most of the votes for PIS in Kaszubia probably came from people attracted by the party's nationalist, pro-Catholic stance, I hoped that the anti-corruption campaign it promised was also appealing. PIS was promising to take on what they saw as the entrenched national *układ* [cabal] of self-serving old guard administrators, police, courts and businessmen. *Express Kaszubski* had no national agenda but it was fighting the local *układ*.

It wasn't long before *Express Kaszubski* received a visit from a former officer in the ZOMO (*Zmotoryzowane Odwody Milicji Obywatelskiej*), the Communist-era riot police set up in 1956 and trained by the East German *Schutzpolizei* for the 'protection of the nation.' They were called out whenever miners, shipyard workers or students went on strike. If rubber truncheons and shields did not break up the protesters, the ZOMO could deploy water cannons, tear gas, live ammunition and armoured personnel carriers mounted with machine guns. On several occasions they gunned down unarmed protestors, most notoriously at the Wujek coal mine in southern Poland in 1981, when they killed nine and injured more than twenty. As Solidarity grew and the ZOMO were called out to more and more protests, they became known as the 'beating heart' of the Communist Party. Their brutality and immunity from prosecution after killing or maiming demonstrators helped speed the collapse of Communism. In the autumn of 1989, after Solidarity had routed the Communists in elections, ZOMO was disbanded.

The former ZOMO officer who turned up at the *Express Kaszubski* offices was furious. We had published a story about his teenage son, Robert, killing a sixty-year-old pedestrian while driving at nearly ninety kilometres an hour in a built-up area, more than twice the legal speed limit. He had been convicted and given a small fine and a suspended jail sentence. The court also suspended his driving licence for two years. But, as our story had reported with indignation, the teenager was still driving pending an appeal to a higher court. His father handed Janusz a police report saying that his son was innocent and that the blame lay with the pedestrian. Why were we trying to stop his son driving? Why, he shouted at Janusz, our editor, were we even reporting the case at all? His son was innocent. The police report said so. Janusz told him that his son had been convicted and sentenced by a court. The more he tried to reason with the man, the angrier he became. As he stormed out of the office, he threatened us with reprisals from 'organs of the state' if we continued reporting the matter. The public prosecutor would be in touch with us. When Janusz recounted the confrontation, I told him to write it up exactly as it had taken place. We ran the bylined story under the headline '*Express* journalist threatened.' Marcin satirized the encounter with a drawing of a bespectacled reporter working on his laptop with a large black outline of a person with menacing hands behind him.

We ran two boxes next to the main story. In the first, Michal Jaszewski, legal advisor to the national journalist's association (*Stowarzyszenia Dziennikarzy Polskich*), said that *Express'* first report had been accurate and legally sound. Our newspaper had every right to raise the issues we had aired. Furthermore, it was a criminal offence to knowingly give journalists incorrect information (the man's son was not, as he claimed, innocent) and to threaten them.

The other box dealt with a curious aspect of the case that excellent reporting by Janusz had uncovered. Police officers who arrived at the scene of the accident had reported that neither the teenage driver nor the victim, Józef Koss, seemed to have been drinking. However, when the case came to court, police claimed that Koss had been drunk at the time of the accident. A blood test, they said, had shown

197

the pedestrian had a 1.7 promil alcohol level, which is more than eight times over the legal limit for driving. It would have been immediately clear to the investigating officers at the scene that Koss had been drinking. The defence argued that his alleged inebriation was as much a factor in the fatal accident as the driver's speeding. However, Koss's wife told the court her husband had never been drunk in his life and had just left the family home when he was knocked down and killed. When asked by Janusz how the former ZOMO officer had a police report saying his son was innocent, a spokesperson said this had been issued during an early stage of the investigation. Just why, she couldn't say. The hospital in Gdańsk where blood is sent for sampling could find no record of the test that had shown Koss had an alcohol level of 1.7 promil. It looked like a glaring case of police incompetence or something much more sinister.

To complete our coverage and make it clear that *Express Kaszubski* had not been intimidated, I wrote a piece for our editorial page. 'If your husband or wife was hit and killed by a teenager driving at approximately twice the legal speed limited you'd be pretty upset,' I started off.

'You'd be even more upset if nearly a year later the same teenager was still at the wheel of his car and his penalty for killing your loved one amounted to no more than a small fine and a suspended jail sentence. The teenager's father stormed into the *Express Kaszubski* office this week to complain about our reporting and threatening us with reprisals. We don't like being threatened and we don't like people like Mr B who suggest they are so well connected with various organs of the state that they will make life tough for us if we continue our reports. To Mr B we say we know you were a member of the ZOMO which for many years oppressed Polish people fighting for a more open, decent society. We accept that you continue to have friends in positions of power. But we don't care. We care that your son is still driving and Mr Koss's life has been valued so cheaply. We'll report this story as fully as it deserves.'

None of the town's other newspapers ran the story or displayed any solidarity over the threats to unleash 'organs of the state' against us. But that was typical. They were also very circumspect in their reporting of another important story that was unfolding. Mayor Gołuński was under investigation by the *Agencia Bezpieczeństwa Wewnętrznego* (ABW), Poland's internal security agency, on suspicion of corruption by a public official. The ABW, roughly equivalent to America's FBI, had raided his house early one morning and taken away documents. Since the arrival of Mr Ziobro as Justice Minister in the PIS government, the ABW had been beefed up and had become more proactive. While other newspapers waited passively for official statements, we set about fleshing out the meagre information released by the ABW or the council. We quickly established that the investigation centred on procurement and tender irregularities during the building of a new school at Staniszewo, a village in the area. It seemed that the main contractor had won a supplementary two hundred thousand złoty (about fifty thousand euros) tender for work on gutters and drainage. This tender was won by the contractor after the official opening of the building. However, photographs we published of the official opening showed that, at the time of the tender, the guttering was already in place, as were the manhole covers for the drainage system.

Despite our photographic evidence, the council claimed the work had been done after the official opening. We sent reporters to ask local people if they had seen any work in progress after the official opening, or if they had noticed the mounds of earth one might expect if drains were being dug. They all said no, as did teachers at the school. Moreover the *dziennik budowy*, a daily record of work done that is required on all public works, seemed to have disappeared in mysterious circumstances. It was difficult not to conclude that taxpayers were paying twice for the same work and that someone was pocketing two hundred thousand złoty.

199

It was a great local news story. Our digging provided us with a succession of front page scandals which boosted circulation. We posed questions to the council and to Mayor Gołuński, few of which were answered convincingly. We provided the mayor with space on our editorial page for a rambling and confusing explanation of everything that had gone on in Staniszewo. I wrote an open letter to the mayor headlined: 'Where is the daily building record, where is the money?' We never got an answer.

The letter ran with Marcin's cartoon of the mayor with a long Pinocchio nose leaning against a sign indicating that digging work was in progress. The mayor was growing used to being pilloried by us. In another editorial I accused him of lying, under a headline which said simply: LIAR. This was in connection with a claim he had made in stories which appeared in the town's other newspapers that the council had just laid two hundred and fifty metres of new asphalt in the village of Pomieczyńska Huta. Since the village is close to us and I went there regularly to recycle bottles and plastic, I wondered where this new asphalt was. Investigating, I found just ninety-three metres of new asphalt. 'It would be nice to be able to believe that the mayor of Kartuzy simply can't count and that he made a mistake,' I wrote in my editorial. 'But it is sadder and more sinister than that. The mayor lied. And he did so deliberately. Elections are looming, and the mayor is trying to hoodwink voters so they give him another term in office.'

We also took the mayor to task for not responding to specific questions about a wide range of topics. Like officials in the Communist era, he hid behind smokescreens of billowing verbiage. His responses reminded me of a letter the well-known Polish writer Tadeusz Konwicki had once received from the attorney general's office and which he republished in his memoir *Wschody i zachody księżyca* [Moonrise, Moonset]. Konwicki had written to the attorney general asking for the release of a dozen or so people arrested and held without trial in 1980. 'I respectfully inform you,' the letter from the attorney general's office read, 'that the persons mentioned in the letter are under arrest for the present, charged with committing specific crimes: in Ziembiński's case those described in Article 270, paragraph 1273, paragraph 1276, paragraph one and in connection with Article 10 of the Criminal Code. The following apply to the other persons – Article 123 with Article 128, paragraph one; 123, 133, 270, paragraphs one and two, 273, paragraphs one and two; 276, paragraphs one and three; 282 in connection with Article 10 of the Criminal Code.'

'Now it's clear,' wrote Konwicki. 'Now I understand everything.'

After a succession of similarly worded letters from the mayor I wrote a piece for the paper announcing that *Express Kaszubski* was gifting Mr Gołuński a copy of Kafka's *The Castle* to remind him of the kind of bureaucratic dissembling he routinely engaged in. We also donated a second copy to the public library and invited subscribers of our newspaper to read it and have sympathy for Kafka's poor land surveyor as well as all those who tried to get straight answers from the *gmina* of Kartuzy.

We also cheekily challenged him over council advertising, none of which was finding its way to our newspaper. Despite the fact that we claimed the largest and fastest-growing circulation of any of Kartuzy's newspapers, the council refused to advertise with us. All council ads appeared in the three papers which continued to publish council press releases and fawning, sycophantic pieces about public officials. In an open letter we offered to carry council advertising free of charge for a year, pointing out that not only were we the most widely read newspaper in the area but also that our generous offer would enable the council to use the savings on worthwhile local projects. Council advertising continued to go to other newspapers, but we had exposed the cosy relationship between public officials and our rivals.

When one newspaper published a picture of the mayor alongside a prominent local businessman at a pre-election event sponsored by the businessman's hardware company, I wrote a leader saying it demonstrated that crony capitalism was thriving in Kaszubia. The businessman concerned was at the time trying to buy a small parcel of *gmina*-owned land without the inconvenience of a public tender. He had also had some of his taxes suspended by the mayor. 'Could all these things be connected?' I asked. Within days, councillors voted for the land to be sold by tender. It was eventually sold to the businessman concerned but at a higher price. 'Crony capitalism never works to the advantage of the taxpayer or community at large,' I wrote.

The mayor was not the only public official with whom we crossed swords. One Sunday, a fire destroyed a barn in the nearby village of Prokowo. The village's volunteer firemen had been slow in getting to the fire because some of the volunteers had been drinking after church and were sleeping it off. When they reached the fire, they found that they didn't have the right key to open the water hydrant. Eventually professional fire fighters arrived from Kartuzy to put out the blaze. Since it was in a barn and there were no injuries, it wasn't a big deal. But the fact that the volunteers had arrived late without the right key was disturbing. What if it had been a house fire and there were children inside? I got one of our reporters to write to the local fire chief, Edmund Kwidziński, to ask why the volunteers had turned up without the standard hydrant key.

The reason for writing rather than phoning was that public officials are required by law to respond to written queries. Mr Kwidziński, once a card-carrying member of the Communist Party, wrote back to say that not only was it not true that the volunteers had arrived without a key, but *Express Kaszubski* should in future contact him to establish the veracity of stories prior to publication. Eyewitnesses and members of the volunteer fire force all said there had been no key. 'Mr Kwidziński is lying,' I wrote in my leader that week, 'and he knows that we know he is lying.'

Taking on public officials in this way was not something a local newspaper in Kaszubia had ever done. The local *układ* consulted their lawyers and issued threats about court action. The threats came to nothing because I made sure our reporters checked and cross-checked their stories and consulted me on the more controversial ones. I didn't mind who or what we accused people of as long as we could support our claims with hard, incontrovertible facts. On several occasions I spiked stories that didn't pass muster. At other times my staff felt that I pushed too hard and was 'un-Polish' in the way that I attacked some officials, particularly the mayor. Friends warned me that there could be repercussions. At a party in Sopot, a woman I knew well asked why I was risking my safety and perhaps that of my family. 'You could get hurt you know,' she said. 'Is it worth the risk?'

Since this warning came just after the murder in Moscow of crusading journalist Anna Politkovskaya, it was something I had already considered. I often wondered whether I might get beaten up, or worse, for my crusade against corruption and the vested interests of the old order. Sometimes when I cycled deep into the forests around us, I thought how easy it would be to stage an 'accident'. The police had certainly not been impartial or professional when Plichta hit me over the head with a fence pole. I had no faith in the office of the public prosecutor or, indeed, any branch of local government I'd had dealings with. An 'accident' could easily become no more than 'death by misadventure'. The local *układ*, its feet planted firmly in the Communist past, certainly had the means to falsify or suppress evidence, intimidate witnesses and use legal technicalities to their advantage.

There was also a lot the local *układ* could do short of removing me permanently from the scene. Polish law allows for pre-trial detention of up to two years, longer in special circumstances, and many public prosecutors use it as a means of extracting 'confessions' or simply to punish people they lack evidence to prosecute in court. Bureaucrats, public prosecutors and judges are never held accountable for wrongly depriving people of their liberty. As a result, more than ninety-five per cent of requests by public prosecutors for pre-trial detention are approved by judges. In less than half of such hearings, is the accused represented by a lawyer.

Among the many miscarriages of justice that made front-page news in national newspapers before I took on the local *układ*, was the case of Lech Jeziorny and Paweł Rey. The two entrepreneurs from Kraków were detained for nine months without trial in 2003 while prosecutors hunted for evidence they had acted illegally in a complex management buyout of a slaughterhouse. They were bankrupted by this pre-trial detention and faced another seven years of investigation after their release. All the charges against them were then dropped without apology or compensation for the time they had spent in jail. The public prosecutor who led the case is still working. Another businessman, Roman Kluska, was also bankrupted by a tax investigation that courts later ruled to have been improper. He had to post more than two million euros in bail to avoid lengthy pre-trial incarceration. Kluska received a derisory 1,250 euros in compensation from the government for his unlawful arrest. Mitch Nocula, an American businessman who had to close down his machine tool business when inspectors wrongly accused him of using illegal software, received just 315 euros in compensation.

Some fifty government departments and agencies can carry out checks on businesses in Poland. They range from tax and customs departments to labour inspectors, public health officials and child welfare workers. There is even an agency charged with, amongst other things, controlling the font size of alcohol levels on wine bottle labels. Given that tax law alone amounts to hundreds of pages of often obscure and sometimes contradictory regulations and procedures, there is probably not a totally compliant company anywhere in Poland. If an excise tax sticker fell off a single bottle of the hundreds of thousands of bottles that Wine Express imported each year, technically I exposed myself to criminal charges. Worse, the public prosecutor could have me locked up while he investigated, arguing simply that I was a flight risk unless jailed. This may seem like something from the theatre of the absurd, but a restaurant owner client of ours had to surrender his passport when inspectors found that tax labels had fallen off half a dozen bottles in a fridge. It wasn't that the tax labels had disappeared. Condensation in the fridge had loosened the labels and they had fallen to the bottom of the fridge. Had common sense prevailed, he'd have been told to glue them back on. Instead he was charged with the criminal offence of excise duty avoidance and had to surrender his passport while the case meandered through the regional court. The value of the missing excise labels was less than two euros.

While I wasn't ever detained on absurd charges, it was worrying to think that it might happen and that I could spend weeks, if not months, sharing a squalid three-square-metre cell with other prisoners before a court ordered my release. That nothing like this had happened so far and that there had been no direct threats against me or the family, probably gave me a greater sense of security than was warranted. 'You know Małgosia,' I said to the friend who had warned me at the party about the dangers of being a crusading publisher, 'I'm doing my thing with the newspaper because I want my children – and yours – to grow up in a better, less corrupt country. I think they would be disappointed in me if I wanted anything less for them.'

It was a vain little speech, the kind of words pounded out on a noisy typewriter by the writer Herman Mankiewicz, who won an Academy Award for the screenplay of *Citizen Kane*. I did want to make my small corner of Poland a better place in which to live, but it was arrogant of me to suggest that Ania and the children cared anything about local politics or that they would have volunteered themselves as hostages to my crusade. I would have been less cavalier had I been able to watch the film *Układ Zamknięty* [Crooked Cabal], a chilling political thriller by Ryszard Bugajski in the style of Costa Gavras's *State of Siege*, *Z*, and *Missing*. It was released long after I had launched *Express Kaszubski*, but was inspired by what had happened to Jeziorny, Rey and others just before I became a publisher. When heavily armed police battered down a door in the film and pinned one of the entrepreneurs and his pregnant wife to the floor with guns to their backs while their children looked on, I shivered inwardly. Even more disturbing was the scene in which one of the businessmen was raped in prison. But most distressing of all was the running dialogue between the public prosecutor and the regional tax collector as they stitched up the entrepreneurs. It was frightening to think that public officials could be so corrupt and so immune to censor of any kind. It is such a powerful film that even Poland's president, Bronisław Komorowski, was moved to declare it essential viewing for officials with power over other people's lives. It would be even better if Poland took this often misused power away from prosecutors by making pre-trial detention illegal.

I don't know whether being a foreigner helped keep me out of jail on trumped up charges. Perhaps my ceaseless self-publicising helped. I took every opportunity to publish pictures in *Express Kaszubski* of myself with ambassadors, politicians, senior government officials, film stars and business leaders. I wanted the *układ* to know that I had good connections, people I could turn to at a national level if anything untoward happened to me.

By now my crusade had received good national press coverage, including a five-page piece in *Press*, a glossy media, advertising and public relations monthly with a wide circulation. The article, headlined '*Prywatne łamy*' [Private column] chronicled my fight with the local *układ* and ended with a question about possible repercussions that was not dissimilar to Małgosia's. 'Look,' I had answered, 'A lot of my friends died covering wars in different parts of the world. Should I not at least have enough courage to take on the local *układ*?'

As we moved into the second half of 2006, the ABW passed on its evidence on contracts and tenders for the school at Staniszewo to the public prosecutor in Tczew, a city on the Vistula River about fifty kilometres from Kartuzy. It was up to the prosecutor to decide whether to indict the mayor for mismanaging public funds or announce there was no case to answer. Weeks went by without a decision. The prosecutor seemed to be dragging his feet. I was concerned there would be no decision prior to the local government elections in November, when Mayor Gołuński would be seeking a second term in office. He was campaigning vigorously. While we published stories about vote buying and other irregularities in the previous election, other newspapers were writing fawning pieces that glossed over the fact that the mayor had been the subject of a year-long investigation and might face criminal charges. If the public prosecutor in Tczew delayed the decision until after the election, Gołuński had a better chance of winning.

There was doubtless lobbying going on behind the scenes to get the prosecutor to delay his decision until after the elections. Those doing the lobbying had money at their disposal and probably influential politicians and church figures on their side. As each day passed and there was silence from Tczew, I feared they were prevailing. It seemed unfair to me that voters might go to the polls not knowing whether one of the candidates would be charged with what amounted to corruption in public office. So I wrote to the attorney general, outlining *Express Kaszubski*'s interest in the case and urging him to ensure that the public prosecutor made his decision prior to the elections. 'Voters have a right to know whether one of the candidates faces criminal charges,' I said in my letter. 'The public prosecutor needs either to lay charges or announce that there is no case to be answered.' We published the letter in full on the editorial page of the newspaper.

Finally, just a week or so before polling day, the public prosecutor charged Mayor Gołuński and other council officials on three counts of what amounted to corruption. The *Express* devoted its front page to the charges. We ran a photograph of Mayor Gołuński with a black band covering his eyes. This is standard press practice because Polish law makes it an offence for newspapers to identify people facing criminal charges. We could also not use his full name. It's a farcical law because we could, for example, say that the mayor of Kartuzy, Mieczysław G., has been charged with corruption. By not using his surname we were supposedly not identifying him. By printing a black band over his photograph we were also observing the law. Far from protecting a man and his right to be presumed innocent until proven guilty, this particular law actually made him look like a criminal. The black band across the eyes was an especially powerful image. I knew that publishing the picture on our front page was unlikely to help the mayor's re-election chances.

We had a long debate in the office about whether or not to print a black band across the mayor's eyes. Some of my staff thought it unfair because it would give the incumbent's opponents an advantage. They also reminded me that an accused was innocent until proven guilty. I understood their arguments. But I also remembered all the letters I had received from Gołuński justifying whatever he was doing to harm my interests with references to a string of obscure laws. I remembered, too, how he had arrogantly changed the name of our village without consultation and how the city architect had told me the mayor wouldn't approve my planning application *regardless of its merits*. Mayor Gołuński was the grand master of deviousness and of manipulating laws and regulations to his advantage. This small town villain deserved, in Shakespeare's words, to be 'hoist with his own petard.' Like Hamlet, I could reflect: 'O tis most sweet, when in one line two crafts directly meet.'

SPIRIT OF PLACE

As my fight with Gołuński intensified, and I juggled ownership and hands-on management of *Express Kaszubski* with running Wine Express and Kania Lodge, I somehow found time to pursue another venture. Ripening grapes in Kaszubia was proving more difficult than I had imagined. Perhaps, I thought, it would be easier to make *grappa* from my vineyard than wait for the rare year when the weather was perfect from early spring until late in the autumn and I could make wine. But if I was going to move into distillation, why not use the potatoes that grow so well in Kaszubia's sandy soil and are a staple part of the diet? Vodka produced from potatoes, many people said, was the best of all vodkas. If grapes for wine were so hard to ripen in our region, why not make vodka?

I asked the question after yet another poor summer meant that the birds and badgers again feasted on our grapes. I had recently learned that vodka need not be the colourless, odourless and tasteless spirit that lines supermarket shelves worldwide, the various brands distinguished more by their packaging than their content. Vodka can be as reflective of its provenance as wine, especially when made from potatoes. There are hundreds of varieties of potato, each with its own characteristics and subtle shifts in texture and taste. What the French call *terroir* in relation to wine – soil, drainage, rainfall and sunshine amongst other things – can also help determine what a potato spirit tastes like.

My mentor was Tadeusz Dorda, who owns a distillery in eastern Poland and exports his Chopin-brand luxury vodkas to the United

States and elsewhere. One day at his distillery in Krzesk, Tad (an Anglicised diminutive of Tadeusz) set up a tasting mat with the names of different grains – rye, wheat, barley and oats – to identify which vodka was in each glass. I wasn't looking forward to this tasting because I didn't like vodka. When buying the land for the lodge, I had followed local custom and brought a bottle to the kitchen table each time I sat down to negotiate with one of the farmers. I recalled the detached, antiseptic taste and the furry mouth and splitting headaches that followed. As Tad filled the glasses, I shuddered at the memory of the negotiating sessions. I'll just 'nose' it, I thought, Tad is not going to be offended if I don't drink the stuff.

My interest grew each time I buried my nose in a glass. 'They are all so different,' I told Tad who was ticking off the characteristics of each new glass he poured. 'Now try this,' he said. 'It's a single distillation made from young potatoes.' The *młody ziemniak* [young potato] was indeed astonishing. It had a beautifully perfumed nose, redolent of peaches and apricots with underlying hints of citrus. It was so good that I tasted it, swirling the fiery spirit about my mouth as one would a wine. It was truly regal on the palate and as absorbing as fine cognac. I was amazed. It was unlike anything I had drunk before and seemed too good to be vodka. I wanted to know more and plied Tad with questions.

The potatoes had been picked at the end of June, not in September when potatoes are normally harvested in Poland. They had also been distilled just once and not rectified. Commercial vodkas are distilled and then rectified as many as four or five times in order to remove methanol and other impurities. But was it just the early harvest and single distillation that accounted for the astonishing aromas? Did the particular variety of potato they'd planted have anything to do with the taste? And what about the soil and the amount of rain and how warm it had been during the growing season? Tad didn't know but was interested in my notion that what the French call *terroir* in regard to wine might be relevant to vodka. I already knew that Kaszubian farmers hedged their bets each year by planting potatoes in both sandy soils and clay. If it was a wet year the best crop came from the sandy soils. If it was dry, the clay soils gave the best yields. The soil type also affected the taste of the potato, farmers told me. Could the amount of sunshine and rainfall also influence the taste of the potatoes? They weren't sure. Nevertheless I was excited. Just as great wines were made in the vineyard, perhaps great vodkas were made in the field.

Tad and I set about finding out. Later that year I trucked ten tons of potatoes from Kaszubia to the distillery at Krzesk. The potatoes had been picked more than two months later than those used to make Tad's standout spirit. They were also a different variety. When the new batch was ready for tasting three weeks later, Tad flew to Kania Lodge in his helicopter and we tasted the two together. The late-harvest spirit from Kaszubia was earthy with hints of tobacco, leather and a whiff of forests in autumn on the nose. But it wasn't nearly as good as the early-harvest spirit from Podlasie. The following year the Kaszubian potatoes were picked at the same time as those in Podlasie. Weeks later, Tad flew up with the samples and we invited guests at the lodge to a tasting session in the dining room.

Burying my nose into bulbous glasses to check the aromas of the samples, I found they were different to each other and to those produced the previous year. Instead of peaches and apricots, the predominant aromas of the new vodka from Podlasie were pear and guava. The new vintage from Kaszubia exhibited aromas of apple and capsicum, more like a Calvados than the earthy spirit from the previous year. The potato varieties, *Lord* in Podlasie and

Vineta in Kaszubia, were the same as the previous year. This time though, both had been harvested at the same time. The different tastes of the vintages had to come from *terroir*, the same mix of soil type, aspect, rainfall, temperature and many other things that distinguish one wine from another.

It was exciting to discover that vodka could reflect time and place in the same way as wine. But could we sell small-batch specific vintage vodka like this? There were plenty of commercial vodkas on the market that were spiced up and given a taste with flavourings of one kind or another. Poland's *Żubrówka*, for instance, owes it specific flavour to long stems of bison grass. None, however, got its flavour from the variety of potato and the field in which it was grown.

I have always started ventures on gut feeling rather than surveys or careful number crunching. If an idea is dwelt on for too long, reasons can always be found not to pursue it. I liked the idea of selling vodka based on time, place and *terroir*. There was one problem though. The European Union defined vodka as a spirit with less than ten grams of methanol per hectolitre of one hundred per cent volume alcohol. The number is completely arbitrary. Under the same EU legislation, cognac is allowed up to 200 grams of methanol, grappa 1,000 and fruit spirits 1,200. The problem with the low number for vodka is that the only way to reduce the methanol to the required level is to rectify it several times after the initial distillation. This strips out the methanol, but also all the natural flavours.

Since the European Union methanol level for vodka clearly has nothing to do with health concerns, it is puzzling why it legislated in this way. Traditionally, vodka has had taste and a spirit of place. In the seventeenth century there were scores of vodka distillers in nearby Gdańsk alone. All would have been closed down under current European legislation. Each made something subtly different from its competitors, all with considerably more than ten grams of methanol. What we were making at Krzesk was much closer to traditional Slavic vodka than anything sold by the big spirits companies which dominate the alcohol business. The only way they gilded this neutered product was by putting it in a fancy bottle, giving it a glamorous name and spending lots of money on marketing. Keeping artisanal producers out of the market probably suited them well.

The European Union's legislation seemed as unjust to me as the mayor of Kartuzy's decision to change the name of our village without consultation. I couldn't take it to task, as I had done with the mayor, in a local newspaper like *Express Kaszubski*. I could, however, make its regulations regarding vodka look as arbitrary and ridiculous as they were. What we were producing was defined by the EU as a spirit drink, not the easiest thing to market in the highly competitive spirit world. But we had a story to tell and stories, many people in marketing contend, are just as important as the product. We would put the words 'Spirit Drink' on the back label as required by law. We would also use standard vodka bottles. It might not be vodka, and it was clearly labelled that it wasn't in the narrow legal sense, but it would look like vodka. It would also taste better than most vodka on the market and we would tell people why.

Tad wasn't ready to start marketing the small-batch spirit drink being produced at Krzesk. I was keen to start and with my eldest son, William, created a company to tackle the British market. We had identified Britain, London in particular, as a good place to test our belief in the product. We registered Vestal Vodka as a trademark, taking the name from Vesta, the Roman goddess of purity. It was nicely alliterative and went well with the large 'V' that would go on the front labels.

William was soon knocking on the doors of London's top bars, clubs and stores, a small suitcase in one hand. Inside, the three 'vodkas' nestled in a polystyrene-foam cut-out. One was made from rye and distilled and rectified to meet EU requirements. The other two were 'spirit drinks' made from young potatoes grown in Podlasie and Kaszubia and distilled at Tad's nineteenth-century distillery in Krzesk. The potato vodkas had about one hundred grams of methanol per hectolitre, half that of cognac and just ten per cent of what was allowed in grappa. These were our premium 'real' vodkas and William told the story as he poured tasting shots for potential clients and listened to them murmur approvingly. Soon we were in places like Harvey Nichols, the Groucho Club and Waitrose. Simon Difford, the Robert Parker of the spirits business in Britain, gave Vestal rave reviews and a rare five-plus score to our second vintage. Stories began appearing in mainstream newspapers. William quickly became so well known that Casio hired him to advertise their G-Shock watches. Advertisements in national daily and Sunday newspapers pictured William in a clubby setting with two bottles of Vestal in one hand and the battered sample suitcase in the other. The text read: 'I relate to the G-Shock ethos of never, never giving up. Setting up a new business is something you have to be relentless about.' Whether or not it boosted sales of G-Shock, it was priceless publicity for Vestal.

As sales grew, my son was approached by angel investors interested in buying into Vestal Vodka. 'Great,' I told William when he phoned with news of an offer. 'But not yet. We need to build turnover first to make the price of any equity much higher. Go back to them in a year or two when you'll need the capital to take Vestal to the next level.'

While William launched Vestal in France and Germany, I looked after the business in Poland. We had the labels printed in nearby

Gdynia and presentation boxes made by Wojciech, the carpenter from nearby Pomieczyńska Huta. A local photographer took all our publicity shots and much of the back-room administration and accounting was done by the Wine Express staff. The potatoes were grown by three local farmers, one of them Staszek Frankowski from the family who had been with us at Kania Lodge from the beginning. I worked with the growers to choose the fields in which the potatoes were planted, believing that well-drained, south-facing slopes produced tubers with the most character and taste. I was with them in the fields when we picked in late June or early July and trucked the potatoes off to the distillery. The farmers all thought it was a pity to pick the potatoes so early when they were the size of golf balls. They were pleased, however, with the premium prices they received.

The new venture was creating jobs and bringing money into the area. Most people were pleased, but there was still resentment. I learned this when I suggested that Vestal Vodka would make a great local story for Kartuzy's newspapers. I had Teresa tell journalists that potatoes grown in a small Kaszubian village were being turned into a high-end regional vodka which was selling in one of London's most fashionable department stores and in top bars and clubs. Moreover, it was probably the first Kaszubian vodka to be produced and exported since before World War II. No one wanted to run the story. Although they didn't say why, I knew it was because I was the outsider who had taken on the local *układ* with my own newspaper. Even worse, I seemed to be winning the fight.

NOT GUILTY
AS CHARGED

When Mayor Gołuński suffered defeat at the polls, he reacted as graciously out of office as he had as the incumbent. He sued me. Lodging a private case against me in the criminal division of the District Court in Gdańsk, he claimed that I had 'publicly accused him of conduct that lost him the public confidence required to hold the post of Mayor of Kartuzy.' This, the charge sheet noted menacingly, was contrary to Polish Criminal Code Article H2 in conjunction with Article 12. If I was found guilty, I could spend as much as twelve months in jail.

It is common practice in libel cases in Poland not to claim damages for oneself but to ask that, if found guilty, the defendant pay a set sum to a registered charity. The ex-mayor was seeking fifty thousand złoty (about 12,500 euros) and had designated an old people's home near Kartuzy as the beneficiary. I was flattered that the ex-mayor was claiming he lost the election because of me and my newspaper. *Express Kaszubski* had worked hard to make local officials accountable, publishing stories that few local newspapers in Poland would have touched. Since I had personally checked all stories of a political nature myself, I was confident that we had not libelled the mayor. But what if the court decided that I had? And what if the judge hated journalists or foreigners and was closely connected in some way to the old order? If guilty, would I just be fined and given a criminal record? Or might the judge sentence me to a term in jail to punish me for my outspokenness and send a message to other meddlers? If *Telewizja Polska* could

217

be so partisan and unfair in relation to me, why not this court as well?

My concerns were not eased by Andrzej Drania, my urbane and clever lawyer from Gdynia. The case, he told me, was less clear-cut than I thought. In fact, he didn't fancy my chances of winning it. He pointed out differences in Anglo-Saxon and Polish libel law that meant I had trodden on dangerous ground in some of my opinion pieces. 'Perhaps,' he mused one day in his wood-panelled office with its dramatic posters of sailing ships in high seas, 'we should use your less-than-perfect command of Polish in your defence.' This seemed evasive and almost underhand to me. But it was tempting. My lawyer thought the ex-mayor had a case. The prospect of a jail sentence, however unlikely, terrified me. Still, I couldn't be so craven and cowardly. 'No Andrzej, this is about freedom of the press and people's right to know what elected officials are up to. We'll fight it on these grounds. I don't want to win this on an obscure legal technicality.'

Before coming to Poland I had never been arraigned before a court on charges of any kind, criminal or civil. But as I sat in the dock in the district court in Gdańsk on the first day of my trial for criminal libel, I realised that I was becoming as comfortable in the austere, slightly intimidating surroundings as an old lag with a long criminal record. Perhaps too comfortable; on the first day Judge Małkowska reprimanded me for slinging my coat over the back of the dock rather than checking it in at the cloakroom.

I knew that the first day would establish little more than who my mother and father were, how much I earned and to which strata of society I belonged. Courts had moved on from assigning you to the working class, *inteligencja* or aristocracy, but now pigeon-holed you on the basis of your educational qualifications. I knew this already because my wife and I were in the midst of another long-running case, this one now in its eighth year, regarding the part of the meadow which Ania's uncle Leszek had misappropriated and refused to return.

For various legal reasons, we could not fight that case on the basis of misappropriation. We therefore sought a court ruling that, as we owned half of the disputed parcel as well as all the land around it, the tiny piece in dispute should be turned over to us on the grounds that it was unmanageable with two owners. There was provision in Polish law for this, and we had paid for a surveyor's report which suggested this was practical and desirable. A judge from the local administrative court in Kartuzy had been appointed to the case and she'd made a visit to Kania Lodge to view the land in question. I showed her the meadow down by the lake and pointed out that all the fields and forest around it belonged to us, explaining how we had bought the meadow to create a contiguous parcel of land around the lodge. She was non-committal, which was fine. However, when we walked back to the Kania Lodge car park, she looked around at the three buildings and waved an arm to take them all in. 'So this is all yours?' she asked Ania in a manner which suggested disapproval. 'You have quite a lot, don't you?' Actually we had about the same amount of land as most local farmers, far too little to make a living from farming. The fact that we had invested time, effort and money into developing our small amount of land into a going concern didn't register with people steeped in the politics of envy and confiscation, as most people who had grown up in the Communist era were. I didn't know the judge's background or who she was connected to in the local community, but her remarks worried me.

In our submissions to the court, Ania and I had already stressed the extent of our investment and the benefits the lodge brought to the local community in jobs, taxes and money spent in the area by visitors from around the world. We had also made the point that

219

we lived on the property the whole year round, not just a few days each summer as Ania's uncle, Leszek, did. Leszek's wife, who was listed as a co-owner with her husband, was an even less frequent visitor. We calculated that she had actually spent about five days in their summer house during the past ten years. To reinforce this point, we had taken pictures of Leszek's run-down, scruffy summer house with its rubbish-strewn yard and overgrown garden. We pointed out that he lived and worked in Gdańsk, where he was the owner of a small business. Leszek was determined to hold on to the land, not because he needed it for any imaginable purpose, but in order to spite us. His was the politics of envy that had destroyed the rural infrastructure after 1945. '*Mało masz?*' [You have too little?] the Communists muttered as they evicted owners from their properties. They then ruined them all, sometimes slowly, but often almost overnight. '*Mało masz?*' Leszek asked Ania as she pressed him to return the land without a lengthy legal battle.

My hopes that the court in Kartuzy might see the logic of our arguments were soon dashed. After her visit, the judge decided that, not only would she not issue an order for Ania's uncle to sell the piece of land to us, but we would have to sell our share to Leszek. The grounds for this astonishing decision seemed to be that, as we had much more land than Leszek, he deserved full ownership of the disputed piece. It did not seem to matter that he didn't live in Sytna Gora, contribute anything to the local community or have any use for the piece of land. No questions were asked about what he owned elsewhere or the value of his house and business in Gdańsk. The fact that we had what the judge called 'quite a lot' was justification for taking it. Ania was devastated. 'How could they give it to him?' she complained. 'The first thing I see from the window when I wake in the morning are beech trees which now belong to someone else.' The decision seemed so unfair that

I wondered whether it had more to do with local politics and the power of the *układ* than with the law.

We appealed against the judgement, which a higher court overturned on the grounds that the law had been inappropriately interpreted and applied. The case was sent back to the local court in Kartuzy for trial under a new judge. The process of getting the opinions of surveyors and other land-use experts started all over again, and the case inched its way slowly through court in tandem with the libel case the former mayor of Kartuzy had brought against me. It was clear from the outset that this time the court's preferred way of resolving the land issue was to divide the property, giving each joint owner an equal share. This didn't make much sense to me, since it would give Leszek a tiny plot of about two hundred and fifty square metres, not much bigger than an average house, right in the middle of our property. It was too small and too close to the lake to build on and would immediately create a new problem, that of access.

The only way of reaching it would be through our land and an access road would further compromise the integrity of our property. There were long arguments about both the practicality and desirability of dividing up such a small plot of land with no legal access except through our land. One surveyor called to the witness stand conceded that, while something as small as a match-head could technically be divided, it didn't make much sense to divide this piece of land into such small parcels. But another testified that it was big enough to divide and the question of access was another matter to be dealt with separately. I could see that the judge was pleased with this expert opinion and that a decision to divide up the land was the most likely outcome.

The question was how to divide it up. The most logical way was to divide it in a straight line from the top of the escarpment to the lake. This would mean that both parties would get a small but equal amount of forest, meadow and lake front. We reluctantly accepted this as the best we could expect. But Leszek wouldn't agree. He wanted all the lake front, the most desirable part of the land, and stubbornly refused to yield even when the judge told him that it would be a mistake on his part not to go along with the surveyor's suggestion. 'You could lose everything,' the judge told him. This seemed such a clear, unequivocal warning that I was astonished when Leszek, bristling with self-importance, reiterated his demand for a larger share of the lake front. As he made his final submission, moustache quivering, I pictured him standing before a Polish *sejm* in the seventeenth century and shouting '*nie pozwalam*' [I don't permit]. 'He's blown it,' I told Ania outside the courthouse after the judge had set a date when he would deliver the judgement. 'He's too stupid and greedy to compromise. I wouldn't be surprised now if the judge gives the whole lot to us.'

That is exactly what happened two months later when the judgement was read out in a second floor courtroom. Only Ania and I were present to hear the judge say that, since Ania's uncle had declined the court's proposal for a division of the land, he was ruling that Leszek be required to sell his share to us. There couldn't have been a better outcome for us. We had steeled ourselves to losing part of the land we had bought and paid for and been tricked out of by Leszek. But now we were getting it all back. Our long, stressful fight had been worth it. He appealed but a higher court upheld the judgement and, more than twelve years after we first took the case to court, we had finally won. There could be no more appeals. The land was ours.

The long-running hearing of the former mayor's case against me was, coincidently, drawing to a close at the same time. In another court, Gołuński had been found not guilty of the charges of improper conduct by a public official, brought against him by the public prosecutor. Other officials in the council were, however, found guilty. Emboldened by the judgement in regard to himself, Gołuński and his lawyer attacked me for using the word 'corruption' in stories about the former mayor. Corruption, they argued, was almost exclusively understood as the acceptance of bribes by public officials. By using the word in connection with the former mayor, I had defamed him and diminished his credibility in the eyes of voters to such an extent that he was not re-elected. I argued that corruption was a much broader church than simply the taking of bribes, and included things like buying votes, crony capitalism and deliberately misleading people through manipulated plebiscites and other things. Anyway, I had never directly accused Gołuński of corruption and challenged them to find a single direct accusation in any stories or editorials printed in *Express Kaszubski*.

Since he had been investigated for nearly a year by the ABW in connection with murky public tendering, an investigation that included the removal of documents from his home and office, my questions about his propriety seemed reasonable and fair. While the ABW investigation was going on, the newspaper *Dziennik Bałtycki* had run one of its silly plebiscites which claimed to show that Gołuński was one of the region's most popular politicians. Attacking the plebiscite in an editorial and referring to the ABW investigation, I suggested that it was too early to determine whether the mayor was one of the most popular, or most corrupt, local officials.

Gołuński's lawyer, a young man named Roman Nowosielski, repeatedly pointed out that Article 212 of the Polish Criminal Code did not require a person subject to libel to have been humiliated in the eyes of the public or to suffer a loss of public credibility. There just had to be a possibility of this happening for the offence to be committed. In other words, Gołuński didn't need to prove that he had suffered any actual harm as a result of anything we had published. It was enough to establish that articles had the potential to cause him harm. Nowosielski also made much of the fact that the former mayor had not been investigated for 'corruption' by the ABW but rather for abuse of power in relation to tender proceedings. This seemed like semantics to me and to Transparency International, the Berlin-based organisation which tracks corruption worldwide and which I had frequently quoted in my editorials. Abuse of power in relation to tender proceedings was, simply put, corruption.

For me, the most interesting and revealing part of the trial came during the cross-examination of witnesses. Gołuński produced three who testified that articles and editorials in *Express Kaszubski* had been a major factor in the ex-mayor's failure to win re-election. Each of the witnesses wanted to dwell on the fact that we had published a picture of Gołuński with a black band over his eyes, one of them saying that this was 'the final nail in his coffin' during the elections. Each time they brought this up the judge reminded them that another court had already decided in my favour on this matter. A fast-track election tribunal had heard the case immediately after we had published the picture and before voters went to the polls. What we had done, the tribunal ruled, was in keeping with Polish law.

After each witness had testified, it was our turn to cross-examine them. Andrzej, my lawyer, cut an imposing figure in court. Sartorially resplendent in pin-striped suit and immaculately-pressed white shirt beneath his open, green-hemmed black lawyer's cloak, he exuded confidence as well as a firm grasp of the issues and the relevant legal statutes. He had helped me prevail in several other cases, and I was always pleased to have him on my side, no more so than in this case. 'Did other newspapers publish stories saying that Mr Gołuński had been investigated by the ABW and charged with a criminal offence?' he asked each witness in turn. They weren't sure, and their memories needed jogging. Andrzej artfully reminded them that stories reporting these facts had appeared elsewhere. 'But other newspapers were not as aggressive as *Express Kaszubski*,' ventured Ryszard Mielewczyk, a retired teacher who had been deputy mayor during Gołuński's time in office. 'But did they say he had been investigated and charged?' Andrzej asked. 'Yes,' he admitted.

When my turn came, I asked each of the witnesses for an example of an article or editorial that had accused the ex-mayor of corruption, or one which had been factually incorrect. Beyond remembering the story we had run with the picture of Gołuński with the black band over his face, they could not be specific. 'My friends and I thought the aggressiveness of the newspaper was quite immoral,' Adam Wieczorek, a pensioner in his seventies, told the court. 'People believed that what was written could be true and the stories contributed to the defeat of Mr Gołuński in the elections.' I pushed him to give me an example of a story we had published that was not true. He could not, and instead wandered off into generalisations, contradicting himself by saying that virtually no one read our scurrilous newspaper while at the same time opining that it had a big influence on the election result.

Mr Wieczorek also ventured the opinion that, in an ideal world, no newspaper would have mentioned that the mayor was facing criminal charges relating to municipal tenders until the case had been heard and a judgement reached. This kind of control over news had been widely practised during the Communist era. Some people still hankered after the dark days when misdeeds could be covered up. This is what the ex-mayor's case against me and my newspaper amounted to. It was a challenge to the right of the press to probe the actions of public officials and inform people about what was going on in their community.

After the cross-examination, I felt that the witnesses called by Gołuński had done much more for my cause than for his. They had admitted that other newspapers had published stories recording, however cursorily, that the ABW was investigating the mayor and that the public prosecutor had charged him with a public offence. They had also conceded that they could not name a specific story or editorial which was factually incorrect. My witnesses, on the other hand, helped me establish two important facts. The first, Mariusz Kasprzak, a councillor and at one time the manager of my newspaper, was able to confirm that he and other councillors had stepped in to prevent the mayor from selling municipal land to a local businessman without first organising a public tender. The second, Wojciech Drewka, editor-in-chief of *Express Kaszubski*, strongly refuted Gołuński's claims that the newspaper had refused to run rebuttals and replies from him. In addition to producing responses from Gołuński which we had published, Wojciech told the court that we had actively encouraged people of all political persuasions to air their views on our editorial page.

While both Mariusz and Wojciech were giving evidence, I could hear an agitated Gołuński commenting sotto voce on what they were saying, at one stage uttering the word 'liar' to something Wojciech had said. This earned him a rebuke from the judge, one of an increasing number he was now receiving as he sought to dominate proceedings in the same way he had once run council meetings. The judge was clearly becoming tired of his interventions and out-of-order comments. They could not have been helping his case. His agitation, I suspected, stemmed from the fact that he knew the case wasn't going well for him. The political comeback he hoped to make depended on his defeating me in court and on his triumph being widely publicised, something the sycophantic local press in Kartuzy would happily do.

Poles tend to love victims, real or imagined, and Gołuński needed to become one to regain credibility. It would be helpful if he could demonstrate that his downfall had been the result of the machinations of an evil foreigner. It would have served his purpose better had I been German or Russian, the traditional creators of Polish victims and martyrs. But even one from distant New Zealand would suffice in closed, inward-looking Kaszubia.

The ex-mayor's case had been further damaged by the fact that we were able to inform the court that Grodzki, the former city architect, had recently been charged with corruption by the public prosecutor. The corruption charges stemmed from events that took place while Gołuński was mayor, and Grodzki reported to him. Grodzki had been the man who had visited me at the lodge to tell me that Gołuński would make sure I didn't get building permission for a new warehouse, regardless of the merits of my application. I had long suspected Gołuński and Grodzki of working hand in hand, and was not surprised when, after a lengthy investigation by the ABW, the public prosecutor had charged Grodzki with corruption. He was subsequently acquitted for lack of evidence.

Wojciech was now not only editor-in-chief of the newspaper, but the proprietor as well. After the elections in which Gołuński had been ousted, I had taken stock of things and decided that *Express Kaszubski* was probably never going to be viable as weekly newspaper. The problem was that, while it had easily the largest circulation, it was just one of four newspapers in a town with a catchment of around fifty-thousand people. All the others would continue to receive advertising from their backers regardless of how few readers they had.

Classified advertising was drying up worldwide, which meant we could not count on hundreds of individuals placing advertisements each week. This made us dependent on advertising from local businesses. But the owners of many of these businesses were friends of the public officials we were exposing. They were never going to advertise with us. Our advertising revenue had in fact grown month after month for more than a year but then we had stalled. There was clearly not enough neutral, non-partisan advertising to support a local newspaper like ours. To fill twenty-four pages with original, interesting news required three full-time reporters as well as part-timers and contributors. We had two people selling advertising space, another making up pages, and yet another taking care of our reception desk and keeping the books for the accountants who did our tax returns once a month. Printing the paper was not cheap and neither was distribution to far-flung small towns and villages. Attempts to boost circulation in the major population areas by using paper boys with smart red *Express Kaszubski* jackets and caps had fallen foul of Polish labour laws which make it illegal to employ minors in any capacity.

The answer, I decided, was to take the paper online. That would immediately strip out more than half of our costs. If we could continue to count on the existing level of advertising then we would do better than break even. By being able to get news out instantly rather than once a week, we could dramatically increase our readership and distribution. This would make the online newspaper an attractive place to advertise, even for those who didn't like us. Advertising seemed a much more promising source of revenue than getting people to pay for access to our stories. As elsewhere in the world, people were reluctant to pay for online information, including news stories.

We spent several weeks preparing everything for an online *Express Kaszubski* and each week told readers what was coming up. When we were ready, we published a final edition of the weekly paper. I felt sad holding it in my hands. It had been a feisty little paper and better content-wise than probably any other small-town newspaper in Poland. I was going to miss the smell of newsprint and the pleasure of leafing through the latest edition to see how everything looked in print.

The number of unique visits to the new *Express Kaszubski* site grew exponentially over the first few months, altering the economics dramatically. An online newspaper, especially the first in the region, could make a real go of things. It might even make money. As soon as I could see that the business model was viable, I decided to offer the paper as a going concern to my staff. The newspaper had taken more of my time than I had bargained for. The wine company and Kania Lodge needed more of my attention than I had been giving them. More importantly, I felt that the fight against corruption and lack of transparency that plagued many areas of government in the region was better fought by someone from the region than by an ageing foreigner.

Having shown the journalists how to do it, I wanted to see if they would take on the responsibilities and risks themselves. If they wanted to make Kartuzy a better place in which to live, they needed to fight for transparency and integrity in public life and stand up to the bullies from the old guard. Since I was prepared to transfer ownership of the newspaper and its title for the symbolic sum of one złoty (about twenty-five cents), there wasn't much of a financial risk. It was instead a challenge, and I was open to offers and suggestions. In the end, Wojciech Drewka, not without misgivings, decided to take up the challenge. When all the paperwork had been completed, I went to the newspaper offices for the last time as proprietor, signed the change of ownership documents and pocketed the one złoty coin.

Five years later, Wojciech was the last witness in the court case Gołuński brought against me. The judge set a date in August for her verdict. I was a little more confident than I had been in the beginning that the decision would be in my favour. So was my lawyer, cautioning however that it could still go either way. In my view Nowosielski had been unable to demonstrate that I had defamed Gołuński in any way. What we had written in the news columns of *Express Kaszubski* had been accurate and properly sourced. Being investigated by the ABW and charged with a criminal offence had probably cost Gołuński credibility with voters. But voters had a right to know what public officials were up to, and it was a newspaper's job to keep them informed. The questions I had raised in editorials had been valid and Gołuński had been given every opportunity to respond.

Gołuński was not in court for the judgement. I sat opposite a stony-faced Nowosielski as Judge Małkowska ruled that I was not guilty of the charge and that costs in the case were to be borne by the ex-mayor. I had been vindicated. It was the verdict I had hoped for but feared I might not get. So uncertain was I of the outcome, that I had already talked to Andrzej about the appeal process. That would not be necessary now. I had taken on the local *układ* in the news and opinion columns of a newspaper I had launched and financed for exactly that purpose. We had won and we had done so fairly and squarely. It was good for Poland and it was good for journalism. It was especially good for me. I wouldn't be going to jail or have a criminal record.

Since the case had essentially been all about the role of the press in the new Poland, I was curious to see how other newspapers in Kartuzy covered it. The silence said everything. Apart from *Express Kaszubski*, not one of the town's newspapers published a word about the outcome of the trial. Later they ignored the fact that a higher court upheld the judgement on appeal and that the ex-mayor had been ordered to pay me some 2,500 euros in costs.

Even *Dziennik Bałtycki*, which had quoted Gołuński extensively as the trial proceeded, made no mention of the outcome. I was not surprised. While I'd owned the paper I had exposed that newspaper's cosy relationship with Gołuński and other public officials and had campaigned to stop it running blatantly misleading opinion polls. The cravenness of their coverage of anything connected to the local *układ* had persuaded me to start *Express Kaszubski* in the first place. The continued cravenness and sheer lack of professionalism at *Dziennik Bałtycki* and other local newspapers made it one of the best investments in time and money I had ever made. I was sorry in some ways that I wasn't still the proprietor. Had I been, I would have sat down immediately and fulminated against the dishonesty and cowardice of the local press.

A PATCH OF PURPLE THYME

After Gołuński lost his case against me, other things began to unravel. Our neighbour Gienek Plichta, the man who fifteen years earlier had tried to block access to our property, offered to sell me the access road and a field next door to Kania Lodge. This was the man police had refused to prosecute after he struck me on the back of the head with a fence pole, drawing blood. This was the same man who had appeared on television soon after being convicted of assault and sworn that he would never sell a square centimetre of Polish soil to a foreigner like me. 'Who runs this place?' he had asked rhetorically, thumping the table for emphasis in a television interview as he implied that I was a grasping predator about to gobble up half the country and enslave the population. It was all theatre of course, staged and directed by the xenophobes who ran Polish state television in Gdańsk and applauded by a small audience of bigots and rednecks from Poland's primitive far Right. In reality it had nothing to do with patriotism and honour. It had been all about shaking me down, telling me that I was an outsider subject to their whims rather than to Polish law or, indeed, common sense.

The field next door to the lodge that Plichta was now eager to sell was a small island in the middle of the nearly ten hectares of land I had bought over the years. There was a covenant on this particular piece of land, making it impossible for Plichta to sell it for anything but agricultural purposes. That made it valuable only to me since no one would pay a premium for land on which it would be difficult to build. Of course that is not how Plichta saw it. For him it was the most valuable piece of land in the world, everyone was interested in it, and I would have to pay a very high price to get it. I let him know that I didn't much care whether I bought it or not and then made him wait before getting down to serious talks. He was selling because he needed the money. I was prepared to pay the going rate for the land, not the prince's ransom he wanted. After months of negotiations, he agreed on a sum that was half the original asking price.

During the negotiations, I cruelly calculated for him just how much money he had lost in possible earnings and in legal fees, court cases, and fines during the eighteen years he had harassed us. It was enough to have built a new barn or completely renovated his house. He would even have had money left over to buy a new car. He readily admitted that other people had encouraged him to make trouble for us. He felt cheated by them. They had not been working in his interests, he admitted sheepishly, but had their own agendas. He wouldn't name those who had been most active in encouraging him, but did not jump to the defence of anyone when I rattled off the names of those in the local *układ* I believed to have been culpable. It was clear, I told him, that they had either lost interest in him or were no longer in a position to help. Blaming others was easier than admitting his culpability. Plichta was never going to apologise for being a willing dupe but it didn't matter. I now had a neighbour who knew he had been used and, more importantly, one who no longer had any desire to harass us.

Plichta was not selling to atone for anything in the past but because it was becoming ever harder to live off a small parcel of land. During the Communist era it had been possible to eke out a living on a just few hectares. It was a precarious, hand-to-mouth existence, especially in Kaszubia where the land was poor and families were large. The staple diet was milk and potatoes. Eggs provided much of a family's protein. Many children went to school hungry, and children and adults alike wore ragged, frequently patched clothes throughout the week, dressing up only for church on Sundays or for special occasions like weddings or funerals. Children's clothes and shoes were mended and passed down to the next sibling. Houses had little furniture, all of it old, worn and tired, and children would often sleep three to a bed beneath lumpy and stained old duvets. A smell of sour milk and cooking fat pervaded houses, few of which had bathrooms of any kind. The toilet was in the yard, and families bathed once a week in a tub in the kitchen.

While the poverty was grinding during the Communist era, peasant farmers at least had title to their land and could pass it on to their children. They also had a roof over their heads, something which would have been hard to come by if they had had the inclination or skills to migrate to a city. Farmers also didn't have to look for customers for the cash crops they produced as the state was obliged to buy from them anything they produced. They had also become used to the rhythm of subsistence farming, the ploughing and tilling of the soil with their plodding draught horses, the planting of rye and potatoes in spring and late summer and the autumn harvests when the whole family dug potatoes or collected sheaves of rye from the harvester and arranged them in stooks. Tethering cows in tiny meadows and feeding pigs and poultry in barns were also part of the rhythm of things, passed on from generation to generation. Some could imagine no other life.

The collapse of Communism not only opened up new opportunities, it created new imperatives. Once the subsidies had been removed, prices went up significantly. There were now property taxes to pay and charges for rubbish collection, along with stiff fines for the disposal of refuse in local forests. Prices of milk, grain and meat came down as the market was opened up and imports flooded in. The tractors that everyone had bought when they sold me land ran on diesel and needed oil changes and repairs from time to time. Those who had bought cars had to pay ever higher amounts for road tax and insurance. All of this required more cash than a subsistence farm in Kaszubia could generate. Every family needed at least one person with a job away from the farm to survive. Men found work as building labourers in Gdańsk and Gdynia, their wives and daughters went off to work in shops in nearby Kartuzy. Some found employment with me and I quickly became the largest single employer in the area. At one stage nearly every household in the village had at least one person working at Kania Lodge or Wine Express. When Poland joined the European Union in 2004 many of the younger people went off to work in Britain. Some have yet to return. Three of Janek Frankowski's five children have worked for years in England. One of Staszek Frankowski's daughters found work as a housekeeper/nanny in the south of France.

Outside jobs and remittances have vastly improved living standards in the village. Each house now has a bathroom and a flush toilet. All have stoves and fridges in their kitchens, and living rooms and bedrooms have furniture that has been bought new rather than having been inherited from a parent or relative. The exteriors of all the houses have been plastered and painted, and some families have two or even three cars. Diets have changed too. Where once potatoes and homemade bread were the staple carbohydrates, many people now eat pasta. The big bread loaves that were once baked in the wood-burning stoves in everyone's kitchen have given way to bread rolls bought from nearby shops and bakeries. Everyone eats more meat. People are getting fatter.

Growing prosperity has meant that most young people are no longer interested in taking over and running the family farm. It is hard work, and it doesn't pay. I suspect that the current fifty-year-olds, people like the Frankowski brothers and Plichta, will be the last generation to farm the land around Sytna Góra as their fathers did. I have already bought land from one farmer who no longer owns a horse or a tractor and has no interest in planting potatoes. Another leases his fields to Janek Frankowski. A third grows nothing and just ploughs his fields to be eligible for a European Union subsidy. Plichta's son Marcin, now in his early thirties, no longer even helps his parents to harvest the rye or bring in the potatoes. He certainly won't be ploughing fields and mucking out barns when his parents pass on. Plichta admitted this to me when he offered to sell me the field. 'Why should I let my son inherit it when all he'll do is sell it?' he told me. 'It's better that I sell it now so that I can use the money in my old age.'

Plichta's decision to sell made 2012 a very satisfying year for us. We had won two important court cases. No one in local government was trying to make life difficult for me in the hope of some personal reward. It was a good feeling. There were occasions over the years when I would gladly have sold up and gone back to being a correspondent or tried my luck in some other country which was ranked several dozen places above Poland in international corruption and ease-of-doing-business tables. What kept me going were inherent stubbornness and the realisation that only a small part of my problems was the result of being a foreigner.

Many of my Polish friends have also fought hard against unfriendly and obstructive bureaucrats to build successful businesses. Poland's dramatic development over the past twenty years has come about in spite of, rather than having been due to, government at any level. Thanks largely to these entrepreneurs,

Poland had the fastest growing economy in Europe during the first stages of the recent recession. But my admiration is greatest for someone who is not a businessman but a man whose long struggle with the sluggish, unhelpful lower levels of Polish bureaucracy has been sustained by a dream rather than by personal profit. The legacy of Jerzy Limon, professor of English Literature at the University of Gdańsk and the director of the Gdańsk Shakespeare Theatre, will be shared by the city of Gdańsk and the whole of Poland. Two decades ago, at about the time I was dreaming of creating a world-class lodge on a lake in the middle of Kaszubia, Jerzy dreamt of building a Shakespearean theatre in Gdańsk on the site of a seventeenth-century theatre where Shakespeare's plays had once been performed, often by travelling English actors.

His was the bigger and much more worthy dream of course. It is finally coming to fruition in a gleaming thirty-million-euro theatre designed by an eminent Italian architect, Renato Rizzi, and funded partly by the European Union. Its outstandingly clever interior design enables the central space to be used both as an Elizabethan stage and as a more traditional Italian-type theatre with the proscenium at one side of the square. Rizzi's dual functionality is made possible by a hydraulic system which enables the Elizabethan stage to be lowered to floor level and the space filled with seats for the audience. The theatre's roof also opens up so that performances can be staged in the open air. It will be a breathtakingly stylish building and one of the best Shakespearean theatres anywhere in the world. Already Gdańsk has an annual Shakespeare festival each summer, drawing performers from all over the world and enabling audiences to watch Hamlet being performed in Korean, Russian, Romanian and Danish, as well as in Polish and English.

The festival has drawn famous actors and directors to Gdańsk, amongst them Peter Brooks and Andrzej Wajda. Early on, Jerzy persuaded Prince Charles, heir to the British throne, to become the Gdańsk Shakespeare Theatre's patron. Jerzy laughs when he tells me how he naively wrote to Prince Charles c/o of Buckingham Palace in 1990 and how a year later he equally naively rode roughshod over protocol and sent a personal invitation to the Prince to visit Gdańsk. When matters of protocol were set right and the invitation was delivered through the office of the Polish president, Prince Charles visited Gdańsk and has been the patron ever since. Jerzy has also received generous support from the long-standing mayor of Gdańsk, Paweł Adamowicz, and from leading regional political figures as well as the minister of culture, Bogdan Zdrojewski. Getting their support and that of the good and great of Polish culture, proved a lot easier than dealing on a day-to-day basis with the local bureaucracy.

When the first performance is staged in the new theatre few people will have an inkling of Jerzy Limon's battles over the years with several layers of Polish bureaucracy, almost all of it venomously hostile, obstructive and totally disinterested in the consequences of their pettiness. 'There are some flaws in the contract with the architect,' one bureaucrat told him. 'It's not our job to tell you what they are. The project can't proceed until they are corrected.' At one stage, he was threatened with arrest and jail because one set of bureaucrats couldn't understand the payment process in regard to the architect and assumed, wrongly of course, that Jerzy was on the take.

Would he have launched the project so enthusiastically in 1990 if he'd known of the bureaucratic battles in store? 'It was better not to know,' he replied after some thought. 'Our lack of knowledge and experience enabled us to create something that the more knowledgeable wouldn't have attempted.' I was at the ground-breaking ceremony, itself a bit of theatre with mechanical diggers playing the leading roles, and wondered whether there were any petty bureaucrats in the crowd and what their thoughts might be. But then I realised that they are such unimaginative people that they are incapable of thinking laterally, that their thought processes revolve around ticking boxes, feeling important and interpreting procedures in as unhelpful a way as possible. They were not interested in the consequences of their interpretation of rules, regulations, by-laws, or planning procedures. They were not there to help anyone wade through thickets of bureaucratic red tape. They were there to boss people around, to establish their own importance and to protect the privileges that went with their jobs. Whether Gdańsk got a world-class theatre was immaterial to them, regardless of the fact that this was their city, where their children would grow up.

Jerzy's doggedness mirrors that of Stefan Sutkowski, who in an earlier era had battled personal hardship and the dead hand of Communism to turn the Warsaw Chamber Opera into one of the most remarkable opera companies in the world. Like Jerzy Limon and the Shakespearean links with Gdańsk, Sutkowski was building on Warsaw's long association with opera. It started in the seventeenth century, when famous Italian soloists often performed there before going elsewhere in Europe. Many works were specially written for the Warsaw stage. Sutkowski set up the Warsaw Chamber Opera in 1961, but when government support was withdrawn three years later he spent almost a decade begging and borrowing money to keep his dream alive. Eventually he persuaded the government to finance it as a state theatre and it has flourished, staging one of the world's finest Mozart festivals each summer.

A few miles away from the Gdańsk theatre is a new deep-water container port capable of handling the largest ships in the world and a staggering eighteen thousand containers. Not only are the ships huge, but they sail to Gdańsk from China and South Korea in just thirty days. The port is owned by the Macquarie Group, an Australian company with investments in ports, airports and roads around the world. It spotted the opportunity of turning Gdańsk into the major port of the Baltic region, serving not just Poland but Central Europe, Ukraine and Russia, whose Baltic ports are often frozen in winter. Until it was built, most container cargo bound for Poland was shipped through Rotterdam or Hamburg. From there it was either trucked directly to its destination in Poland or trans-shipped in smaller vessels to the ports of Gdynia and Gdańsk. Shipping a container from the Far East directly to Gdańsk instead of through Hamburg or Rotterdam can reduce the cost by twenty to thirty per cent and eliminate the carbon dioxide emissions of thousands of trucks driving halfway across Europe.

Since import duties are assessed and paid at the port of entry in the European Union, it is in Poland's interests to import directly through Gdańsk. But Polish bureaucracy is so obstructive and petty that importers, me included, sometimes choose Rotterdam or Hamburg as the port of entry. Poland loses out every time a cargo is not shipped through Gdańsk or some other Polish port. Surprisingly little is being done to streamline bureaucratic procedures so that Poland, rather than Holland or Germany, benefits from EU import duties. Jerzy Limon is right when he says that Polish bureaucrats either don't see or don't care about the consequences of what they do. Sadly, no political party has had the gumption to take them on.

While some things have not changed much in the two decades I've been in Poland, others have. My son Harley, the boy whose nappies I once hand-washed with lake water, turned nineteen in 2012 and left for university in Britain. He is studying architecture in Aberdeen at a university named after Robert Gordon, an Aberdonian who became prosperous as a merchant in Gdańsk during the late seventeenth and early eighteenth centuries. His brother, Alexander, has also gone to Britain to study architecture Many of his classmates are also now at universities abroad, mainly in Britain but also in the United States and Australia. Their parents' and grandparents' generations had no opportunities to study abroad and counted themselves lucky to even be allowed to make a brief visit to any country outside the Soviet sphere.

On my daily summer bike rides, outings that take me through villages with names like Garcz, Sianowo and Kolonia, and fields of rye and oats, I sometimes wonder what the future here will bring these two sons. Not long ago on turning eighteen, they would have been whisked off to two years military service. They would have been bullied because of their family background and fed endless Communist claptrap by sadistic propagandists. As a father I'd have had to tell them to go along with things, not draw attention to themselves and not to trust anyone. Surviving, I would have told them, is what these two years are about. Seventy years ago if I hadn't been smart enough to see what was coming, they might have found themselves in the German army on the Russian front, bewildered, frightened teenagers like so many of their countrymen who were devoured by the era's despots. A century and a half ago, they could have been riding off from the family home to do battle against the Tsar in one of Poland's failed uprisings.

In another age they might also have watched the family home go up in flames as one invader or another passed through Poland. They may have finished up in a German or Russian prison or simply been taken to a forest and shot. They may also have found themselves, like so many Poles in the nineteenth and twentieth centuries, forced to flee abroad and endure the exile's *tęsknota* or homesickness. In Philip Marsden's book *The Bronski House*, which unpicks the history of a land-owning Polish family who fled to

Britain to escape the Russians during World War II, there is a poignant passage as the widow Helena realizes the finality of the tragedy:

> So the most feared and the most appalling thing happened. We fled Mantuski [the family home], left our beloved Mantuski. The house rebuilt by Adam [her dead husband], the precious rooms, the carpets, the furniture and books – all gone. Our beloved staff, the dogs, the herd bred carefully over seventeen years, the forest, the bees, the orchards, the dreaming river, all gone. We are homeless, beggarly, broken. No Poland. No Mantuski.

Harley and Alexander have grown up in a golden age for Poland, probably the most gilded two decades the country has known in three centuries. The world is open and accessible in a way that was unimaginable when their mother was their age. Both sons have already been to most countries in Europe and as far afield as China, Australasia and Africa. Just before finishing school, they flew to Iowa in the US with their Polish school team of problem-solving thespians for an international competition. Not only have Europe and the world opened up for young Poles, it has also shrunk. Our children can fly directly to London, Paris, Rome, Berlin, Barcelona and Stockholm from the airport at Gdańsk, just twenty-five kilometres from the lodge. The terminal is a soaring glass and steel building handling more than three million passengers a year and as many as sixty flights in a single day. In summer, charter flights deliver local tourists directly to Greece, Turkey, Spain, North Africa and Egypt. When I first came to Poland the terminal was not much bigger than a potting shed in the garden of a London house. On a very busy day there might have been five flights.

There are supermarkets, shopping malls and convenience stores that stay open all night. In the malls are the usual fashion names found in America or Britain as well as names that might surprise first-time visitors. My mother once said that she'd happily live in Poland if Marks and Spencer and Boots were present. Marks and Spencer is now here, and there is a branch opposite our wine store in Gdynia. Car showrooms are full of the latest models. Fast food restaurants, gas stations and digital advertising screens at intersections characterise the new Poland. Another restaurant seems to open every week in Gdańsk. Wine bars offer increasingly interesting lists. Coffee shops sell latte, mocha and macchiato, words that would have meant nothing to earlier generations of Poles. Newspapers bulge with advertisements for new apartments and houses built by private developers. Many of these new homes are as fancily finished as in richer parts of Europe. Private medicine has taken hold and one can visit a doctor in a smart, modern medical centre or have a knee operation in a private hospital and be home before lunch the following day.

All this makes living in Poland much easier than it was two decades ago and the abundance and availability of so much is a visual rebuke to the inefficiencies and outright failures of the Communist era, a time when people queued every day for a loaf of bread, needed a coupon for meat or petrol and had to bribe someone to obtain the few bags of cement required to lay a garden path. Our children's generation cannot imagine how grey, melancholic and dispiriting it was. Even for us the memories are fading, bleached by distance and disbelief that it could ever have been so petty, mean and forced. Who, now, could imagine turning in their passport after a trip abroad or carrying a folded bag at all times just in case something appeared in a shop? Who could imagine armed soldiers in the rear of an aircraft, or such poverty in villages that not a single house had a bathroom and children wore ragged, passed-down clothes and sometimes went hungry?

I have assimilated enough of Poland's historical experience to wonder whether the golden era of the past two decades is not just a flicker of sunshine on Polish shores. You can change systems, but you can't do much about geography. Poland remains between Germany and Russia. While both its once-meddling neighbours are preoccupied with other interests, geography might once again become Poland's curse. Being part of a functioning union of European states is Poland's best guarantee of security in the early part of the twenty-first century. Any unravelling of the union, whether it starts in Greece or Portugal or somewhere else, should worry Poland more than just about any other nation in Europe. Yet Poles can be ambivalent about Europe and sometimes hostile.

Just before the referendum in 2003, when Poles voted on whether or not to join the European Union, our son Alexander's primary school religion teacher urged the class to tell their parents to vote 'No'. Accession to the European Union, she told the eight-year-olds, would lead Poland into moral bankruptcy, destroy families and create a godless society. More than twenty per cent of voters either agreed with this or had other reasons for not wanting Poland to become part of Europe. Fortunately, seventy-seven per cent of voters said 'Yes' to the Union and Poland joined in 2004. Ania protested against the religion teacher's airing of her political views, and Alex has not since been to a religion class.

There are an uncomfortably large number of people in Poland who not only hate the European Union but Russia as well. In fact they seem to hate everything that does not conform to their narrow, bigoted and minority view of what Poland and Polishness are all about. On Independence Day in 2012, far Right groups mustered some twenty thousand people in Warsaw for an alternative rally to the official celebrations nearby which drew ten thousand. Above the crowd at the far Right rally rose a sea of red and white Polish flags interspersed with placards and banners targeting leftists, homosexuals and Jews. One group tried to set an EU flag alight. 'We are at war for Poland,' roared one of the speakers. 'We will take Poland back.' Since Poland's current government is centre Right and fairly conservative on social issues, the far Right is truly xenophobic, ultra-nationalist and hateful.

Hatred for Russia is historically more understandable, but no less rational. Since the plane crash at Smolensk in 2010 which killed Polish President Lech Kaczyński and the other ninety-four passengers, there has been an unseemly and sometimes nauseating campaign by the dead president's brother Jarosław and his political party to link the crash to a conspiracy between the Russians and the current Polish government. I say 'unseemly' because the official enquiry blamed poor weather conditions, pilot error and inadequate airport facilities. The nauseating bit is that Law and Justice (PIS), the main opposition party, has woven the crash into its political broadcloth. The party leader, Jarosław Kaczyński, says his brother and the other crash victims were 'murdered' and continually calls for the present government's resignation. Other members of PIS repeatedly accuse Prime Minister Donald Tusk's government of complicity in covering up Russian responsibility for the crash, which they claim was an assassination.

To reach this conclusion, one would first have to believe that the Russians cared enough about Lech Kaczyński to want to remove him, especially since opinion polls at the time showed that he had little chance of winning the next election. One would also need to believe some really implausible scenarios, amongst them that the Russians sneakily laid down a thick blanket of fog at the precise moment the Polish plane was due to land and that they then tricked the pilot into attempting a landing. Disturbingly, opinion polls in late 2012 suggested that one in three Poles suspects both a plot and a cover-up. The conspiracies and betrayals that litter Polish history have given rise to, and perpetuate, a cult of martyrdom, a sense that the outside world is always ganging up on a tiny coterie of brave and saintly true believers in the heart of Europe. Anyone who opposes their xenophobic outlook is not a true Pole. That was how the far Right justified the killing of Poland's first president, Gabriel Narutowicz, in 1922. This cultured technocrat was from a distinguished Polish-Lithuanian family. His father died in a Russian prison following his participation in the 1863 uprising, one of several Polish attempts during the nineteenth century to throw off the Russian yoke. Yet he was branded a traitor and a Jew in a scurrilous campaign by the Right to prevent his taking office. Five days after he was sworn in, he was shot dead.

Nearly a century after Narutowicz's assassination, the far Right in Poland remains violent, anarchic and politically incoherent. Not long after right-wing protestors battled with riot police on Poland's Independence Day in 2012, police arrested a radical nationalist who was an admirer of the Norwegian mass murderer Anders Breivik and who was planning to blow up the Polish Parliament with four tons of explosives. After his arrest, the forty-five-year-old scientist from a university in Kraków told prosecutors that his motives were xenophobic and anti-Semitic. The people now ruling Poland, he said, were foreigners and not true Poles.

I reflected on this and other things one sunny autumn day when the thermometer rose unexpectedly to nearly 20°C and I was returning to the lodge on my bike after a twenty-kilometre ride. As I crested the hill on the driveway we had paved immediately after Plichta sold us the road, I realised that it was well over twenty years since I first came here and dreamt of building a lodge. It was now nearly twenty-five years since Communism collapsed and twenty-seven years since Ania I were married in the gothic cathedral in

Oliwa, near Gdańsk. Both of us had lived here far longer than we had lived anywhere else in our lives. Our two children have never had another home. If I have ever belonged anywhere, it must be here.

I paused near where the old birch tree once cast its shadow over the road. It has gone, cut down when Plichta sold us the road. The driveway is now flanked by oak trees I planted on adjacent land a decade earlier, trees that one day will cast long shadows over the road. Beneath the avenue of trees is a wide green lawn stretching for more than one hundred metres. From the crest of the driveway where I had stood nearly two decades earlier and watched the little red bulldozer dig the foundations of Kania Lodge, the view was now partly obscured by our house. It was no longer possible to see the vineyard from this vantage point, or the meadow for which we fought so long and where I learned of my father's death. I could not see the tennis court which I built with the inheritance from my grandfather who had made his money in India or the gardens where Ania has toiled so creatively, doggedly and successfully. Nor could I see the old beech trees which skirt the escarpment dropping down to the lake or the wild cherry trees which blossom with such abandon each May.

But I could still see where the bulldozer once worked and the tiled roof of one wing of the lodge. Further on the sun dances mischievously on the rippled surface of The White Lake, the welcoming body of water that brought us here in the first place. Behind it, the forest retreats in serried ranks of dark, smoky green, like a medieval army. Off to the left the sheep are grazing in a field that a New Zealander would call a paddock. On sloping land above it is the mixed deciduous and coniferous forest we planted shortly after arriving. Only this morning I had picked mushrooms there, mostly *maślaki*, slippery jacks in English, but some handsome ceps as well. Badgers and foxes have made their homes there, and jays glide silently from tree to tree.

Off to my right from where the birch tree once stood there is a spreading patch of wild thyme with tiny purple flowers. When the time comes, I have told my children, spread my ashes here on the spot where once I had felt a frisson of fear about risking all on a whimsical venture in a rural backwater on the very fringes of Europe.